NOT TRIVIAL

*How Studying the
Traditional Liberal Arts
Can Set You Free*

NOT TRIVIAL

*How Studying the
Traditional Liberal Arts
Can Set You Free*

Laurie Endicott Thomas

Freedom of Speech Publishing

Not Trivial
How Studying the Traditional Liberal Arts Can Set You Free
By Laurie Endicott Thomas

Book designer, David Moratto

For more books like this one,
visit Laurie Endicott Thomas's Web site at: www.not-trivial.com

Printed in the United States of America.
The publisher offers discounts on this book when ordered in bulk quantities.
For more information, contact Sales Department, Phone 815-290-9605,
e-mail: sales@FreedomOfSpeechPublishing.com

Freedom of Speech Publishing, Leawood, KS 66224
www.FreedomOfSpeechPublishing.com

ISBN: 1938634993
ISBN-13: 978-1-938634-99-4

This book is dedicated to the 31 Boston schoolmasters who explained in 1845 that direct instruction in intensive phonics is the only intelligent way to teach children to read English. They were right, and the matter should have been settled then. This book is also dedicated to Rudolf Flesch, who explained in the 1950s that our educational system's refusal to use intensive phonics for reading instruction explained why millions of American children were failing to learn to read.

Contents

Acknowledgments

I'd like to thank my mother, Ruth Endicott, for teaching me to love books, and my father, Bill Endicott, for teaching me to look words up in the dictionary when I write, even if I think I already know what the words mean. I also owe them a debt of gratitude for making the sacrifices to finance my university education. I also have to thank my dear husband, Geoffrey Thomas, for his unfailing support and guidance.

This book came about because my steadfast friend Marjorie Winters suggested that I write a grammar column for the *American Medical Writers Association Journal*. Those articles allowed me to pass along lessons that I learned from Caroljean Ellis in my early days as an editor. While I was doing research for those articles, I read David Mulroy's invaluable book, *The War Against Grammar*. That book encouraged me to expand the scope of this book from explaining the causes of bad writing to explaining the breakdown of civility in our society.

For giving me insight into the philosophy of education, I have to thank my friend Howard Ozmon. I had the privilege of copyediting one of the early editions of his classic textbook *Philosophical Foundations of Education*. Bruce Deitrick Price's Improve-education.org Web site and John Taylor Gatto's book *The Underground History of American Education* also helped to shape my understanding.

I also have to thank my friends Sarah Mercuri and Sheila and Tony East, who patiently listened to me babble on while I was developing the ideas that went into this book. John Lenz, Charles Courtney, and Peter Geidel read early drafts of several chapters and gave me valuable advice. Don Potter read the entire book and gave me comforting reassurance that it is on the right track. I also owe a debt of gratitude to Bonnie Rathgeber McGhee and Carol Boyer for their invaluable help in proofreading.

I also want to thank the excellent teachers I had when I was a student in public schools in Ohio, Wisconsin, and New Jersey. I hope that this book gives today's schoolteachers the roadmap they need for achieving their mission as teachers.

PART I: *Literacy*

Teaching children to read should be as easy as A, B, C. Young women with little more than a primary school education themselves once had great success in teaching reading, using little more than Webster's blue-backed speller and the Bible. Yet today, millions of people who grew up in the United States are functionally illiterate, even though they have spent up to 13 years in schools that were staffed by college-trained, licensed teachers. What is going on?

Lots of people want to blame the students and the teachers. However, I think we should look at the methods that the teachers have been taught to use. As Rudolf Flesch explained in his 1955 bestseller *Why Johnny Can't Read,* American schools had started using a method of reading instruction that doesn't work. His 1983 bestseller *Why Johnny Still Can't Read* explained that the ineffective method was still being used 28 years later. It's still being used today.

Why would anyone force teachers to use a teaching method that doesn't work? The answer to that can be found in a bestseller from 1845: *Narrative of the Life of Frederick Douglass, an American Slave.*

> Very soon after I went to live with Mr. and Mrs. Auld, she very kindly commenced to teach me the A, B, C. After I had learned this, she assisted me in learning to spell words of three or four letters. Just at this point of my progress, Mr. Auld found out what was going on, and at once forbade Mrs. Auld to instruct me further, telling her, among other things, that it was unlawful, as well as unsafe, to teach a slave to read... It would for-ever unfit him to be a slave. He would at once become unmanageable, and of no value to his master. As to himself, it could do him no good, but a great deal of harm. It would make him discontented and unhappy.

In short, education can prepare you for either freedom or slavery. The kind of education that was designed for free people was called the liberal arts. To study the liberal arts, you must first learn to read.

The Studies That Are Appropriate for Free People

I f you are a storybook character, it's easy to solve the problem of lousy public schools. All you have to do is lie about your address, so that your child can get into one of the good public schools that serve the rich neighborhoods. That's what Johnny Nolan did in the novel *A Tree Grows in Brooklyn*, which was about the struggles of an Irish immigrant family in Brooklyn in the early 20th century. Of course, that trick seldom works today. Nowadays, some school district administrators spy on children to figure out where they live, and some parents have even faced criminal charges for lying about their address to get their children into a better public school.

In the land where every man is supposedly created equal, the public schools have never been created equal. Children who grow up in neighborhoods with good schools have a much better chance of getting a good education, which has always been the ticket to the American Dream. On the other hand, children who grow up in neighborhoods with poor schools will face a lifetime of struggle. Sometimes, the quality of the schools varies dramatically between neighborhoods that are right next door to each other.

Many people struggle to afford a house or apartment in a neighborhood with good public schools, to give their children the best possible start in life. Many parents view this sacrifice as an investment because a good education will help their children get good jobs when they grow up. At the same time, a growing minority of families in the United States are choosing to educate their children at home. Some of these families are dissatisfied with the quality of the education in their local public schools. Others are mainly concerned about how their children's education will affect the children's spiritual or moral development. They want their children to grow up to be not only knowledgeable and wise but also good.

All of these families are grappling with age-old problems. Education helps people develop the skills and earn the credentials they will need to make a living, but it also helps to shape their lives in many other ways as well. The education that is provided to children will also have an influence on the kind of society they go on to create.

In ancient times, when slaves did much of the work, there were two different kinds of education: mechanical arts (*artes mechanicae*) and liberal arts (*artes liberales*). The mechanical arts were the skills that were needed in some sort of work, such as agriculture, blacksmithing, weaving, or trade. In the ancient world, these skills were considered servile, which literally meant appropriate for servants or slaves. In ancient Rome, even many doctors and accountants were slaves. The liberal arts, on the other hand, were literally the studies that were considered appropriate for freeborn men. They prepared a young man for public service, such as a career in the Senate.

The liberal arts were intended to help a man figure out the truth for himself and to enable him to express his views persuasively. They were also intended to instill public virtue: the willingness to set his own selfish desires aside when they conflicted with the needs of his community. Thus, the liberal arts were intended to prepare a man to become a good person and a good citizen.

I say "man" and not "person" because the liberal arts were not originally considered appropriate for women and girls, or even for all men. A liberal arts education was generally reserved for the sons of the wealthy and powerful. These privileged few made up the ruling elite, who had supposedly been chosen by God to rule over everyone else. (The word *elite* comes from the French word meaning chosen.) The rest of the population could get, at best, some training in the mechanical arts. Instead of being taught how to use independent judgment, they were given "Noble Lies"—what we now call propaganda—to keep them in line.

Who should get a liberal arts education, and who should get nothing but a mechanical arts education and propaganda? How you answer that question says a lot about how deeply you are committed to democracy.

If you really want to have government of, by, and for the people, you will want everyone to have a liberal arts education. On the other hand, if you want to preserve the privileges of a ruling elite, then you provide a liberal arts education only to the sons (and maybe now the daughters) of the elite, with maybe a few extra spaces open to strivers from the middle class. Of course, you would also need to provide enough education to the children of the middle class so that they could go on to serve as middle management in the corporations and other institutions controlled by the truly powerful. These white-collar workers could then be expected to use their education to cling to their privileged position within the status quo, not to serve the general population by pursuing radical reform.

Support for the liberal arts both reflects a society's existing political system and affects its political future. The liberal arts were important in ancient Athens, a society in which all adult male citizens were expected to serve in juries and in the Demos, which was an assembly where all matters of interest to the community were discussed. The liberal arts were also highly regarded in Rome, especially during the period of the Roman Republic, when the government was run by officials elected by the people. The liberal arts fell out of favor in Europe during the Dark Ages, when the people were ruled by crowned heads instead of being governed by officials whom the people elected. Fortunately, the ancient pagan writings on the liberal arts were preserved in the Muslim world, where independent scientific and philosophical inquiry were still widely accepted and supported.

Interest in the liberal arts began to revive in Europe during the High Middle Ages, when a growing and increasingly urbanized population demanded a more highly educated, professional clergy. During that period, several monastic and cathedral schools developed into the first true universities. The universities at that time were largely pre-professional schools, training young men for careers as theologians, lawyers, and doctors. Like training in the mechanical arts, this early university training was intended to teach students the skills they would need on the job. However, the training for the learned professions is a lot different from the training that one needs to become a butcher, a baker, or a candlestick-maker. To prepare students to participate in theological, legal, or scientific debates, the medieval universities revived the liberal arts.

The ancient liberal arts curriculum was divided into seven subjects that were sorted into two groups. The first group was called the trivium (three courses) because it consisted of the three arts of discourse: grammar, logic, and rhetoric. The other four subjects (the quadrivium) were the arts of number: mathematics, geometry, music, and astronomy.

The trivium consisted of subjects that any educated person was expected to have mastered. If something was trivial, there was no need to explain it to an educated person. Mathematicians still use the word *trivial* in that sense. However, the overwhelming tide of English usage has swept the word in a different direction. It is now generally used to mean unimportant facts, such as the answers in the game Trivial Pursuit.

I wrote this book because I think that grammar, logic, and rhetoric are not trivial in the modern sense. I believe that if we wish to have anything remotely resembling freedom and democracy, then we all need to have solid basic skills in those disciplines by the time we leave public school. These are the disciplines we need in order to discuss important issues and reach consensus like civilized adults, instead of just screeching at each other like monkeys or hurling abuse at each other like schoolyard bullies.

Lately, political discourse in the United States seems to have been getting worse and worse. Part of the problem is that many of us were taught in childhood that it is impolite to talk about religion or politics. Many of us were also taught that it is impolite to talk about money and sex. Unfortunately, this means that people end up believing that it is impolite to talk about what they think is true, about what they think is good, and about what they want out of life. If polite people refuse to talk about those things, then impolite people will dominate those discussions. Yet democracy is based on the idea of people having discussions and reaching consensus about important topics. If you cannot have serious, productive conversations about important topics, you cannot have a democracy. The liberal arts are important for democracy because they help people develop the skills that they need in order to have meaningful conversations about important topics.

What irks me about the political speech I hear and the political writing I see is that so much of it is sophomoric. Sophomoric means "conceited and overconfident of knowledge but poorly informed and immature." The word implies that the person isn't necessarily stupid but has an incomplete education. I hear uneducated people make sophomoric remarks on talk radio, but I have also read many sophomoric remarks in my university alumni magazine. So the problem isn't necessarily a lack of schooling. It's a lack of training in the specific skills that one needs to be wise and reasonable.

A surprisingly large number of the Founding Fathers had a liberal arts education. In those days, a liberal arts education was called a classical education because it was based on ancient Greek and Latin language and literature. Their education inspired them to break free of a monarchy and found a republic modeled on that of Rome before the Caesars. A classical education was a luxury that only gentlemen could afford, partly because the books were expensive and partly because that kind of study took time that could be spent learning something more immediately practical. Why learn Latin, which nobody speaks anymore? Why not learn French or Spanish instead? Why not learn accounting or engineering, which can help you make a good living?

Education in the United States has undergone profound changes since the Revolutionary War days. Back then, a Harvard man was expected to be able to translate portions of the Bible from the original Hebrew or Greek into Latin. Today, nobody aside from a few classics majors and divinity students can do that. Back then, Benjamin Franklin's lightning rod represented the cutting edge of high technology. Since then, science has advanced at breathtaking speed. There's simply so much more to learn these days. So I'm not going to argue that everyone needs to study Greek or Latin. Nor do I particularly care whether people can read Aristotle in Greek, as long as they learn to think logically and make reasonable arguments.

There are two possible explanations for why the liberal arts are not central to the education of everyone in a democracy. Either the liberal arts have been lost in the shuffle or they have been deliberately neglected. With so many pressing issues being addressed in education, it's easy for some things to get lost in the shuffle. However, it's clear that the liberal arts have often been deliberately suppressed. As manufacturing started to shift from households and small workshops to factories, the factory owners started to think of public schools as a way to transform the children of independent-minded farmers into obedient mill hands. Instead of using public education to promote equality and democracy, many educational reformers in the 19th century wanted to make the United States more like Prussia: undemocratic, regimented, anti-intellectual, and militaristic.

One of the big advocates of Prussian-style education for children in the United States was Horace Mann. He was also a strong advocate of what has been called the "whole-word" or "look-and-say" method of teaching children to read. Instead of learning to sound out a word letter by letter, children were expected to learn to recognize entire words, as if we used pictograms instead of a phonetic alphabet to write English. The look-and-say method is a ridiculous way to teach someone to read English. No meaningful research has ever supported it, and real-world experience, particularly in California, suggests that its results have been disastrous. Nevertheless, the look-and-say method is still widely used in public schools throughout the country, especially in the poor neighborhoods. It is now called balanced literacy. Why has this problem been allowed to persist? Perhaps it's because it was harming the children of the working class in public school while having no effect on the wealthy children, whose parents can afford private tutoring to undo the damage caused by bad teaching methods.

The quality of public education eroded still further in the mid 20th century, when a powerful faction of English teachers decided that it was bad to teach grammar in grammar school. The reasons that were given for refusing to teach grammar were as ridiculous as the reasons that had been given for not teaching children to sound out the letters when they are learning to read. The results were similarly dismal. Yet this problem has been allowed to persist for decades. Why? Again, I suspect that it's because it was harming working-class children. Savvy middle-class people could put their children in a private school or hire a tutor. Of course, the elite were still sending their children to prep school, where they learned French or even Latin grammar.

I have long been painfully aware that even many educated people in the United States have a poor grasp of English grammar. As a medical editor, I've had to spend countless hours correcting the grammar of educated people, including medical doctors. When most people think about grammatical errors, they worry about things like double negatives (as in Mick Jagger complaining that he can't get no satisfaction) or nonstandard conjugations of verbs (as in people saying "I seen" instead of "I saw"). Personally, I couldn't care less about such things, which often are simply differences in dialect. I'm far more worried about problems that affect meaning.

People who don't understand the mechanics of how English sentences are put together have trouble understanding long, complicated sentences. They struggle when they try to learn a foreign language. They have trouble understanding logical arguments. They find it hard to express any subtle or complicated idea in plain English. Often, their writing is so bad that I wonder what goes on in their minds. I'm not just talking about high school dropouts. I have seen atrocious writing coming from people who have been through college and even professional school.

When I have had to train other editors and writers, I found that many of them had never learned some basic grammatical principles that I learned in seventh grade, even though some of those poor souls had been English majors. I was able to help them improve their writing skills dramatically within a matter of days, just by having them review the parts of speech and teaching them some of the basic rules of English syntax. Eventually, I started explaining those rules in a column on grammar for the *American Medical Writers Association Journal*.

The best time to teach grammar is during childhood. Children learn languages and language-related skills much more easily than adults do. If children are deprived of the opportunity to study grammar in childhood, they may suffer the consequences for the rest of their lives. This seems to me to be a grave injustice and a threat to democracy.

The study of logic also has important political implications. In a dictatorship, the people are supposed to believe whatever the dictator tells them. They are not supposed to try to figure out whether the Party Line makes sense and is supported by the available evidence. In other words, they are not supposed to use logic.

Even in societies that are not dictatorships, some people are attracted to antidemocratic political movements. Sociologists have found that these authoritarian followers tend to be less logical in their thinking than the average person. Authoritarian followers tend to believe that something is true because some authority figure said it and to believe that something is good because some authority figure endorses it. If a demagogue can persuade enough authoritarian followers to fall into line, their entire society can descend into a totalitarian nightmare.

Logic is part of the scientific method. Besides making observations, scientists must think logically about what they observe. Industry and the military need people who can think that way, because scientists and engineers come up with new inventions and solve various kinds of technical problems. However, scientists and other people who are trained in logic sometimes apply their logical minds in ways that are inconvenient to the leaders of their society.

During the Cold War, we in the United States would hear a lot about the dissident scientists in the Soviet Union. However, the West had its fair share of dissident scientists. For some reason, we Americans heard surprisingly little about them. In 1945, a group of scientists, engineers, and other experts who had worked on the Manhattan Project established the *Bulletin of the Atomic Scientists*, to warn the public that the atomic bomb that they had just invented posed a threat to the survival of humanity. Since then, the *Bulletin of the Atomic Scientists* has attempted to warn the public about other dangers, such as climate change. However, its circulation was always small—only about 15,000. It's now getting a wider reach through the Internet. However, if the general public is unintellectual and has a poor science education, warnings from dissident scientists will be ignored.

The third branch of the trivium is rhetoric, which is the art of persuasive speech and writing. It's the most clearly political of the disciplines in the trivium. The ancient Greeks and Romans who wrote the basic texts on the subject viewed it as a political art that was necessary for the proper functioning of their society.

When modern people think of the art of persuasion, they may think of advertising and public relations. Those are the approaches used by corporations and wealthy people. However, ordinary people can also use speech and writing to persuade other people, occasionally using their skills to build powerful grassroots democratic movements. When I tried to think of examples of people who had done that, three names sprang immediately into my mind: Mohandas K. Gandhi, the Rev. Dr. Martin Luther King, Jr., and El-Hajj Malik El-Shabazz (Malcolm X). To my horror, I realized that all three men were eventually assassinated. Maybe it really is no accident that the trivium isn't widely taught to the children of the oppressed!

Many people have complained about problems in our public education system in the United States. However, I think that many of them are proposing a cure that's far worse than the disease: to destroy public education in favor of state-subsidized but church-run and/or racially segregated private schooling. I think it would be far better to preserve and strengthen free public education, which I consider the bedrock of democracy. In addition to providing better and more evenly shared funding for public schools, I think we need to rethink how we decide what gets taught, and how it gets taught. At present, those decisions are made largely at the state or local level, often by people who have a limited education and an anti-intellectual political agenda. The people who make curriculum decisions can do great harm, and yet they can never be sued for malpractice.

The liberal arts were largely invented about 2400 years ago for preparing young men to participate in Athenian democracy. Some of the texts that were written back then have been used until modern times to help prepare young men to participate in a democratic or republican form of government. Some of the principles that were taught back then would be useful in solving our current problems.

From a 21st-century perspective, the obvious flaw in Athenian democracy is the fact that only the male citizens got to participate. Women and slaves were systematically excluded. Over the past few hundred years, there has been a general international trend toward extending voting rights and other civil and human rights to everyone, not just to the nobility or to native-born male property owners who were members of an established church. In that context, we need to think about how to extend the kind of education that is appropriate to freeborn people (i.e., the liberal arts) to everyone in society.

The ancients felt that the purpose of a liberal arts education was to cultivate wisdom and virtue. Today, educators talk about developing higher-order thinking skills and character, but they mean exactly the same thing. In educational circles today, the usual debate is about how much time to take away from teaching basic skills to teach higher-order thinking skills. That debate makes no sense to me. You cannot exercise higher-order thinking skills unless you have some basic facts to think about. How could you collect those facts and express your ideas about them if you cannot read and write? Wouldn't it make more sense to help children build their basic skills as efficiently as possible, so that they can then use those skills to do something interesting and meaningful?

I hope that this book will encourage people to go to the library or the Internet and find some resources so that they can brush up their own skills in grammar, logic, and rhetoric. This kind of study will help them develop wisdom and improve their ability to persuade other people. I hope that they then use those skills to work toward improving the curriculum at their own local public schools, and then to join a larger movement to improve public education and political discourse in the United States as a whole.

CHAPTER 11

Learning to Read

In ancient Rome, the liberal arts were the studies that were considered appropriate for free people. In contrast, slaves were taught only the mechanical arts and the servile arts. Even today, debates about education are really debates about freedom and equality. If you want to live in a free and democratic society, then you will want every child to study the liberal arts. But if you want to make sure that slaves stay enslaved and that poor people stay poor, you will allow them to learn only the servile arts and the mechanical arts. The easiest way to keep an unequal society unequal is to make sure that only a privileged few get a liberal arts education.

The easiest way to prevent people from studying the liberal arts is to keep them from learning to read. A person who cannot read cannot study the liberal arts. There are two basic ways to keep people from learning to read. One is to keep them from going to school. The other is to make the schools so ineffective that children could spend years in school without learning to read.

If you prevent children from going to school, their parents quickly figure out that you are their enemy. They might even fight you. At the very least, they'll end up marching in the streets, singing "We shall overcome." If, on the other hand, you work behind the scenes to undermine the quality of their schools, the people might end up blaming themselves, their children, or their children's teachers for the children's failure to learn. A wealthy person could even end up being praised for donating to educational charities, even as those charities work behind the scenes to undermine public education.

The history of the United States provides clear examples of three basic kinds of educational policy. Colonial Massachusetts created universal free public education because its leaders wanted everyone to learn to read well enough to understand the Bible. In contrast, legislatures in many of the Southern states before the Civil War made it illegal to teach any black person to read or write at all. With the rise of industrialization, some members of the wealthy elite used their philanthropy to gain influence over the teachers' colleges. The teachers' colleges then trained teachers to use ineffective teaching methods. In 1900, if someone couldn't read, it was usually because he or she had never been to school. Today, millions of Americans are functionally illiterate even though they have spent as many as 13 years in public school.

When the Massachusetts Bay Colony was first chartered in the 1620s, it was supposed to be just a trading company. However, some of its shareholders were members of the Puritan reform movement within the Church of England. These Puritans realized that they could turn their trading post into a refuge where Puritans could escape religious oppression. They believed that in Massachusetts, Puritans could build a community that would provide an example of godliness—a City on a Hill—for the rest of the world to follow.

The shareholders in the Massachusetts Bay Company believed that their City on a Hill could fulfill its religious mission only if its citizens could read the Bible and understand Calvinist theology. They also believed that their colony could survive and prosper only if its citizens worked together in harmony. To promote this harmony, the shareholders decided that the colony would have a democratic system of government.

To make sure that everyone could read the Bible, the colony's General Court passed laws that promoted universal education. A law passed in 1642 required all parents to make sure that their children learned to read. A law passed in 1647 required any town with a population of at least 50 families to hire a teacher at the town's expense. Towns with a population of at least 100 families also had to hire a schoolmaster to prepare the more promising boys to go to Harvard College, where they would be trained for the ministry.

Although Massachusetts passed laws requiring that all children be taught to read, many of the Southern states before the Civil War made it illegal to teach any black people to read. The reason was quite simple. Black people who could read and write could (and often did) use those skills for their own purposes. They could forge passes or even organize slave rebellions. Although the ability to read and write could make an individual slave more productive as a worker, the existence of literate black people, enslaved or free, posed a threat to the entire slave system and even to the lives of the slaveholders.

Even after slavery was abolished, the wealthy landowners and the emerging industrialists in the South still wanted to keep black people "in their place." The purpose of depriving black people of political and social rights was clear. It kept wages low and profits high, and it often let the exploiters and their enforcers get away with murder. Throughout much of the South and even in many places in the North, black children were sent to inferior, segregated schools. Many of the schools for black children in rural areas were in session only when there wasn't any field work to be done. As a result, black children were systematically deprived of the kinds of educational opportunities that were routinely provided to the white children in their communities.

In much of the South, literacy tests were used to keep black people from registering to vote, which meant that black people couldn't elect someone who would improve their children's schools. The fact that blacks weren't registered to vote also meant that they couldn't serve on juries, which meant that trials involving black plaintiffs or black defendants were heard by all-white juries. If you have any doubt that this oppression was motivated by economics, consider this: the civil rights movement was allowed to gain traction only after Southern plantation owners started to use machines instead of human beings to pick cotton.

The US Constitution's Fourteenth Amendment, which was ratified in 1868, declares that no state shall deny to any person in its jurisdiction the equal protection of the law. Yet it took almost 90 years for the Supreme Court to decide that this Amendment meant that segregation in public schools was unconstitutional. Even after the Supreme Court decided in 1954 that school districts should stop sorting children by race, segregation persisted, especially in the North. Because of problems such as job and housing discrimination, black and white children tend to live in separate neighborhoods and go to different schools. This de facto racial segregation is a serious and persistent problem in public schools in the United States.

To see how badly this problem of separate and unequal schooling has infected public education, even in the North, read Jonathan Kozol's classic book *Death at an Early Age: The Destruction of the Hearts and Minds of Negro Children in the Boston Public Schools*, which was published in 1967. What's especially shameful is that the horrors he described in the book were happening in Boston, whose founders had believed in universal free public education and whose citizens had once played such a prominent role in the movement for the abolition of slavery.

In 1991, Kozol wrote *Savage Inequalities: Children in America's Schools*, which showed how little the situation had improved in the intervening years. Racial segregation and unequal educational opportunities were still common in the United States. Kozol noted that the schools of Camden, New Jersey, had a budget of only $3000 per child per year. Meanwhile, school districts only a few minutes away by car had budgets of $8000 or even $14,000 per child per year.

The question of who gets to go to school where, and how the schools are to be funded, is still a hot political issue. Another question, one that cuts across race and class lines, is the question of how the children are to be taught. The most hotly debated issue is how children should be taught to read, since reading is the skill that children must learn before they learn nearly anything else. The perennial debate over how to teach children to read has been called the Reading Wars. The opening shot was fired in the 1840s, and the wars continue to this day.

For the past 3500 years, children who spoke languages that are written with an alphabet (instead of with characters that stand for whole words) have been taught to read by learning the sounds associated with each letter of the alphabet. The children are then taught how to blend those letter sounds into syllables. The children could then use that knowledge to read any word they see, just by sounding out the letters. Children could also use that knowledge to figure out how to spell any word that they know.

In many languages, the spelling is so simple and predictable that it takes only about three months for a child who can speak that language to learn to read and write. However, it takes about two and a half years for a young English speaker to learn to read English fluently. That's because each vowel in English can be pronounced several different ways, and because English has many irregular spellings. English also has many loan words from foreign languages. Thus, it's no wonder that spelling bees are held only in English.

Despite the irregularity of English spelling, it is far, far easier for an English-speaking person to learn to read English than it is for someone in China to learn to read Chinese. Instead of using letters that stand for sounds, Chinese uses complicated characters that stand for words. Chinese people are considered literate if they can recognize 2,000 Chinese characters. A highly literate Chinese person may know 20,000 characters. Yet an English-speaking third-grader who knows how to use the rules of phonics can easily read and write tens of thousands of English words.

It's hard enough for Chinese speakers to learn to read Chinese characters, but it would be far harder for an English speaker to learn to read English words as if they were Chinese characters. That's because Chinese characters were originally based on meaningful drawings. In contrast, the shapes of English words are not meaningful or interesting. Furthermore, the shape of an English word can change dramatically because of changes in case and typeface. Consider the word *great*, which looks radically different in different typefaces:

Great *great*
GREAT ***Great***
great great
great 𝔊reat

A child who has been taught to recognize the word as a shape might have no clue that all of those different shapes represent the same word. In contrast, a child who has been taught to recognize letters and to sound out words can easily adapt to different typefaces and scripts.

Many of the children who were initially taught to memorize words as shapes eventually figure out how to break the phonetic code. They may notice that various letters or letter combinations are predictably associated with particular sounds. From then on, they go on to sound out the words, just as if they had been taught to do so from the beginning.

Unfortunately, some children don't realize that they're supposed to analyze the sounds of the words, or they may have trouble doing it. Those children might not notice that letters make up a code that represents sounds. Thus, those children don't break the code on their own. They end up learning only a few hundred words per year, which means that they will end up functionally illiterate. This fact explains why so many millions of native English speakers in the United States remain functionally illiterate despite having spent so many years in school.

In 1998, the National Academy of Sciences published a report titled *Preventing Reading Difficulties in Young Children*. Its main conclusion was that "Adequate progress in learning to read English (or any alphabetic language) beyond the initial level depends on having a working understanding of how sounds are represented alphabetically." The authors went on to explain, "There are three potential stumbling blocks that are known to throw children off course on the journey to skilled reading. The first obstacle, which arises at the outset of reading acquisition, is difficulty in understanding and using the alphabetic principle—the idea that written spellings systematically represent spoken words."

Nevertheless, many educators over the years have argued that children *shouldn't* be taught the alphabetic principle. In 1844, Horace Mann, who was First Secretary of the Massachusetts Board of Education, argued, "No thorough reform will ever be effected in our schools until this practice [of beginning with the alphabet] is abolished."

Why did Mann come to such a bizarre conclusion? Mann had never taught primary school and thus had never taught anybody to read. Furthermore, he evidently misunderstood some of the strategies and tactics that had been used successfully for 200 years to teach children in New England to read English. After all, the 1840 census showed that only 1.1% of the Massachusetts residents over 20 years of age were illiterate.

In his *Seventh Annual Report to the Massachusetts Board of Education*, published in 1844, Mann said that German and Dutch children are not taught the names of the letters of the alphabet but are taught the sounds of the letters. Then the children are taught to sound out the words letter by letter. Mann claimed that this method, called phonics, would not work in English because English vowels can have too many different sounds. Thus, he thought that children should be taught words first, then letters. Mann got this idea from Thomas Gallaudet, who was using what are now called "sight words" to teach deaf-mute children to read.

It's hard to believe that Mann thought that phonics wouldn't work. Phonics was the method that had enabled Massachusetts to achieve nearly 99% literacy. *The New England Primer* had started out by teaching children the sounds of the letters and then included a *syllabary*, which showed the children how to combine letters into syllables. After the Revolutionary War, Noah Webster's blue-backed speller used the same approach. It became a bestseller, second only to the Bible.

The Association of Boston Schoolmasters responded politely but firmly to Horace Mann's theory: "We love the secretary but we hate his theories. They stand in the way of substantial education. It is impossible for a sound mind not to hate them."[1] They explained,

> Education is a great concern; it has often been tampered with by vain theorists; it has suffered from the stupid folly and the delusive wisdom of its treacherous friends; and we hardly know which have injured it most. Our conviction is that it has much more to hope from the collected wisdom and common prudence of the community than from the suggestions of the individual. Locke injured it by his theories, and so did Rousseau, and so did Milton. All their plans were too splendid to be true. It is to be advanced by conceptions, neither soaring above the clouds, nor groveling on the earth—but by those plain, gradual, productive, common sense improvements, which use may encourage and experience suggest. We are in favor of advancement, provided it be towards usefulness.

The Boston schoolmasters were right. Mann's method did not work nearly as well as the traditional method. The matter should have been settled right then and there. Unfortunately, Mann had the last word. He had enormous influence on who got to teach at the normal schools that were being established to train teachers. Thus, the whole-word method never really died. It was like embers that continue to smolder unnoticed, just waiting for the opportunity to burst into flame.

To understand why Horace Mann was so influential and how he used his influence, it's important to understand the politics of his day. The 1830s were a time of social reform movements in the United States, and particularly in Massachusetts. A temperance movement to fight alcoholism sprang up, as did a movement for the abolition of slavery. During the 1830s, Massachusetts also undertook a major reform of its educational system, largely because the Congregational church was disestablished in 1833.

An established church is a church that has some official status with the government. The established church might not run the government (as in a theocracy), and the government might not run the established church. Nevertheless, the established church typically gets financial support from the government, and the established church and its members have special privileges. For example, one might have to belong to the established church to vote or go to school or hold public office, or the established church might run or staff the schools.

In Massachusetts, the Congregational church was the established church. In the early days, each town in Massachusetts was organized around a Congregational church. Each Congregational congregation was self-governing, and it had the power to hire and fire its minister. Although the Congregationalist churches weren't bound to any particular articles of faith by any civil authority, they tended to espouse an orthodox Calvinist theology. This theology was expressed in the *New England Primer*, which was widely used for teaching children to read.

Although the Massachusetts Bay Colony was originally founded as a Puritan religious community, the power of the established church eroded over the years. With the growth of other Protestant denominations in New England, especially during the Second Great Awakening, came pressure to disestablish the Congregational Church in Massachusetts. Since the Congregational churches had served as the religious wing of local governments, this meant that there was an opportunity to break the Calvinist monopoly on public schooling and to replace it with a nonsectarian Protestantism. Thus, it isn't surprising that many of Horace Mann's key supporters were Unitarian or Episcopalian.

Horace Mann advocated widespread reforms within the educational system of Massachusetts. Mann persuaded the business community in Massachusetts that spending more public money on schools would be a good investment. He persuaded the taxpayers of Massachusetts to fund more and better schools, with better-trained teachers and a wider curriculum, and to enable children to stay in school until age 16. The kind of school that Mann advocated was called a common school because it was nonsectarian and open to children of all classes and religions. In addition, Mann advocated the establishment of normal schools, which were schools to train the people who would go on to teach in the common schools. Mann also tried to ban the use of corporal punishment in the schools. As you can see, many of the reforms that Mann advocated were good and probably were badly needed at the time. Yet some of the reforms that he advocated were downright disturbing.

In 1843, Mann went to Europe to visit schools, particularly in Prussia, and he advocated that Massachusetts adopt the Prussian model of education. In retrospect, it's shocking that someone would argue that a highly literate and remarkably democratic society like the Commonwealth of Massachusetts should remake its educational system to be more like Prussia's.

The Prussian educational system was part of a system of social reforms that were undertaken in response to Prussia's humiliating defeat by Napoleon's forces at the Battle of Jena-Auerstedt in 1806. These reforms transformed Prussia from a feudal society into a modern state. The purpose of the Prussian educational system was to train young men for the military and the bureaucracy and to instill in the general population unquestioning obedience to the King. As Johann Gottlieb Fichte explained, "The schools must fashion the person, and fashion him in such a way that he simply cannot will otherwise than what you wish him to will." In other words, the purpose of Prussian education was to eradicate free will by eradicating freedom of thought—the exact opposite of the purpose of the liberal arts. The goals of Prussian education would have been deeply offensive to the average New Englander.

A Prussian-style education not only suppressed independence of mind, it taught children to submit to authority figures and adhere to an institutional schedule. It thus would presumably turn them into docile and compliant factory workers. This aspect of the Prussian educational system had particular appeal to the owners of the growing textile industry in Massachusetts.

When the textile factories in Lowell, Massachusetts, first opened, many people believed that the industrial revolution would be kinder, gentler, and more civilized in New England than it had been in Britain and France. Most of the employees at Lowell were girls and young women, and the "Lowell girls" were expected to go to church and have proper morals. Although these girls and women worked an average of 73 hours per week, they were given opportunities to attend concerts and lectures. In 1840, a local Universalist minister even organized a monthly magazine written by and for the Lowell girls. Yet the Lowell girls used their writing and speaking skills for their own purposes, such as organizing strikes for higher pay and better working conditions.

In 1845, some female textile workers from Lowell organized the Lowell Female Labor Reform Association, which sent petitions signed by thousands of textile workers to the Massachusetts legislature to demand a 10-hour workday. This movement even spread into neighboring New Hampshire. In this context, Horace Mann's call for a system of education that would turn the children of the independent-minded New England farmers into unthinking robots found a warm reception among the mill owners.

Although many of the reforms that Mann advocated were beneficial and badly needed, others posed a serious threat to literacy and even to democracy. Unfortunately, the people whose children would be affected didn't always get a chance to discuss these policies in public forums, in the democratic New England tradition. Instead, many of the policies were spread by indoctrinating the aspiring teachers in the normal schools.

The Boston schoolmasters were right and Mann was wrong about the value of phonics instruction in English. That fact was clear enough in the 1840s. It became increasingly obvious as the scientific evidence piled up in later years. The whole-word approach to teaching reading was not only less effective than phonics but actually harmful.

It seems odd that a system of reading instruction that was discarded as worthless in the 1840s would become the dominant method of teaching reading in the 20th century. What's even odder is that this method of teaching reading would persist despite the rise of the social sciences, which documented how harmful that method is.

Study after study showed that the whole-word method is ineffective and harmful, and that intensive phonics is the only reasonable approach for teaching children to read English. Unfortunately, decisions about educational policy are driven more by political concerns than by scientific understanding or concern for children. I'll explain in Chapter 20 the reasons why phonics was abandoned in favor of whole-word reading instruction. In Chapter 3, however, I'll start to explain what the trivium is and why it's important.

Reference

1. *Penitential Tears; or, A Cry From the Dust, by "The Thirty-one," Prostrated and Pulverized by the Hand of Horace Mann, Secretary, &c.* Boston, MA: C Stimpson, 1845.

PART II: *The Trivium*

The traditional liberal arts curriculum was broken down into seven subjects. The three verbal arts (grammar, logic, and rhetoric) were called the trivium. Those three subjects have to be introduced in that order.

Grammar is the study of how to combine and alter words to make meaningful sentences. You need to understand some grammatical principles in order to study logic, which deals with how to put those sentences together into arguments. The study of logic enables you to base your opinions on facts and to use logical arguments to persuade other people.

Rhetoric is the art of persuasion. Logic (*logos*) is one of the three means of persuasion. The other two are character (*ethos*) and emotions (*pathos*). People who have studied logic and rhetoric are better able to persuade others. Perhaps more importantly, they are more likely to demand logical arguments and less likely to be swept away by a charismatic leader who plays on their emotions. That's why the liberal arts have always been valued in societies with a democratic or republican form of government and suppressed by tyrannical governments. It's also why the liberal arts have traditionally been taught to children who are expected to grow up to be somebody and withheld from those who are expected to be nobody.

CHAPTER III

Grammar, Freedom, and Humanity

T he classical liberal arts curriculum began with the trivium, which consisted of the three verbal arts: grammar, logic, and rhetoric. The ancient Romans called the these disciplines the liberal arts because they considered those studies to be appropriate for free people, as opposed to slaves.

What does it mean to be free, and what does it mean to be a slave? Here's how I look at it: To be free means to be treated as a human being, and to be a slave means to be treated like an animal. Animals can be bought and sold and literally cannot speak for themselves. For the first fourscore and nine years of US history, men, women, and children could be sold at auction, just like horses or cattle. In many places in the United States, state and federal government officials offered a bounty for killing Indians, just as they offered bounties for killing undesired animals, such as wolves. In other words, slaves were treated as if they were domestic animals, and Indians were treated as if they were wild animals.

As anyone who has studied the Reconstruction era of US history can tell you, freedom means more than the abolition of chattel slavery. The 13th Amendment's abolition of slavery was an important milestone on the road to full human rights for everyone in the United States. We still haven't arrived at that destination. The 13th Amendment merely outlawed one of the ways in which human beings were being treated like animals. It didn't ensure that everyone would be treated as fully human.

The study of the liberal arts promotes freedom because it enhances some uniquely human abilities. In fact, the ability to understand grammar is a sharp, bright line that divides *Homo sapiens*, or modern humans, from all other living species. The liberal arts are the studies that enhance these natural, uniquely human abilities. That's why children who are expected to grow up to be *somebody* have traditionally been schooled in the verbal arts, while those children who are expected to be *nobody* have not.

Although the ability to grasp grammatical concepts is natural and uniquely human, the study of these concepts is artificial. Such studies are a product of civilization. Many modern educators ignore this fact. They expect that children will develop high levels of verbal arts spontaneously, without direct instruction. Thus, they have fought against deliberate instruction in the verbal arts. In short, they are opposed to civility itself. The word *civility* originally meant training in the humanities. Merriam-Webster's Web site defines *civilization* specifically as the stage of cultural development at which writing and the keeping of written records is attained.

Children normally acquire their native language simply by hearing it being spoken around and to them. Deaf children and the hearing children of deaf parents automatically pick up sign language in a similar way. This ability to acquire a language is uniquely human. When people tried rearing young chimpanzees as if they were human children, the chimpanzees never learned to talk. Even when researchers went to great lengths to try to teach some sort of sign language to chimpanzees and gorillas, none of the apes ever grasped the basic grammatical concepts that are easy for nearly any human child to understand.

Back in the 1960s and 1970s, several groups of researchers tried various approaches for teaching chimpanzees and gorillas to use language. It would have been physically impossible for the apes to speak English; an ape's voice box simply cannot make many of the sounds in the English language. (The ability of the human voice box to make so many different sounds comes at a heavy price. We are far more likely than chimpanzees or gorillas to choke to death.) So instead of trying to teach apes to speak English, some of the researchers tried to teach them American Sign Language. Other researchers tried to teach apes to manipulate tokens or use a keyboard with various kinds of symbols. Although the researchers got the apes to make certain kinds of gestures or to press certain keys on a keyboard to get certain kinds of rewards, no ape has ever been able to use anything remotely like human grammar.

When I say that apes can't use grammar, I don't mean that apes say "he don't" instead of "he doesn't." I mean that the apes could never figure out a way to show which noun represents the subject of a verb and which represents the direct object and so on. Apes have never been able to express who did what to whom, or when something happened, or how long it took. Apes have never been able to clarify whether they were asking for something to happen, asking whether it already happened, or merely saying that it did happen. Apes can't explain that they meant that something would have happened if something else had not happened. To express ideas like that, one needs grammar.

American Sign Language is a real language because it allows a human being to express such ideas. ASL has its own grammar, which is different from English grammar. Anyone who can speak more than one language knows that the rules for putting together a sentence are different in different languages. One of the reasons for learning the grammar of your native language is to make it easier to learn additional languages. For example, if you already understand the concept of grammatical case, you'll have a much easier time learning German or Latin.

Although people have taught chimpanzees and gorillas to mimic some signs that came from American Sign Language, the apes didn't actually succeed in using that language. For example, if I were to befriend Tarzan's chimpanzee friend Cheeta* and teach him the signs for "Laurie," "Cheeta," and "banana," I can expect him to generate strings of signs such as this:

---

* Both Tarzan and Cheeta are fictional characters. So is Jane. No actual ape-men, apes, or love-interests were inconvenienced in any way in the production of this chapter.

Laurie banana Laurie banana Cheeta Laurie give.

If Cheeta were to do that, I'd guess that Cheeta wanted me to give him a banana. Of course, it's a safe bet that Cheeta would always be pleased to receive a banana. If a dog paws at her feed bowl, I'm pretty sure that she would like to be fed, but dogs always seem to be thrilled whenever food goes into the bowl. Even if a dog figures out that pawing at the bowl prompts a human being to put food in the bowl, it doesn't mean that the dog is using language.

Dogs can't use nouns and verbs. A noun is a word that expresses a person, place, thing, or idea. A verb is a word that expresses action or a state of being. The only part of speech dogs seem to use is interjections. Gary Larson once drew a *Far Side* cartoon in which a scientist had invented a dog-to-English translator. It revealed that a dog's barks, when translated into English, meant "Hey! Hey! Hey! Hey! Hey!"

Even if Cheeta the chimpanzee could make the signs for "Laurie," "banana," and "give," he'd still have no way of expressing the idea "Cheeta gave Laurie two bananas yesterday" or "Cheeta usually gives Laurie two bananas every morning." He could never use the signs to express the idea "I will gladly give you two bananas tomorrow if you give me one banana today." In other words, he can't express the tense and aspect of a verb or the mood of a verb.

Grammatical tense expresses whether the verb refers to an action (or state of being) in the past, present, or future. Grammatical aspect expresses other features of timing, such as whether the verb refers to a one-time event, to something that happens repeatedly or habitually, or to something that continues up to a certain point: "I had been giving him bananas until I ran out of money."

The mood of a verb reflects the speaker's attitude toward the verb. Is the speaker making a statement of fact, issuing a command, asking a question, or making a conditional statement or a statement contrary to fact? Consider the difference between these two sentences: "Give me the banana!" "I would have given you the banana if you had asked nicely." A human being who can speak any natural language, including American Sign Language, can easily express ideas like that. Chimpanzees and gorillas simply cannot express ideas like that, no matter how hard you try to teach them to use signs. I wonder whether apes can even think thoughts like that.

I'm not sure how Cheeta would have dealt with pronouns, but Tarzan certainly had trouble with them. In the movie *Tarzan of the Apes*, when Tarzan first meets Jane, she says, "Thank you for saving me!" and points to herself. Tarzan then points at Jane and says, "Me!" Then there follows a comedy of errors in which Jane tries to explain that when she says "I" or "me" she means Jane, but when Tarzan says those same words, they mean Tarzan. Pronouns have no meaning of their own. They take their meaning from their context.

I wouldn't be surprised if all natural human languages have pronouns, which are words that stand in for a noun. School-age children who are native speakers of English may have trouble figuring out when to say "I" as opposed to "me"; but they rarely if ever have trouble figuring out whether to say "I" as opposed to "you." That's because the "I-me" distinction is a matter of grammatical case, which is never marked in English nouns, whereas the "I-you" distinction is a difference of person, which is of tremendous importance in any language.

Of course, you can go only so far with using just nouns, pronouns, verbs, and interjections. If you want to provide more information about those nouns and verbs, you need to use modifiers. To modify means to change, and grammatical modifiers change the meaning of some other element in the sentence. There are two main kinds of modifiers: adjectives and adverbs. Adjectives modify nouns and pronouns. Adjectives answer such questions as *which one? what kind?* and *how many?* Adverbs are far more versatile. They can modify verbs (including infinitives [e.g., *to go*] and participles [e.g., *going* and *gone*]), adjectives, other adverbs, prepositions, phrases, clauses, or whole sentences. Adverbs pose or answer questions like *how, when, where, why,* or *how often?*

An adjective or adverb is a single word. Sometimes, you can have a string of words that behaves as if it's a single word. A string of words that behaves as a grammatical unit is called a phrase. A prepositional phrase, such as *in the tree*, consists of a preposition (e.g., *in*) and a noun phrase (*the tree*). The preposition links the noun phrase to the rest of the sentence. A prepositional phrase can modify a noun (the <u>chimpanzee</u> *in the tree* is eating bananas) or a verb (the chimpanzee <u>was eating</u> *in the tree*).

A clause is a string of words that includes a subject and a predicate and that makes up part of a compound or complex sentence. A compound sentence contains two or more independent clauses, which are clauses that could stand on their own as sentences. Here's a sentence with three independent clauses: "I came, I saw, and I conquered."

Notice that "I conquered" was connected to the other two clauses with a conjunction, which is the last remaining part of speech in English. Conjunctions can be used to connect words, phrases, clauses, and sentences. The coordinating conjunctions (*and, but, or, nor, for, yet, so*) are used to connect elements that are of equal rank. In contrast, the subordinating conjunctions, such as *if*, are used to connect a subordinate clause to a main clause. "If Cheeta asks nicely, I'll give him the banana." Because of the subordinating conjunction *if*, the first clause can't stand on its own as a sentence. It is therefore a subordinate or dependent clause. "I'll give him the banana" is an independent clause because it can stand alone as a complete sentence. A sentence is considered complex if it contains a subordinate clause and an independent clause. In addition to the coordinating and subordinating conjunctions, there are some conjunctive adverbs that work to connect clauses and sentences. Examples include *however, nevertheless,* and *therefore.*

In this chapter, I've just reviewed all of the eight parts of speech in English and some of the basic grammatical concepts that I think everyone ought to know. In Part VI of this book, I'll explain how to use these concepts to become a better writer. These concepts really aren't that hard to understand, especially for children. Just as learning a foreign language is easier for children than for adults, learning grammatical concepts is much easier during childhood.

Most schoolchildren learn what nouns and verbs are, and that they should use the plural form of a verb with a plural form of a noun, but that's about as far as their formal education in grammar goes. They might never learn how the order of the elements of a sentence can affect meaning. Consider the word "only." It can be an adjective, and adverb, or a conjunction. Putting that one word in a different position within the sentence can dramatically change the meaning of the sentence.

- Only I ate the cake. (No one else had any.)
- I only ate the cake. (I didn't buy or bake it.)
- I ate only the cake. (I didn't eat anything else.)
- I ate the only cake. (There weren't any other cakes.)

When I was in grammar school, I learned how to recognize the eight parts of speech and how to diagram sentences. Those skills, plus the touch typing skills I learned in a ninth grade typing class, have been the most valuable skills I ever learned in school. My skill in typing helped me get summer jobs when I was in college, and today it helps me write much faster. My grammar skills helped me get a job as a medical editor, which led to a career as a medical writer. Unlike most of the people who work as editors, I wasn't an English major. In fact, I never took even a single English class in college. I got advanced placement credit to fulfill my English requirement and took courses in German and Spanish instead.

When I started working as an editor, I was shocked to discover that many highly educated people had failed to learn things that I had learned in seventh grade. I found more than typographical errors and the occasional noun-verb disagreement in the manuscripts I was editing. I found that writers often didn't know the real meaning of the words they used. They used nouns and verbs that didn't work together, such as giving a direct object to an intransitive verb. The verb tenses they used didn't always match the timing of the events and states of being they were describing. They misplaced and dangled their modifiers. They used pronouns but didn't make it clear what nouns the pronouns represented. They were often so careless with their conjunctions and prepositional phrases that their sentences were confusing or nonsensical. Sometimes, I'd find one or more of these problems in nearly every sentence in a manuscript.

Bad writing can be unpleasant to read; but as long as the writing is about some commonplace subject that you already understand thoroughly, you can use your pre-existing knowledge of the subject to figure out what the writer meant. Unfortunately, you're out of luck if you have to learn about a subject from a badly written article or book. It's like trying to grope your way in the dark through an unfamiliar building. To enable readers to understand what an author was trying to say, I often had to edit the manuscripts heavily.

Many of the authors were shocked by how heavily I edited their manuscripts. Sometimes, they wanted to know why I had made certain changes. When I explained the grammatical problems I was trying to solve, they were mystified by terms such as *intransitive verb* or *dangling participle* or *absolute phrase* (I'll explain all these terms in Part VI). Hardly any of them had ever been taught to diagram sentences. It wasn't that they were uneducated people. Most of the authors were medical doctors or veterinarians. The problem was that they'd been deprived of proper grammar instruction.

I found that it was worthwhile to take the time to explain why certain kinds of changes were necessary. Sometimes, after I explained the problem that I was trying to solve, the author would come up with an even better solution. Usually, the author's next manuscript would be much cleaner.

A few years later, after I was put in charge of training editors and proofreaders, I found that the best way to train new employees was to have them spend their first few days on the job reviewing basic grammatical concepts and learning how to diagram a sentence. Then I'd teach them a few practical rules, such as that one should avoid putting a potentially adjectival prepositional phrase directly after a noun unless it is supposed to modify that noun. After I taught people those rules, their writing skills improved dramatically, practically overnight. So when someone tries to tell me that teaching people grammar doesn't improve their writing skills, all I can say is that it does when I'm doing the teaching.

Shortly after I'd started working as an editor, I met a young woman who was teaching English at a prestigious private school run by Quakers. (It always struck me as odd that the plain people ended up running fancy private schools.) Hopeful that I had met a kindred spirit, I asked her if she was teaching her students how to diagram sentences. I was shocked by her response. She pulled herself up to her full height, looked down her nose at me, and said, "We don't teach children to draw sentences, we teach them to write sentences."

Stung by her tone, I said, "I hope you reconsider. As a technical editor, I'm finding that many educated people don't know enough about sentence structure to write clear sentences." I then went on to describe some grammatical problem that I'd been seeing a lot. At that point, the look on her face changed from contempt to fear. It suddenly dawned on me that despite her bachelor's degree from a prestigious university, she didn't understand what I was saying, even though I was explaining something that I'd learned in seventh grade. I realized that she couldn't teach her students much about grammar even if she wanted to, because she'd never learned much about it herself.

Since then, I've realized that there has been, as David Mulroy put it, a war against grammar instruction in schools. A few years ago, I met someone who was teaching English in a public high school. When I asked him whether he teaches his students to diagram sentences, his eyes opened wide and he said, "Absolutely not. If an administrator walked past my classroom and saw even a fragment of a diagram on the chalkboard, I'd be fired."

Even without any formal instruction in grammar, nearly all young children figure out how to use all of the parts of speech in their native language to generate meaningful sentences. Some people have argued that since nearly all children have this natural ability, there's no need to bother with teaching them grammar. But would those same people say that since nearly all children spontaneously learn how to run and jump and throw things, there's no need for athletic coaches? Of course not. Such an argument would be dismissed as idiotic.

Just as coaching is necessary to help athletes develop their athletic skills, formal instruction in grammar and writing is needed to help children develop their verbal skills. Children who have never been taught grammar are likely to have poor reading comprehension, poor skills in logic, poor writing skills, and difficulty in learning a foreign language.

In the mid 1990s, I met a linguistics professor. I asked him why English teachers stopped teaching children to diagram sentences. He said that it was because diagramming the sentence doesn't necessarily clarify its meaning. For example, if you diagrammed the sentence "The pastor married the woman," the diagram wouldn't tell you whether the pastor became the woman's spouse or merely performed her wedding ceremony. I responded, "But that's a stupid reason. The point of the diagram is to show the grammatical relationships within the sentence, not to tell you what the words mean."

He laughed and said, "You asked me *why* teachers have stopped teaching students to diagram sentences. You didn't ask me for a *good* reason not to teach it!" I asked him if there were any good reasons, but he couldn't think of any.

Many people oppose formal instruction in grammar because they think that grammar is boring and that boredom makes children unhappy. Those same people don't think that it's boring for a child to spend hours bouncing a ball and trying to throw it through a metal hoop. Children willingly spend lots of time doing such tasks if the tasks are part of a game. The real question is how teachers and parents can harness children's play drive to help children develop the skills that they will need in adulthood. After all, isn't that the function that play normally serves for the young of any species whose behavior isn't driven purely by instinct?

Many people think that pointing out a child's mistakes will destroy the child's self-esteem and motivation. If that were true, then children would hate video games. Video games relentlessly punish the player for making mistakes, and the game almost always ends in some sort of deadly disaster. Somehow, children manage to enjoy the game despite the inevitable setbacks and defeats. If they are allowed to continue playing the game, they eventually develop high levels of skill. Why can't this same principle be used to help children develop skills that matter?

Some nonprescriptivists claim that grammar lessons are simply a way to impose an arbitrary set of rules on other people, forcing people to learn "the language of the oppressor." Thus, they oppose grammar instruction in principle (even though they themselves use grammatical Standard English). Yet as Andrew Kern explained,

People coming to America and people for whom standard English is not their common idiom need to learn standard English grammar and vocabulary because it gives them access to the entire corpus of writings written in standard English. Those multi-culturalists who argue that these children should not be "compelled" to learn standard English (though for some reason they think it just that they be compelled to attend school) are causing the very thing they claim to oppose: alienation and exclusion. Every country in the world seems to see the practical value of standard English except the US. If I were a white supremacist, I would pour my resources into backing these naive multi-culturalists and preventing minority students from disadvantaged communities from learning standard English. What a simple way to "keep them down."[1]

There's a kernel of truth in what these nonprescriptivists are saying. The ways in which Standard English differs from nonstandard varieties of English are arbitrary, and there's no reason why any variety of English should be considered superior to any other. As I explain in more detail in Chapter 23, I don't think that we should do anything to give anyone the idea that Black English or Appalachian English or Broad Scots is in any way inferior to Standard English. Instead, we should be teaching people how the varieties of English differ, so that people can understand each other better and appreciate a broader range of English literature. We also need to provide training in English as a second dialect to any child whose first language is a nonstandard dialect of English, just as we teach English as a second language to children whose first language was Spanish or Chinese. The point isn't to stamp out Spanish or Chinese but to give children more options in ways to express themselves.

It should have been obvious that the decision to stop teaching grammar in grammar school, like the decision to stop teaching children to sound out the letters of the words when they are learning to read, would have harmful effects. Even those educators who weren't clever enough to predict the harmful effects of those policies should have been able to notice the harmful effects in retrospect. So why didn't the people who were making educational policy notice the problem and take corrective action? Did they want students to fail?

In this context, I think it's important to keep in mind a rule that has been called Heinlein's razor: *Never attribute to malice that which can be adequately explained by stupidity, but don't rule out malice.* People who don't have a science education can easily misunderstand scientific research. They may even have difficulty in learning from their own experience. As a result, they may have trouble in figuring out why things happen. Consequently, they may have a particularly hard time in figuring out what effects a policy is likely to have, or even in noticing what effects the policy has had. In other words, a poor science education can cause even well-meaning people to support harmful policies. On the other hand, people who supported anti-phonics or anti-grammar policies because they knew that those policies would have harmful effects on children should definitely be considered malicious. Perhaps the naïve multiculturalists are getting support from malicious white supremacists. Stranger things have happened.

Giving children a strong grounding in the basic skills in reading and grammar doesn't necessarily make them unhappy or turn them into bigots. However, refusing to help children develop solid basic skills does set them up for frustration and failure in higher education and in adult life. As I'll explain in later chapters, grammar is a fundamental discipline that you need in order to learn other kinds of skills. If you can't figure out the grammatical structure of sentences, you'll have trouble in learning to think logically. If you can't think logically, you'll be easy prey for con men and dishonest politicians.

Reference

1. Kern A. The war against grammar. Quiddity. November 2, 2007. http://quidditycirce.wordpress.com/2007/11/02/the-war-against-grammar

CHAPTER IV

Grammar, Rules, and Personality

Grammar is the study of how words are altered and combined to form meaningful sentences. Every language has its own grammar—its own set of rules. I suspect that many people's feelings about grammar have a lot to do with their feelings about rules in general.

People with an authoritarian follower type of personality like to follow and enforce clear sets of traditional rules. That's why the arguments for grammar instruction often sound politically conservative. In contrast, people with a bohemian type of personality tend to resent rules and distrust the people who make and enforce them. That's why so much of the anti-grammar rhetoric sounds liberal or leftist. In other words, people on both sides of the debate over grammar seem to be motivated by political ideology. However, I think that many people on either side of the debate misunderstand the political significance of grammar lessons.

Bohemians realize that grammatical rules are social conventions and that some social conventions are used for bad purposes. For example, people who speak a nonstandard dialect may be treated unfairly. Bohemians are afraid that teaching grammar to children would reinforce children's biases against people who speak nonstandard English. Nevertheless, a population needs to have some social conventions if any meaningful communication is to take place. The story of the Tower of Babel provides a vivid metaphor of what happens if people have no common language. When God took away the people's ability to understand one another, they had to stop building their tower to heaven. Without at least some social conventions, you can't communicate well enough to achieve any common purpose.

Authoritarian followers do realize that children benefit from learning grammatical principles. However, children often benefit from that sort of education in ways that undermine the power of traditional authorities. That's why student radicals are often such a thorn in the side of authority figures.

When I was a child, my parents sent me to school to learn things and to learn how to do things. My parents believed that schools are supposed to teach children how to read and how to express themselves effectively in writing and in speech. Learning the grammatical rules of a language helps children communicate with other people who speak that language. Learning the rules of Standard English has become particularly important. Mastery of Standard English enables children to communicate with educated people from all over the world.

There has always been a need for people to communicate with people who grew up speaking some other language. The traditional solution to this problem is the development of an international language—a lingua franca or bridge language. After the Alexander the Great's conquests, Greek became the language of commerce and government throughout his empire. Greek remained the international language of scientists and philosophers during the Roman Empire. During the Middle Ages, Latin became the international language of European scholars and scientists. In the late 17th century, the English scientist Isaac Newton wrote his *Philosophiæ Naturalis Principia Mathematica* in Latin. In the mid 19th century, however, the English scientist Charles Darwin wrote his *On the Origin of Species* in English. By the mid 20th century, English was firmly established as the international language of science, aviation, shipping, and many other fields.

Since Standard English has become such an important international language, I think that it's important for children in the United States to learn it. However, I think that it's also important for them to learn other languages and to respect other varieties of English, along with respecting the people who speak them.

For years, I've worked as an editor in medical publishing. That means that I've spent countless hours imposing not only the rules of Standard English but the rules of the American Medical Association's *Manual of Style* on the manuscripts that landed in my inbox. Some of the rules I've had to enforce are arbitrary, such as using American spelling instead of British spelling. For example, I'd have to change "haemoglobin" to "hemoglobin" and "oestrogen" to "estrogen." I've also had to apply consistent rules for how to present numbers and units of measure. For example, I'd have to change "one milligram" to "1 mg." However, the major problems that I dealt with were problems that affected the meaning of the sentences. My most important responsibilities were to make sure that the authors succeeded in saying what they intended to say and to make it as easy as possible for the readers to figure out what the authors meant.

I've worked for a company that published a psychiatry journal. I've also worked for a pharmaceutical company that was doing research on antidepressant and antipsychotic medications. Somewhere along the line, I made a stunning discovery. I realized that my responsibilities, as spelled out in my job description, matched the symptoms of a mental illness that I don't have: obsessive-compulsive personality disorder.

According to the fourth edition of the American Psychiatric Association's *Diagnostic and Statistical Manual*, obsessive-compulsive personality disorder is "a pervasive pattern of preoccupation with orderliness, perfectionism, and mental and interpersonal control, at the expense of flexibility, openness, and efficiency, beginning by early adulthood and present in a variety of contexts." In other words, this diagnosis is a label given to annoying, moralistic, mean-spirited, overly picky control freaks.

Obsessive-compulsive personality disorder (OCPD) is not the same thing as obsessive-compulsive disorder (OCD), even though the name is similar and the symptoms of the two conditions overlap. People with OCD have unwelcome thoughts that they often realize are irrational. They engage in ritualistic behavior, such as excessive hand-washing, to try to relieve the stress caused by these unwelcome thoughts. Mr. Monk from the television show *Monk* provides a sympathetic portrait of someone with a comically exaggerated case of OCD. In contrast, the people with OCPD think that their thoughts and behaviors are correct, and they can become aggressive to the people who don't meet their persnickety standards. Dana Carvey's character The Church Lady from *Saturday Night Live* has a comically exaggerated case of OCPD, especially when she's doing her "superior dance."

People with OCPD might have an urge to correct other people's grammar. However, it's only to satisfy their own need for orderliness and control and to indulge their urge to punish the unworthy. People with OCPD can become aggressive against people who don't meet their high standards.

Personally, I never viewed editing as a way to put other people down. While I'm working on a manuscript, the author is nowhere in sight. It's as if I'm doing a homework assignment from English class. Because most of the material I've edited was written by medical doctors or veterinarians or scientists, I did not feel superior to the authors. If any of them expressed chagrin that I had to edit their work so heavily, I'd point out that in a sane and rational world, I fix grammatical errors and they prescribe drugs and perform surgery. They always seemed to appreciate that perspective!

People with OCPD like to issue corrections to other people for minor or imaginary transgressions. On the other hand, people with narcissistic personality disorder can't tolerate corrections from anyone. In Greek mythology, Narcissus was a beautiful but callous young man who had broken many hearts. To punish him, the goddess Nemesis lured him to a pond, where he fell in love with his own reflection. Unable to tear himself away from his reflection, he eventually died and was transformed into the flower that bears his name. Modern psychologists and psychiatrists use the term *narcissistic* to describe selfish, egotistical jerks. People with narcissistic personality disorder have unrealistically high opinions of their own abilities and performance. They can respond with anger (narcissistic rage) if they are given any criticism or any feedback that is less than worshipful.

As an editor and proofreader, I have had to find and correct other people's mistakes. Consequently, I have occasionally had to deal with temper tantrums from authors who were shocked at how heavily I had to edit their work. Typically, my boss had assigned their work to me because it needed heavy editing or because my boss knew from experience that the author was prone to throwing tantrums. Fortunately, I was trained to suggest no editorial changes to someone else's work unless I could explain why each change was necessary.

When an author expressed anger that I'd edited his work heavily, I'd simply offer to go through the manuscript with the author line by line. Then, I'd explain each problem that I'd identified and why I had recommended that solution. Occasionally, the author would suggest an alternative solution to a particular problem, and I'd take that suggestion whenever possible. However, the main effect was that my explanations of grammar rules would defuse the author's anger.

I think that there were three reasons why I was successful in getting authors to accept my suggested editorial changes. One was that I made it abundantly clear that I cared deeply about their work and wanted it to get the widest and most sympathetic readership possible. Second, I helped the author to understand that there are objective standards that need to be followed in technical writing. If you make sloppy mistakes when you are writing about some commonplace subject, your readers will be able to use their common sense to figure out what you really meant. Unfortunately, your readers won't have that luxury if you are writing about something that they don't already understand. The third reason for my success was that I use terms like *intransitive verb* or *dangling participle* as if everybody knows what those terms mean. I think a lot of people would rather stop arguing with me than reveal that they have no idea what those terms mean.

When I teach adults about things like intransitive verbs and dangling participles, their writing improves dramatically. Yet the antigrammar warriors want me to believe that teaching those concepts to children doesn't help and may actually be harmful. In other words, the antigrammar warriors are making an extraordinary claim. They would have to provide extraordinary evidence if they want me to believe it. In fact, they haven't provided any persuasive evidence, which tells me that they are being irrational. When people argue about whether to teach grammar, they're seldom having a rational conversation about what happens when a child is taught how to diagram sentences. More often, they're really expressing how they feel about authority and the very existence of rules.

English class (or language arts class, as it is often called) presents a good opportunity for children to learn about rules, communication, and interpersonal relationships. From learning about grammar rules and taking grammar tests and having the mistakes in their compositions corrected, children learn that there are some objective standards in formal writing. From reading a wide assortment of literature, children also learn that some of these rules have changed over time. They learn that even good writers apply different kinds of rules in different kinds of work. These lessons help children develop broad-mindedness, tolerance, and mental flexibility—which are precisely the traits that adults with obsessive-compulsive personality disorder have failed to develop.

I think it's important for children to be taught that there are clear, objective standards in Standard English and what those standards are. In contrast, advocates of "whole language" make arguments like this:

> For some teachers, the most difficult aspect of creating a Whole Language writing program is knowing when to correct children's writing. Whole Language kindergarten teachers are aware of their children's need to communicate effectively, and they know that through daily exposure to "correct" or effective oral and written communication, their students will not only be receptive to suggestions for improvement, but will reach a stage where they themselves insist on correct writing.[1]

Would anyone dream of using this kind of approach to coaching a children's sports program? Could you imagine a sports program with no scorekeepers or timekeepers? Could you imagine a sports coach limiting his or her coaching to the occasional suggestion? Could you imagine a coach refusing to have children do drills in the fundamentals of a sport, and expecting that children should just spontaneously grasp the difference between good and bad form from watching television or from watching the teams who beat them? Of course not. A coach who followed that kind of recipe for failure would not be tolerated, because most people think that sports are important. Unfortunately, too many people think that the verbal arts are not important.

Why should schools spend money on sports programs, since so few children go on to a career in professional sports? The answer is simple: people believe that sports programs "build character." Sports programs are supposed to teach lessons about sportsmanship, fairness, honesty, teamwork, and the importance of discipline and hard work. However, some kinds of moral lessons can be taught only in an academic setting. People cannot take a meaningful part in a democratic society unless they learn certain kinds of academic disciplines.

David Mulroy is a classics professor at the University of Wisconsin-Milwaukee. His book *The War Against Grammar* explains that the abandonment of grammar instruction in public schools in the United States has led to a serious decline in the verbal aptitude of American college students. Students are finding it far more difficult to study foreign languages — especially highly inflected languages like Latin. They even seem to have difficulty in understanding complicated sentences in English. To gauge how bad this problem is, he asked the students in his elective mythology course to write out the literal meaning of the following sentence:

> When in the Course of human events, it becomes
> necessary for one people to dissolve the political bands
> which have connected them with another, and to assume
> among the powers of the earth, the separate and equal
> station to which the Laws of Nature and of Nature's God
> entitle them, a decent respect to the opinions of mankind

requires that they should declare the causes which impel
them to the separation.

None of the students seemed to know where this sentence came
from. (It's the first sentence in the Declaration of Independence.)
Many of the students seemed to think that the sentence was about
the breakup of a romantic relationship. Others wrote long, flowery
passages that seemed to be free-associations on some of the more
colorful words in the passage. Only a minority of students could
figure out what the sentence meant: that when people are breaking
political ties, they should explain why they are doing so. Mulroy
pointed out that to understand the literal meaning of the sentence,
the reader has to know enough about English grammar to identify
the sentence's main clause. Unfortunately, many students don't even
know what a clause is.

Mulroy explained that since people who haven't studied grammar are so poor at understanding complicated sentences, they end
up fixating on some of the individual words. If you can't understand
the literal meaning of what someone else is saying, then you can't
really address the strengths and weaknesses of the other person's
line of reasoning. All you can do is get picky about some of the words
that the person uttered and attack him or her personally. Mulroy
pointed out that many schoolchildren are actually being encouraged to try to figure out another person's "hidden agenda" or "point
of view or bias." This approach is a shocking departure from the
traditional rules for how to discuss things in public.

According to *Robert's Rules of Order*, which is the traditional
American guidebook for how to hold public meetings, "It is not
allowable to arraign the motives of a member, but the nature or
consequences of a measure may be condemned in strong terms. It is
not the man, but the measure, that is the subject of debate." By
encouraging children to engage in ad hominem (toward the man)
arguments, we've turned our backs on something that used to be a
basic principle for how to treat one another in public. In Chapter 1,
I complained that Americans have taken to screaming nonsense at
each other like monkeys, and hurling abuse at each other like

schoolyard bullies. What's alarming is that this obnoxious, paranoid behavior is being reinforced by what children in the United States are being taught in "language arts."

If you cannot understand the literal meaning of other people's sentences, you will not be able to understand their arguments. You will thus be immune to reason. You will be unreasonable. By depriving children of grammar instruction and teaching them to ignore what someone is saying and instead to imagine that person's "hidden agenda," we are actually teaching children to be unreasonable. I find that to be a troubling development. If we cannot reason with each other, how can we achieve anything through democratic means?

I wrote this book because I am concerned about the low and possibly deteriorating quality of public debate in the United States. I think that the problem is real and has many causes, but one of the main causes is the abandonment of the traditional trivium (grammar, logic, and rhetoric) in primary and secondary education. We are not teaching children the studies that are appropriate for free people. As a result, people don't know how to participate meaningfully in a free society. Unfortunately, the abandonment of the trivium has made it harder for people to recognize the scope and nature of this problem.

The refusal to teach grammar to children has been a serious problem in the United States and probably also in the United Kingdom. I doubt that this nonsense has been allowed to go on in continental Europe, partly because it is so important for the schoolchildren there to learn foreign languages. A few years ago, a woman who grew up in the Dutch-speaking part of Belgium told me that she likes reading American books because the sentences are so short and simple. She said that compared to books written in Dutch, books written for a US audience seem to have been written for children. Maybe they were.

It's just as easy to write a complicated sentence in English as in Dutch. The difference is that most writers in the United States are under intense pressure to write at a sixth-grade level. The National Library of Medicine urges people who write about health for a consumer audience to write at a fourth-grade level. In particular, the Iowa Board of Health urges writers to use the Fry readability index to measure how readable their writing is. Here's an example of a sentence that was rated as above college level on the Fry index:

> Babies born to women who are covered by one of Iowa's health care programs are covered through the month of their first birthday, provided the baby continues to live with the mother and reside in the state of Iowa.

Here's the same information, written at a fourth-grade level:

> Are you pregnant? Do you get health coverage from an Iowa program? If you do, your baby will also be covered. Coverage will last until the end of the month of your baby's first birthday. The baby must live with you in Iowa.

Of course, I want information from a state board of health to be written so that everyone in the state can understand it. However, I'm afraid that all this "dumbing down" is hiding an epidemic of functional illiteracy in the United States. The fact that the College Board has altered the way it scores the verbal SATs has made it hard for people to see that the problem has gotten worse over time. Young people's verbal skills, as indicated by the SAT, declined after the schools stopped teaching grammar; and the problem isn't due to more people taking the test. Perhaps the worst part of this problem is that the people who have poor verbal skills are unlikely to realize how poor their verbal skills are.

In 1999, Justin Kruger and Daniel Dunning published a controversial article in which they suggested that people who have poor verbal and social skills are generally unaware of how poor their skills are.[2] Not only do unskilled people make mistakes, but their incompetence makes it impossible for them to judge their own abilities. As their skills improve, so does their ability to judge their level of skill. Kruger and Dunning specifically studied the grammar skills of students at Cornell University.

Two things about Kruger and Dunning's article disturbed me. One was the idea that people with poor grammar skills could even get admitted to Cornell, which is, after all, one of the most selective universities in the United States. The second was the idea that a young person could go through all the years of schooling leading up to university without having a pretty good idea of how his or her skills compare to those of other students. Aren't kids getting extensively tested, and aren't the test scores being expressed on a curve?

Young people shouldn't have to depend on their own judgments of whether they are good at something. They should be getting guidance from adults on those matters. However, I'm afraid that many children in the United States aren't getting honest feedback from adults because many adults are afraid that any sort of criticism would undermine the children's self-esteem. This idea is associated with the trend, which has sometimes been taken to absurd lengths, to build children's self-esteem at any cost. I think that this trend is dangerous. Do we really want children to grow up to be arrogant, shameless people who think they know more than they really know? Do we really want a child to grow up to be the sort of person that no one likes or respects?

The people who don't want children to be taught grammar in grammar school argue that teaching children the rules of grammar and having them diagram sentences and do other kinds of drills in grammar would be pointless or even harmful. They argue that pointing out the grammatical and spelling mistakes in a child's writing would scar the child emotionally. Yet those same people never seem to argue that children shouldn't learn rules and do drills in gym class. They don't seem to think that children would be scarred for life if their baseball team lost a game or even if it lost all of its games. The anti-grammar warriors never seem to argue that the children shouldn't learn music theory and practice scales when the children are learning to play an instrument. Why should I believe that the kinds of instruction that are appropriate in a sports program or a band program would be counterproductive in English class? It makes no sense to me!

The debate about whether to teach grammar to children is one aspect of a larger debate that has gone on for centuries: about whether discipline or freedom is better for children. To me, this whole debate makes no sense. It's a false choice, like asking whether being awake or being asleep is better for children. The answer depends on what time of day it is. As I see it, some kinds of discipline promote freedom. For example, by learning the rules of music theory and practicing their scales and chords, musicians develop the ability to play whatever comes into their mind, instead of just reading printed notes off a piece of paper.

The rules of grammar exist to enhance human communication. Without these rules, it would be impossible to construct meaningful sentences. People who have mastered these rules have a much easier time understanding what other people have to say and can express themselves much more effectively. People who have a poor understanding of these rules have trouble understanding anything written at more than a fourth-grade level. Yet in order to participate meaningfully in a democracy, people have to be able to read material that was written for grownups. Grammar can be used as a tool of oppression if people who speak nonstandard dialects of English are treated unfairly. However, the refusal to teach children the rules of Standard English grammar is an even more powerful tool of oppression.

References

1. Raines S, Canady R. *The Whole Language Kindergarten.* New York, NY: Teachers College Press, 1990.

2. Kruger J, Dunning D. Unskilled and unaware of it: how difficulties in recognizing one's own incompetence lead to inflated self-assessments. *J Pers Soc Psychol.* 1999;77(6):1121-1134.

CHAPTER V

Arguments Good and Bad

M any people in the United States were brought up to believe that there's no such thing as a good argument. The term "good argument" sounds to them like an oxymoron, a contradiction in terms — like military intelligence, black light, or jumbo shrimp. They think that an argument is an unpleasant conversation, something that could easily escalate into a physical fight. They believe that everyone should either agree with each other or "agree to disagree" — that nothing productive can come from talking about disagreements. Yet the word *argument* didn't originally mean that anyone was disagreeing with anyone else. The word *argument* came from the Latin word *argumentum*, which meant evidence. An argument originally meant a rational reason for deciding whether to believe something.

In high school English classes, young people should learn the difference between an argument and a debate, as well as the difference between debate and dialectic. An argument is a set of reasons for accepting a particular conclusion. A debate is a contest, with winners and losers. The contestants in a debate offer arguments in support of opposing points of view, for the purpose of persuading the audience. The audience decides who wins. When the debate is among candidates for a political office, the voters decide who wins. Debate can also be a competitive sport in which teams compete to impress the judges with the quality of their arguments and their skill in using the rules of the contest. This sport is considered to be good training for young people who hope to go to law school.

In the United States, we have an adversarial system of justice, which means that our court trials take the form of debates. On one side there are the prosecutors (in criminal trials) or the plaintiffs' attorneys (in civil trials). On the other side are the defendants' attorneys. In a lower court, the judge is supposed to serve as an impartial referee, and the jury decides who wins. In appeals courts, judges make the decision. In contrast, some other countries have an inquisitorial system, in which judges take an active role in investigating the case. Each system has its strengths and weaknesses.

Any adversarial process can easily become ugly. The ugliness comes from the fact that the adversaries want to win, as if they were playing a sport. Competitive debate is a sport that people choose to play. However, court cases are not supposed to be a sport. Most defendants and even many plaintiffs wish that the court case wasn't even happening.

The adversarial nature of a court case can easily lead the participants into temptation. For example, the prosecuting attorney's duty in a criminal case is to serve justice, not to win convictions. Unfortunately, some prosecuting attorneys focus more on winning than on justice. To win convictions, police and prosecutors sometimes plant false evidence against the defendant or hide evidence that would prove that the defendant is innocent. Prosecutorial misconduct is a major cause of false convictions in the United States. Prosecutorial misconduct can also occur in societies with an inquisitorial system.

The focus on winning instead of on truth and justice can cause problems in any kind of adversarial process. No one expects attorneys or the members of a debate team to accept the other side's arguments. Competitive debaters are assigned to a position at the beginning of a debate and stick to that position throughout the entire process, even if they are wrong or their cause is unjust. In other words, they are supposed to be unreasonable. Unfortunately, court cases and debates provide a model of unreasonable behavior that people imitate in other settings. The adversarial model is particularly ugly and unproductive in a social setting because there's no wise and impartial judge to enforce rules of evidence and the rules of civility.

I think that in the United States, there is far too much emphasis on debate and far too little on dialectic. In dialectic, someone offers a thesis, which is an argument in favor of a proposition. Someone else might offer an antithesis, which is a counterargument against the proposition. A thesis or antithesis may be accepted or rejected outright, or parts of both might be incorporated into some new synthesis. Thus, the participants in dialectic can learn from each other and come up with a completely new understanding of the subject. In dialectic, there are no winners and losers, because dialectic isn't a competition. The purpose of dialectic isn't for the One True Faith to prevail against Error. The purpose of dialectic is to help the participants as well as the audience improve their understanding of a subject.

To see how the process of thesis-antithesis-synthesis works, look at the history of 20th century physics. Some ancient philosophers offered the thesis that light behaves like a stream of particles. Others supported an antithesis: that light behaves like the waves on the ocean. The debate between these two sides went on for more than two thousand years. Finally, 20th century physicists worked out a synthesis: a theory that accounted for both the particle-like and the wave-like behavior of light. This synthesis, which is called particle-wave duality, is fundamental to quantum mechanics. In other words, evidence from both points of view went into the development of a more satisfying and more useful theory.

In the case of the particle-wave duality of light, both sides were partly right but neither had a complete view of the problem. It was similar to the fable from ancient India about the blind men and the elephant. Each of the blind men felt a different part of the elephant's body, and thus each one came up with a different idea of the nature of the elephant. The man who felt the tusk thought that the elephant was a spear, the one who felt the trunk thought that the elephant was a snake, and so on. In some versions of the fable, the men end up debating each other endlessly. To me, that is a perfect illustration of how debates can be pointless, as well as unpleasant.

In some versions of the fable, a wise king intervenes to tell them that each is right but only in a limited way. I don't like fables that teach adults that they should depend on the wisdom of a king or other authority figure. If I were to tell the fable, I'd have the blind men listen to each other and work together like reasonable human beings to develop a complete picture of the elephant. In real life, we are all like the blind men, able to perceive only a limited and distorted view of the world.

To engage in dialectic, you must be mature enough emotionally to accept the fact that you could be wrong. You must also be willing to consider the possibility that the ideas and institutions that you hold sacred might be imperfect or even bad. You have to be willing to consider the possibility that someone else might be right—even if that person thinks differently than you do or is of a different sex than you are or comes from a different social or ethnic group. You have to put the quest for knowledge and wisdom ahead of your own ego. If you lack this kind of emotional maturity, you will be stunted in your intellectual and moral development, and you won't even realize that you are stunted.

I think that one of the reasons why politics in the United States has gotten so ugly is that people have never been trained in dialectic, and they have been trained to use debating tactics that are unreasonable. Part of the problem is the kind of training in apologetics that many people receive. Many people are taught in childhood that their own particular, limited view of religion represents the one true faith, which they must impose on other people and defend from any possible criticism. Thus, they may get the impression that narrow-mindedness and fanaticism are saintly. They may get so intoxicated by their sense of theological correctness that they forget to love their neighbor as themselves, as if that were optional.

Of course, fanaticism can be a problem even in a society that is officially atheist. The problem is not the content of the belief system. The problem is arrogance—what the ancient Greeks called hubris. Even people who think of themselves as atheists or rationalists can have a fanatical admiration for some guru or school of thought. As a result, they may enjoy "debates" where they merely hammer away with their official talking points. Their goal is to exert dominance, not to find truth.

Like most educated people in the United States, I was brought up to believe in the importance of free speech and freedom of the press. I was repeatedly told that free and open debate in the "marketplace of ideas" would help people find the best ideas and policies.

I wrote this book to help people understand that freedom of speech and of the press is necessary but insufficient to produce the kind of society that a civilized person would want to have.

We do need freedom of speech and of the press in order to have other kinds of freedom. Unfortunately, freedom of speech doesn't do much good if people can't understand each other or refuse to listen to each other. Freedom of the press doesn't do much good if people can't read. Free and open debate is unproductive if the debates are pointless, nasty games with no rules, no referees, and no sportsmanship.

Conservatives have long complained that the "liberal press" is biased against their point of view. Only recently have prominent liberals begun talking about the influence that the corporations and other institutions that own and control the "marketplace of ideas" work to shape the debates. Journalists often cover stories in ways that distort the public's understanding of an issue.

Unfortunately, journalists can distort the news even through their attempts to be objective and fair. Simply reporting on a subject makes it seem as if it's worthy of attention. Giving equal coverage to two sides of a dispute makes it seem that both have something important to say. But what if the dispute is between the vast majority of the scientific community and one lone crank or a handful of hacks who are being paid by a public relations firm? What if there are more than two sides to a problem? To be able to make sense out of the news takes a high level of literacy and sophistication.

Logic was the second element of the classical trivium. Grammar was the first. You have to study grammar before you study arguments because arguments are made up of sentences. To decide whether an argument makes sense, you need to understand the sentences in it. Once you have the ability to analyze sentences and arguments, you can use it to decide whether what someone is saying is reasonable. This skill is useful in everyday life and is absolutely essential for anyone who is expected to take an active part in public affairs. That's why it's one of the skills that were traditionally reserved for freeborn people, as opposed to slaves. In a free society, these skills should be taught to everyone.

In Chapter 3, I explained that each language has its own set of rules for putting together meaningful sentences. These rules enable a person to say who did what to whom, and how and when and why and even how often it happened. Writers who learn to apply these rules will be much better able to say exactly what they mean. If they want to make a good argument, however, they need to know more than the rules of grammar. They also need to know some rules about how to use evidence and how to make arguments.

Not only are there rules, but there are different sets of rules to be used in different kinds of arguments. The prosecutor in a criminal case has to prove the defendant's guilt beyond a reasonable doubt. However, the decision in a civil case is supposed to be based on the preponderance of the evidence. Even the rules about what kind of evidence you can use are different in law than they are in science, partly because science and the law serve different purposes. The purpose of a legal process is to solve some sort of conflict, but the purpose of science is to improve human understanding. In law, justice delayed can be justice denied. In science, however, decisions often have to be delayed until adequate evidence has been collected.

There are two basic kinds of arguments: arguments about what is true, and arguments about what should be done. Ordinary people encounter both kinds of arguments in their personal lives and in their lives as citizens. Often, the first kind of argument has to be resolved before the second one can even begin. For example, sick people need to know what kinds of medical treatment are effective for their condition, and what the side effects are likely to be, before they can decide what treatment they want to have. Ordinary people need to know something about the issues before they can make informed political decisions.

I think that everyone needs solid training in how to tell good arguments from bad arguments. This kind of training is good for the individual's intellectual and moral development. It helps one find truth and serve justice. That's why the studies that help people develop these skills were considered appropriate for free people, but not for slaves.

CHAPTER VI

Grammar, Logic, and Character

Political discussions in the United States tend to be nasty. Many people believe that this nastiness is natural and inevitable. After all, there's supposedly a "cultural divide" or even a "culture war" in the United States. However, I think it's absurd to imagine that there could really be a cultural divide between members of the same family, and I don't think that cultural differences are ever an excuse for deliberate rudeness.

The cognitive linguist George Lakoff argues that the cultural divide arises largely from people having different views of the ideal family. He says that conservatives tend to subscribe to the strict father model while liberals embrace the nurturing parent model. I use a different family metaphor. To me, American society looks like a dysfunctional family.

A dysfunctional family is one in which some of the grownups misbehave and create pointless strife; meanwhile, children and other vulnerable family members are subject to neglect or even abuse. The dysfunctional family may include at least one adult with a substance abuse problem or a major mental illness. Often, the family includes passive or child-like adults who allow the strife and abuse to go on.

The main problem in a dysfunctional family is a disregard for the rights and needs of some of the family's members. Some family members get special treatment, while others' basic human rights are violated. These problems tend to go unresolved, either because family members deny that anything is wrong or because they don't know how to resolve conflicts.

Within families, inequality based on sex used to be taken for granted. Husbands had power over wives, and sons were treated differently than daughters. Within American society, other kinds of inequality also used to be taken for granted. In 1857, Supreme Court Chief Justice Roger B. Taney wrote that people of African ancestry "had no rights which the white man was bound to respect." From my perspective, it seems that the "culture wars" are not really between people who think that children need discipline and those who think that children need nurture. The conflict is mainly between those who think that all persons are equal and those who think that some persons (especially the imaginary persons called corporations) are, in Orwellian terms, "more equal than others."

From my perspective, it seems that one side of the "cultural divide" consists of people who want to build on the achievements of progressive popular movements: the civil rights movement, the women's movement, the peace movement, the labor movement, the environmental movement, and the movement to end child abuse. The other side consists of people who oppose those movements and want to do what they can to undermine them.

As in many a dysfunctional family, plenty of people in the United States deny that anyone is being treated unfairly. Instead, they feel angry at the people who mention the "elephant in the room." Likewise, the people in dysfunctional families don't know how to resolve conflicts. If a heated discussion breaks out, some people view the existence of disagreement as the problem and insist that "both sides" must be equally at fault. To me, such attitudes smack of denial and codependency.

If we want our nation to become less dysfunctional, we must acknowledge our problems and learn how to resolve conflicts. The first step in resolving conflicts is to achieve a reasonable consensus on matters of fact. To do that, one must learn to engage in dialectic.

To participate in dialectic, you need some sort of training in logic. Before you can study logic, however, you need to understand some basic principles of grammar. That's because grammar deals with how sentences are put together, and logical arguments are made up of sentences.

An argument is made up of a set of statements that can be either true or false. Such statements are called propositions. A proposition has a subject and a predicate. It can be a simple sentence, or it can be a clause within a compound or complex sentence. The verb in the predicate of a proposition can express an action or a state of being, but it has to be in the indicative mood. "Socrates is a man" is a proposition, because it contains a subject "Socrates" and a predicate "is a man" and the verb in the predicate is in the indicative mood. "My dog has fleas" is also a proposition, as is "we all scream for ice cream."

In contrast, a command such as "Shut the door!" is not a proposition. It does contain an implied subject ("You") and a predicate ("shut the door!"), but the verb is in the imperative mood. Commands may be obeyed or disobeyed, but they can't be true or false. This concept becomes important in moral reasoning, as I'll explain in Part V.

Questions aren't propositions. That's because the verb in a question is in the interrogative mood, not the indicative mood. In some languages, such as Welsh or Irish Gaelic, you have to alter the verb itself to show that the sentence is a question. In English, we use word order and a rising tone of voice or a question mark at the end of the sentence instead of altering the form of the verb. "Are you going to Scarborough Fair?" is not a proposition; it is clearly a question because the verb appears before the subject. "You are going to Scarborough Fair" is a proposition. "You are going to Scarborough Fair?" is a question because of the question mark. In speech, you'd indicate that this sentence is a question by the way you say "Fair?" A question may prompt you to answer yes or no, but the question itself isn't true or false.

Statements that have a verb in the subjunctive mood are also not propositions. The subjunctive mood can be used to express statements about hypothetical conditions, wishes, recommendations, requirements, or suggestions. Modal auxiliary verbs such as *can, could, may, might, must, ought, should,* or *would* can be used for this purpose. The subjunctive mood can also be used for statements that are contrary to fact: "If I *were* king of the forest...!"

The truth or falsity of a proposition is called its truth value. If a proposition is true, its truth value is "true." If a proposition is false, then its truth value is "false." Logic enables you to use the truth values that you already know to figure out some of the truth values that you would like to know. You can do this if the propositions are logically related to each other.

The simplest kind of relationship deals with whether the propositions can have the same truth value at the same time. Can all of the statements in a set be true at the same time? If so, they are consistent. If not, they are inconsistent. I have found this concept of logical consistency to be extremely useful in helping me spot mistakes and lies. If someone tells me a bunch of things that can't all be true at the same time, I know that there's at least a mistake somewhere. I may not be able to tell right away which of the statements is false, but I know that something is wrong somewhere. Having the ability to notice logical inconsistency is like having a keen sense of smell. It can warn you that something is rotten.

There are two ways in which propositions can be inconsistent. They can be either contrary or contradictory. If all of the statements in a set can be false at the same time but they can't all be true at the same time, they are contrary. Consider three propositions about an individual named Charley: "Charley is a cat," "Charley is a hamster," and "Charley is a horse." If Charley is a cat, then one of the propositions is true and the other two are false. If, on the other hand, Charley is a dog, then all three propositions are false.

Contrary statements can all share the same truth value, as long as they are all false. Contradictory statements, on the other hand, have opposite truth values. Here are two contradictory propositions: "Charley is a cat" and "Charley is not a cat." You can tell, right off the bat, that one of these statements has to be true and the other one has to be false, as long as both statements refer to the same Charley. You might not know which statement is true; but you know, from the structure of these two propositions, that one is true and the other is false.

If you combine two contradictory propositions into a single proposition — "Charley is a cat and Charley is not a cat" — you have a contradiction. A contradiction is any proposition in the form "A and not A." A contradiction is necessarily false. That means that it is always false under all possible circumstances.

On the other hand, if you combine two contradictory statements with the conjunction *or* instead of *and*, you have a tautology: "Charley is a cat or Charley is not a cat." A tautology is a statement that is always true (necessarily true) because it contains all of the logical possibilities.

Tautologies aren't the only kind of statement that is necessarily true. An analytic statement, which has a predicate that states an idea that's already found in the subject, can also be necessarily true. For example, "All bachelors are unmarried" is necessarily true because the definition of the word *bachelor* is "an unmarried man." In contrast, the statement "All bachelors are married" is necessarily false because it contains a contradiction.

The statement "All bachelors have blue eyes" is a synthetic statement because the predicate contains an idea that isn't found in the definition of the subject. The statement "All bachelors have blue eyes" isn't necessarily true. In fact, it is false.

Some prominent philosophers such as Bertrand Russell have argued that mathematical laws (e.g., the Pythagorean theorem) and mathematical equations (e.g., $2 + 2 = 4$) are also necessary truths even though they are synthetic statements. Outside of mathematics, synthetic statements are neither necessarily true nor necessarily false. A proposition that isn't necessarily true or necessarily false is contingent. To decide whether a contingent statement is true or false, you may have to depend on observation.

An argument is more than a set of propositions. An argument consists of one or more propositions that serve as premises and another that serves as a conclusion. You can't tell from looking at a proposition in isolation whether it is part of an argument or whether it would be a premise or the conclusion. In fact, the conclusion of one argument may be used as a premise in another argument.

An argument is valid if and only if the conclusion is a logical consequence of the premises. To see how this works, look at a classic type of argument, the syllogism. A syllogism includes a major premise, a minor premise, and a conclusion:

Major premise: All human beings are mortal.
Minor premise: All Greeks are human beings.
Conclusion: All Greeks are mortal.

All three of these propositions are true. What makes this argument valid is that the conclusion *has to be true if the premises are true.* The conclusion of a valid argument can be false if one or more of the premises is false. This means that an argument can still be valid even if all of the statements in it are false.

If an argument is valid and all of its premises are true, then it is sound. The conclusion of a sound argument is always true, but the conclusion of an unsound argument can be true or false. To show that an argument is unsound, all you have to do is show that at least one of the premises is false or find an error in the reasoning. If you find either of those problems, you cast doubt on the conclusion.

These concepts of validity and soundness apply only to deductive arguments. A deductive argument, such as a syllogism or a mathematical proof, is intended to establish the definite truth of its conclusion. Inductive arguments, on the other hand, are intended merely to show that the conclusion is *unlikely* to be false, just as a prosecutor tries to prove a defendant's guilt beyond a reasonable doubt. As I'll explain in Chapter 8, it wouldn't be appropriate to describe an inductive argument as sound or unsound. Instead, inductive arguments are generally described as strong or weak.

To make it easier to see the logical structure of an argument, Aristotle used letters to stand for some terms. For example, the syllogism above could be presented as follows:

Major premise: All A are B
Minor premise: All C are A
Conclusion: All C are B.

The classical syllogism is only three lines long. Even so, you need to use some conjunctions to put it together if you wanted to express it in ordinary speech. Here are two ways to state the syllogism in ordinary English:

- **If** all A are B **and** all C are A, **then** All C are B.
- All A are B, **and** all C are A; **therefore**, all C are B.

Notice how conjunctions (*and, if,* and *then*) and a conjunctive adverb (*therefore*) help you figure out that an argument is being made and help you identify the premises and the conclusion.

In the following, I've put together a list of words and phrases that are often used to indicate that a proposition is a premise.

Premise Indicators

Assuming that	For/for one thing
Because	Given that
Considering that	Inasmuch as
Follows from	Owing to
For the reason that	Since

The following gives a list of words that often indicate the conclusion of an argument.

Conclusion Indicators

As a result	Necessarily
Consequently	So
Demonstrates that	Therefore
Ergo	Thus
Follows that	We can conclude that
Hence	Which implies that
Must be the case that	Which means that

Although these indicators can be useful, they don't necessarily prove that a proposition is a premise or conclusion. For example, the "since" in "I haven't seen her since she lost all that weight" just says when something happened (or didn't happen). It's not giving reasons for someone to accept a conclusion. Similarly, if I say "I ate my lunch early because I was hungry," I'm just saying why something happened, not why you should believe something. In contrast, the word *because* is serving as a premise indicator in the following sentence: "Because he arrived late today, and he only arrives late when his train is late, his train must have been late today."

As arguments get more complex, you need to use a lot more of what computer programmers call logical operators: words like *and*, *or*, and *not*. Grammatically, most logical operators are conjunctions. *Not* is an adverb. That's why people who learned the parts of speech and how to diagram a sentence in childhood are ahead of the game when it comes to analyzing logical arguments.

When people are making an argument, they don't always state all of the propositions. According to Aristotle, good speakers often leave out obvious propositions so as not to bore their audience. An argument that has been shortened because one of its propositions hasn't been stated is called an enthymeme. For example, "Socrates is mortal because he is human" is an enthymeme because the proposition "all humans are mortal" has been left unsaid.

Aristotle pointed out that some premises are so obvious that they can be left unsaid. However, a dishonest person might leave out an unreasonable premise, so as to distract attention from it. If you are evaluating an enthymeme, you have to fill in the missing propositions yourself. According to the principle of charity, you are supposed to fill them in with the most reasonable propositions you can think of.

When you are trying to decide whether an argument is sound, you have to pay attention to the form of the argument as well as to the truth value of the premises. Look at what happens when you substitute other words in the syllogism:

> Major premise: All cats are reptiles.
> Minor premise: All poodles are cats.
> Conclusion: All poodles are reptiles.

The conclusion is false: poodles are not reptiles. However, the premises are also false. Cats are not reptiles and poodles are not cats. Yet the argument itself is valid because the conclusion *would be* true if the premises were true. If all cats really were reptiles and all poodles really were cats, then all poodles would definitely be reptiles. Thus, the argument is valid, even though all the statements in it are false. Even though the argument is valid, the fact that one or more of the premises is false makes the argument unsound, which means that the conclusion could be either true or false. This is an extremely important point for people to understand.

When sociologist Robert Altemeyer studied authoritarian followers (i.e., the sort of people who are sympathetic to antidemocratic political movements), he found that authoritarian followers tend to have more trouble than the average person in thinking logically. They tend to decide whether an argument is good or bad according to whether they like the conclusion, not according to whether the premises would actually support that conclusion if they were true. In other words, they seemed to be unaware that the validity of an argument matters.

Here's an example of the problem he pointed out. Consider the following argument:

> All fish live in the sea.
> Sharks live in the sea.
> Therefore, sharks are fish.

People who have high scores on a test for authoritarian values would be more likely than the average person to say that that argument is valid. As Altemeyer explained,

> If you ask them why it seems right, they would likely tell you, "Because sharks are fish." In other words, they thought the reasoning was sound because they agreed with the last statement. If the conclusion is right, they figure, then the reasoning must have been right. Or to put it another way, they don't "get it" that the reasoning matters—especially on a reasoning test.[1]

As Altemeyer points out, the reasoning should justify the conclusion; but to many people, the conclusion justifies the reasoning.

They have trouble deciding whether observable evidence proves something, and they are likely to conclude that some irrelevant piece of information proves something they already believe. For example, if they hear that archaeologists found the ruins of an ancient wall at Jericho in Palestine, they're likely to believe that the finding proves that the story of the Battle of Jericho, as described in the book of Joshua, is literally true—even though the wall in question is from a completely different historical period.

Unfortunately, people who have this kind of trouble with logical thinking tend to believe what they want to believe, and they are highly susceptible to prejudice and Big Lies. Unfortunately, there is no way to reason with them. If they don't like your conclusion, they will think that you and your argument are ridiculous. If you try to reason with them by providing evidence or giving a logical argument, they will likely respond with contempt or maybe anger. This refusal to listen to reason is one of the big reasons why political discourse often gets so ugly.

Authoritarian followers may have strong opinions, but they don't base their opinions on an independent logical evaluation of the evidence. They merely collect their beliefs and attitudes from various authorities. Authoritarian followers generally don't spend much time thinking through their belief system. As a result, they often don't notice or particularly care about inconsistencies in their own belief system. This leaves them open to charges of hypocrisy.

The word *hypocrite* came from a Greek word meaning a stage actor—someone who pretends to be something that he is not. It can also be used to mean someone who pretends to believe something that he or she does not really believe. In the Gospels, Jesus often criticized people for hypocrisy. Some scholars suggest that the heavy use of the word *hypocrite* in the gospel according to Mark was a play on words. They think that the text of Mark, which is the oldest of the gospels, was originally composed for public performance. Thus, the person playing the role of Jesus would be accusing stage actors (literally, hypocrites) of hypocrisy. Thus, the ironic use of the word *hypocrite* may have been a light-hearted way to convey an important message.

The opposite of hypocrisy is integrity, which means wholeness. If you have integrity, then you are what you say you are: you really believe what you say you believe, and you practice what you preach.

Before you can have integrity, you must learn to think logically. All moral codes are made up of rules, often in the form of if-then statements. If you can't think logically enough to follow those rules, then you cannot have integrity. That's why the study of logic was considered to be important for the development of virtue. Of course, you can't begin to study logic until you have mastered some of the basic concepts of grammar. Grammar and logic are fundamental disciplines that students need to master before they can go on to study science, law, or even basic morality.

Reference

1. Altemeyer R: *The Authoritarians*. Winnipeg, Manitoba: Robert Altemeyer. 2006. http://members.shaw.ca/jeanaltemeyer/drbob/TheAuthoritarians.pdf

CHAPTER VII

Definitions and Groups

L ogic deals with truths that spring from the meaning of words. If you want to think logically, you have to think carefully about what words mean. You have to think about the dictionary definitions of a word. You may also have to think carefully about how a particular word is being used in a particular kind of argument. For example, some words can be given a special, technical definition in a legal or scientific discussion. For example, what does it mean to be an adult? In the United States, citizens can vote at 18 years of age; but in many states, you can't buy beer until you are 21 years old. You have to be at least 25 years old to serve in the House of Representatives and at least 35 years old to serve as President.

Definitions clarify how a word relates to other words and other concepts. If you want to make a logical argument, or even just to convey information, you need to think about the definitions of the words you use. You even need to think about the definitions of common words, such as *cheap*. If you say that something is cheap, do you mean that it has a low price or a low value?

There are several different kinds of definition. Consider, for example, the term *starting lineup*. In sports, the term *starting lineup* is defined as the official list of players who will actively participate when the game begins. Although that kind of dictionary definition explains what people mean when they talk about a team's starting lineup, it doesn't tell you who is in the lineup and who isn't. The only way to know that is to look at the list.

The list of players in a baseball team's starting lineup is an example of an extensive definition. An extensive definition creates a set by listing every member of the set. In contrast, an intensive definition doesn't list the members of a set. Instead, it gives you rules for deciding who or what goes into the set and who or what gets left out. The definition of the word *bachelor* is an intensive definition. It says that all adult male human beings except for the ones who are married are included in the set of bachelors.

Sometimes, the truth of a statement depends entirely on the meaning of the words it contains. For example, since the word *bachelor* means an unmarried man, you know that the statement "all bachelors are unmarried" is necessarily true. It's an analytic statement. The predicate simply restates an idea that is already contained in the definition of the subject. Thus, the statement is true by definition. You don't have to look for married bachelors to test the truth of the statement.

You can use a true analytic statement as a premise in an argument. If you know that Fred is a bachelor, you know from the definition of the word *bachelor* that he is an unmarried man.

When you say that Fred is a bachelor, you are saying that he belongs to the category that includes all adult male human beings, except for the ones who are married. To understand categorization, you must understand the difference between concrete objects and abstractions. Traditionally, a concrete object (concretum, plural concreta) was considered to be something that takes up space at a particular time. Of course, quantum physics showed that the conventional concepts of time and space break down when you are dealing with things that are too small to be seen even by a microscope or things that are whizzing past you at close to the speed of light. For everything else, the conventional concepts of space and time still work pretty well.

Unlike a concretum, an abstractum does not exist in any particular time or place but represents a *type* of thing. For example, when Socrates was alive, his body was a concretum because it took up space at that time. However, we could also regard Socrates as a member of various abstract categories and subcategories: he was a man, a human being, a Greek, a philosopher, and so on. In other words, concreta are material things and abstracta are the categories to which we assign those things. Concreta exist in the physical world and abstracta exist in our imaginations. Although abstracta exist only in our minds, we need to use abstracta if we want to make any sort of general statements about things in the material world.

When we say that Socrates was an ancient Greek philosopher, we assign him to an abstract category. We can also assign abstract ideas into other abstract categories. For example, you might consider the labor theory of value to be part of Marxism because Marx wrote about it. Yet you can find the same idea in the works of classical economists, such as Adam Smith. Unfortunately, people often reject a particular idea because of the category to which they have assigned it, instead of evaluating the idea on its merits. Using categorization in that way can create serious problems.

Philosophers have dealt with issues related to the concrete and the abstract for thousands of years. I don't want to get too bogged down in these issues. In this book, I mainly want to explain how a poor understanding of the distinction between the concrete and the abstract leads to political problems. Many of these problems result from how we classify ideas into ideologies and people into groups — and how that act of categorization ends up affecting how people are treated. To explain that, I have to tell you a story about something that happened in medieval France.

In the early 13th century, some of the people in what is now the South of France developed an alternative view of Christianity. They imported some of their ideas about religion along with trade goods from Bulgaria and Armenia, which were then part of the Byzantine Empire. One of these ideas was that the Roman Catholic Church was spiritually, morally, and politically corrupt and shouldn't be given any more money.

As you might imagine, Pope Innocent III was annoyed that some people were disrespecting his authority. He was downright infuriated when those people stopped giving him money. His response was to declare that those ideas, which were assigned to a category called Catharism, were heretical. He then launched the Albigensian

Crusade, offering the lands of the Cathar "heretics" to any French nobleman who could conquer them militarily.

The Albigensian Crusade was officially a war against Catharism. Yet Catharism is an abstractum. It exists only in the mind. You can apply physical force only against concreta. How could you use physical force against ideas, which are incorporeal? You can't. You can use physical force only against people and things. During the Albigensian Crusade, the crusaders killed a great many people, many of whom weren't Cathars. Some of those who were killed were faithful Roman Catholics. Some of them were even Roman Catholic priests.

One of the first battles in the Albigensian Crusade took place in the city of Béziers. On July 21, 1209, the Crusaders ordered the Biterrois (as the inhabitants of Béziers are called) to hand over the heretics or to leave the city before the Crusaders besieged the city and killed everyone. The Biterrois, most of whom were good Catholics, decided to stand and fight alongside their Cathar neighbors. This posed a puzzle for the crusading soldiers. How could they decide who was a Cathar, and thus deserved to be killed, and who was a good Catholic, and thus should be spared?

One of the commanders (the Papal Legate Arnaud-Amaury, Abbot of Citeaux) said for the soldiers not to worry about it. They were to kill everyone; God would recognize his own. When the Crusaders sacked the city, they massacred everyone, including Catholic priests and people who tried to take sanctuary in the Cathedral of St.-Navaire. The Crusaders set fire to the cathedral, which collapsed on the people inside.

The Albigensian Crusade provides a useful model for understanding wars in general. The crusade was launched by a handful of wealthy and powerful people who were greedy for even more wealth and power. That included not only the Pope but the northern French noblemen who coveted the real estate in southern France. Of course, the ordinary foot soldier would get very little from the crusade and would be lucky just to make it home in one piece. Thus, the foot soldiers had to be convinced that they were fighting for some grand purpose—to please God by fighting the Catharist heresy.

If you look at the three groups of people involved in the Albigensian Crusade, you can see that each of the three common theories of the nature of war stems from one of those points of view. The Pope and the nobility of northern France saw the crusade as a political instrument—something undertaken by wealthy and powerful people to enrich and empower themselves further. The foot soldiers were encouraged to view the crusade as eschatological—something that has to do with the ultimate destiny of humankind. The Biterrois doubtless viewed the war as simply a catastrophe—something bad that simply happened to them.

I see the same pattern repeated in modern wars. Wars are planned by rich and powerful people who want to enrich and empower themselves further. However, the people who are doing the fighting must believe that they are fighting for some higher purpose. Otherwise, why would they bother to risk life and limb? To the people who are being targeted, the war is simply a catastrophe.

The justification for the Albigensian Crusade was based on a logical error called reification, which means treating an abstractum (in this case, heresy) as if it were a concretum. Of course, once people are so irrational as to imagine that they are going to war against an idea, they can easily end up slaughtering every human being in their path. This problem is not limited to medieval France. During the Vietnam War, US Marines and Green Berets adapted the Albigensian Crusade motto for their own purposes: "Kill them all. Let God sort them out."

After the terrorist attacks on the World Trade Center and the Pentagon on September 11, 2001, President George W. Bush launched what he called a "War on Terror." When I hear people talk about the "War on Terror," I think of President Franklin Delano Roosevelt's first inaugural speech, which he gave in 1933, in the depths of the Great Depression. Roosevelt told the nation that "the only thing we have to fear is fear itself!" Terror is an emotional state. It is an abstractum that exists only in the mind of the beholder. You can't use physical force against something that exists only in your own mind. You can use physical force only against concreta: people and things.

If terror is a state of mind, what is a terrorist? To decide who is a terrorist, and who is not, we need an intensive definition. US federal law defines terrorism as "the unlawful use of force and violence against persons or property to intimidate or coerce a government, the civilian population, or any segment thereof, in furtherance of political or social objectives." Thus, a terrorist is someone who uses unlawful force and violence for those stated purposes. Yet many of the individuals who have been labeled as "terrorists" have never been involved in using any force or violence against anyone. It would therefore make no sense to call such a person a terrorist. Likewise, it makes no sense to claim that you were acting in self-defense if you attacked someone who posed no conceivable threat to you.

Freedom of conscience and freedom of speech are guaranteed by the Bill of Rights in the US Constitution. Nevertheless, Americans were indoctrinated during the Cold War with the idea that some people, by virtue of their ideas, had no right to live. Americans were encouraged to believe that people in Asia were "better dead than red." This idea was used to rationalize military adventures that were supposedly intended to force people in other countries to accept our system of government—instead of being allowed to rule themselves, which is what democracy is really supposed to mean. Often, there has not been even a pretense of promoting democracy, such as when the United States has supported dictatorships and despotic kings.

Supposedly, the United States was "spreading democracy" by killing communists; but in reality, the term *democracy* means that a population gets to choose not only its elected officials but its own form of government. Unless the people in a country get to rule themselves, they don't have democracy. Democracy is not something that can be imposed on a population from outside. It has to be something that they do by and for themselves. After all, the word *democracy* means that the people rule themselves, instead of having a government imposed on them by soldiers sent by someone else's government. Democracy can't be imported or exported. It has to be homegrown.

The idea that people have no right to exist unless they hold the right ideas has often led to mass murder. So has the idea that people have no rights unless they have the right ancestors. The idea that someone's rights should depend in some way on who his or her ancient ancestors were is called racism.

The older portions of the Bible are full of racist ideas. That's because they were written at a time when societies had grown large enough that social interactions could no longer be regulated by long-standing personal relationships. Instead, they had to be governed by one's status as a member of a larger group. To adjust to that new reality, one had to learn to be kind to people whom one had never met before, as long as the strangers could be identified as members of one's own group. That's probably why there are so many stories about strangers who turn out to be angels in disguise.

Lot was considered a virtuous man because he offered to hand over his virgin daughters to be raped by a mob instead of handing over strangers (who unbeknownst to Lot were angels) to be raped by the mob. For the past few hundred years, many Christians have believed that the story of the destruction of Sodom and Gomorrah is a cautionary tale against homosexuality. However, the prophets thought that Sodom's sin was not homosexuality but inhospitality, along with greed, gluttony, and idolatry.

The oldest books of the Bible describe a society in which people's rights depended on their membership in a group, and the groups were defined in terms of paternal ancestry. The Jews were supposedly descended from Abraham through his son Isaac. According to the Qur'an, Abraham's son Ishmael, by his Egyptian handmaiden Hagar, was the ancestor of the Arabs. In reality, of course, any population has more than one ancestor, and the boundaries between populations tend to be fluid. My own ancestors came from several different nations.

Few Americans understand that not all Arabs are Muslim, and not all Muslims are Arabs. Many Arabs are Jewish or Christian, and many Arab Muslims have ancestors who were Jews or Christians. Likewise, many people who are identified as Jews today are the descendants of converts. Converts to Judaism were so common in the ancient world that the Greeks had a word for them: proselytes. Thus, the idea that a modern-day person's identification as Jewish,

Christian, or Muslim has anything to do with ancient ancestry is hard to swallow.

Many of our political problems in the United States have always had something to do with how we assign people to groups. How do we decide who is American, and who is not? How do we decide who is black and who is white? How do we decide who is a Christian, and who is not? How do we decide who is an American Indian, and who is specifically a Cherokee, and who is not? How do we decide who is a communist, and who is not? How do we decide who is an insurrectionist, and who is a freedom fighter? How do we decide who is an adult, and who is a child? Even a simple question such as who is male and who is female can be hard to answer. Yet until we make clear definitions of the words that we use, we cannot think logically.

CHAPTER VIII

Strong and Weak Arguments

In Chapter 3, I explained that the ability to parse (i.e., to understand and apply grammatical principles) is a thin, bright line dividing human beings from other animals. The ability to parse gives us another ability that is uniquely human: we can use language to reason with each other. I think that's what Aristotle meant when he called man "the rational animal."

When people reason with each other, they give reasons to support their conclusions. When you give reasons to support a conclusion, you are making an argument. Logic is the study of arguments. It helps you recognize whether an argument that involves deduction is valid or invalid. It helps you recognize whether other kinds of arguments are strong or weak, and whether the conclusions of those arguments are likely to be true.

Few people seem to understand how important the study of logic is for improving our interpersonal relationships and our society as a whole. As I'll discuss in Chapter 11, logical reasoning is one of the three means of persuasion. In other words, logic enables you to say something besides "because I said so" or "or else I will hit you" as a means of persuasion. The study of logic can help you avoid making errors in thinking. If your friends have skills in logic, they can use those skills to help you correct your mistakes—at least if you are humble enough to let them. Some forms of psychotherapy are designed to help people to recognize and correct errors in reasoning.

The underlying theory is that irrational thoughts often give rise to emotional and behavior problems.

When people can't use logic, they can't "use their words" like civilized human beings to resolve conflicts. That inability leads to frustration, which fuels anger. When people don't have skills in logic, their disagreements often give rise to name-calling, or worse. That's why the word *civility*, which originally meant training in the liberal arts and the humanities, came to mean good manners.

Many of the Founding Fathers of the United States had a classical education, which gave them training in logic and argumentation. It inspired them to establish a system of government that was based on laws that were created through political discussions. I think that they would be shocked to find that so many Americans now believe that political discussions are, by definition, impolite. The main reason why I wrote this book is to persuade people that the traditional liberal arts give people the skills they need in order to hold productive discussions about serious topics. Such discussions are necessary if people are to work together for any common purpose. In other words, I wrote this book to strengthen democracy. If the public disengages from politics, or if they are misled by propaganda, then their society tends to degenerate into oligarchy or even dictatorship.

Few Americans have had any real training in logic and rhetoric. Most Americans who came of age after the mid 1960s have even been deprived of training in grammar, which you must learn before you can begin to study logic. I think that those facts explain why our political discussions in the United States have become so pointless and ugly.

American public school students may get a little bit of exposure to set theory and if-then statements in math class. They might learn about Boolean operators (AND, OR, and NOT) in a computer class. They might pick up some pointers about grammar and rhetoric in high school if they have a good English teacher. However, there's no systematic attempt to teach grammar, logic, and rhetoric to everyone, even though those skills have been recognized for more than two thousand years as the basic skills that are necessary for democracy.

Many people imagine that illogical thinking is a problem that has something to do with one's position on the political spectrum. Rightists tend to think that anyone to the left of them is illogical. Leftists tend to think the same of anyone to the right of them. Centrists think that anyone who doesn't cleave to the middle of the road is illogical. Of course, when centrists assume that a middle position between two extremes must be correct simply because it is in the middle, they make an error in reasoning called the fallacy of moderation.

Although the kinds of illogical thoughts that an individual has may help to explain why he or she ended up at a particular point on the political spectrum, I think that irrationality is a major problem everywhere: left, right, and center. If you doubt that, try discussing strategy or tactics with people in your own political party. Many people seem rational until you try to tell them something they don't already know or try to get them to change their mind about something. If they can't think logically, then you won't be able to use logic to persuade them.

Logic is one of those subjects that are hard to learn through experience. Logic must be taught. If you want to study logic on your own, you must use some sort of curriculum that includes problem sets with answers, so that you get honest feedback on your level of skill. People who have poor skills in logic are generally unaware of how poor their skills are. That's because their lack of skill makes it hard for them to recognize their mistakes. That problem, combined with arrogance, makes it impossible for them to learn from other people.

There are two basic kinds of logical argument: deductive and inductive. Deductive arguments are intended to establish definite truth. The classic example of this kind of reasoning is the syllogism: "All men are mortal; Socrates is a man; therefore, Socrates is mortal." Mathematical proofs are also deductive arguments.

When you make a deductive argument, you are saying that the conclusion is true *because* the premises are true. If the deductive argument is valid and all the premises are true, then the conclusion is definitely true. Such an argument is said to be sound. A deductive argument that is invalid or contains at least one false premise is unsound. The conclusion of an unsound argument could be true or false.

Inductive arguments, on the other hand, are intended to show that the conclusion is *unlikely* to be false. Inductive arguments are generally used for drawing conclusions from limited information, such as when people base generalizations on their observations. Mathematics may be full of deductive arguments, but most of the arguments in science are inductive. For example, the people in ancient and medieval Europe noticed that all the swans they saw were white. From those observations, they came up with a general rule, "All swans are white." In fact, the idea of a black swan became a metaphor for something that could happen but never does. Then, Europeans found out that there were black swans in New Zealand and Australia. Then, the idea of a black swan came to symbolize the weird things that happen only on the far side of the globe.

Once Europeans found out about the black swans down under, they could no longer honestly say "all swans are white." Instead, they had to add a qualifier. They could say either "*some* swans are white" or "all *European* swans are white." In other words, induction can lead you to create tentative rules, as well as rules that apply in some situations but not in others. The rule about swans being white applied in Europe but not in Australia or New Zealand.

Unless you have seen every swan that has ever existed or will ever exist, you can't be sure about any generalization based on an observation of swans. You can deduce that if something is a swan then it is a bird. However, you can't observe some characteristic that isn't part of the definition of the word *swan* in a group of swans and apply it to all swans with complete confidence.

An argument by induction can sometimes lead to false conclusions. Thus, an argument by induction cannot be described as valid or sound. Instead, people talk about the strength or weakness of an inductive argument. Instead of being described as true or false, the conclusion of an argument by induction may be described as probable or improbable.

To understand how to base decisions on evidence, you need to understand the basic principles of inductive reasoning. One of those principles is the idea of a strong or weak generalization. A generalization is strong if it is generally true, with few or no known exceptions. The more exceptions there are, the weaker the generalization is. For example, if I see that all of the swans on a particular lake are white, I can say "All of the swans on this lake are white." That statement can be true if I can really see all of the swans. However, such a limited generalization is seldom useful. If I wanted to make up a rule that describes all swans, including many that I have never seen, I run the risk that some swans will break that rule.

Biology class provides a great opportunity for students to learn about strong and weak generalizations. For example, in biology class you learn that, by definition, mammals are warm-blooded, furry animal species whose females nurse their young. For more than two thousand years, Europeans thought that all mammalian species give birth to live young. Then, the indigenous Australians taught them that some furry animals, such as the duckbilled platypus, lay eggs. In other words, biology teaches you to be careful about basing generalizations on incomplete evidence. Biology class should give you practice in dealing with strong generalizations (all mammals nurse their young) and weak generalizations (most mammals give birth to live young).

One common form of inductive reasoning involves observing a sample and then generalizing the results to the population as a whole. For example, if you find that x% of a sample has a certain attribute, it might be reasonable to assume that x% of the population that the sample came from has that attribute. You can then use that generalization as a premise in a statistical syllogism: 38% of the US population has O-positive blood; Henry is a member of the US population. Therefore, Henry has a 38% chance of having O-positive blood.

There are many possible pitfalls in inductive reasoning. If you depend on too small a sample, you commit the fallacy of hasty generalization. Even if your sample is large, you can end up with problems if your sample is biased. *The Literary Digest* found that out the hard way. In 1936, *The Literary Digest* ran a poll that predicted incorrectly that the voters in the Presidential election would elect Alf Landon instead of re-electing President Franklin Delano Roosevelt. Although the poll got responses from 2.4 million people, those respondents didn't represent an accurate cross-section of the American voters. The respondents tended to be wealthier than the average American: they could afford magazine subscriptions, telephones, or an automobile even during the Great Depression. Since then, pollsters have developed much better methods of sampling and statistical analysis.

An argument by analogy is another form of inductive reasoning. If you know that two things are alike in some ways, you may suspect that they may be alike in other ways, as well. For example, cats and dogs have many things in common. Thus, if you know how to treat a particular disease in a dog, that knowledge might be a good starting point for figuring out how to manage the same disease in a cat. But as any veterinarian can tell you, cats are not small dogs. For example, some drugs that are well tolerated by dogs are lethal to cats.

The controversy over whether animals should be used in medical research hinges on two kinds of discussion that involve arguments by analogy: scientific discussions and ethical discussions. The scientific discussions deal with the question of whether the results of the animal studies can enable you to predict what will happen in human beings. The ethical discussions deal with the question of how animals should be treated. However, both of those discussions deal with a basic question: to what degree are animals like human beings? How close is the analogy? What do the similarities and differences between humans and other animals imply?

Arguments by analogy are commonly used in legal and moral reasoning. When Americans want to argue that something is evil, they often draw an analogy to what happened in Nazi Germany. As Mike Godwin put it, "As an online discussion grows longer, the probability of a comparison involving Nazis or Hitler approaches 1." Sometimes, people use Nazi analogies in ways that generate more heat than light.

Nazi analogies are based on the idea that several different behaviors can spring from the same cause. As the German poet Heinrich Heine wrote in a play in 1821, "where they burn books, they will ultimately burn people also." More than a century later, the Nazis burned books and then committed human rights violations, including the use of gas chambers and crematoria, on a massive scale. Thus, many people become uneasy when they see the members of some political movement throwing books into a bonfire. Of course, Nazi analogies are sometimes used to defame some tolerant, nonviolent people. That kind of defamation is called a false analogy.

I think that there are two reasons why people overuse Nazi analogies. One is that many people don't know how to make a good argument by analogy. They have trouble making a point-by-point comparison, and they have trouble understanding proportion and context. Thus, they are prone to making false analogies. Another reason for the overuse of Nazi analogies is that few Americans know enough about history to draw any other historical parallels. They know that Hitler was a bad person. Thus, comparing someone to Hitler is just a way of expressing contempt. In contrast, if I compare someone to Tomás de Torquemada, I generally have to explain who Torquemada was and why the comparison is meaningful.

As I explained above, a fallacy is an error in reasoning. There are two basic kinds of logical fallacy. A formal fallacy is an error in the form or structure of the argument. An informal fallacy is an error that arises from the content of the statements in the argument, such as an inappropriate generalization. If you find a fallacy in an argument, it means that you should be cautious about accepting the conclusion. The conclusion might still be true; but even if it is, you need to find a better argument to support it.

Philosophers have named some of the common fallacies (errors in reasoning). I'll explain some of the more common fallacies in the next few paragraphs. Consider this to be just an introduction. I strongly urge people to get a proper textbook and make a serious study of them.

A formal fallacy is an error in the form or structure of an argument. There are several common formal fallacies. An argument from fallacy assumes that if an argument contains an error in reasoning, its conclusion must be false. The appeal to probability assumes that because something could happen, it will happen. People make the conjunction fallacy when they fail to realize that the probability of two things happening together is lower than the probability of either one happening without regard to the other. For example, the set of librarians is larger than the subset of librarians who wear glasses. The masked man fallacy was named for the following example: I don't know who the masked man is, but I know who Jones is; therefore, the masked man is not Jones. The base rate fallacy is when you conclude that an event will occur even though you don't know how common it is. For example, if you get a positive test for a rare disease, you shouldn't automatically assume that you actually have the disease. Tests for rare diseases often produce more false alarms than correct diagnoses.

Propositional fallacies are formal fallacies that result from confusion over the use of words like *if, then, and, or,* and *not.* If the statement "if you build a baseball diamond, then the Chicago Black Sox will come" is true and you do build the baseball diamond, then the Chicago Black Sox will come. However, the statement deals with "if," not "if and only if." In other words, the statement implies that the Chicago Black Sox might come even if you don't build the baseball diamond. If the Chicago Black Sox came and you conclude that you must therefore have built the baseball diamond, then you commit the fallacy of affirming the consequent. If you assume that the Black Sox won't come because you didn't build the diamond, then you commit the fallacy of denying the antecedent.

Syllogistic fallacies result from some defect in a syllogism. Here's an example of the fallacy of the undistributed middle: All cats are mammals; my dog is a mammal; therefore, my dog is a cat.

Informal fallacies are fallacious for reasons other than structural problems with the argument. For example, the argument from ignorance assumes that something must be true because it has not been or cannot be proven false. "Begging the question" means that people assume the very thing that they are trying to prove; this is also called circular reasoning. Some people mistakenly use the phrase "to beg the question" to mean that something implies that a question should be asked.

The fallacy of composition assumes that something that is true of part of a whole must be true of a whole. For example, atoms are invisible to the naked eye; however, the things that are made out of atoms are not necessarily invisible. The fallacy of division assumes that something that is true of a whole must be true of each of its parts. For example, a ship floats on water, but individual pieces from the ship wouldn't necessarily float on water. The fallacies of composition and division are important in politics because they are often used to draw false conclusions about groups and members of groups. For example, the fact that a political party as a whole supports a particular political policy doesn't mean that everyone in that party supports that policy.

The continuum fallacy is a problem in fuzzy logic, which deals with situations where there's no clear boundary between two conditions. The continuum fallacy is sometimes called the bald man fallacy: If a man loses one hair, it does not make him bald. If he loses two hairs, it does not make him bald. However, you commit the continuum fallacy if you assume that a man can therefore never be called bald, regardless of how much hair he loses.

Several common fallacies relate to statements about cause and effect. If you assume that A caused B just because A happened before B, you commit the *post hoc ergo propter hoc* fallacy. If you assume that A caused B because the two always seem to happen together, you commit the *cum hoc ergo propter hoc* fallacy, which means that you falsely assume that correlation implies causality. The fallacy of the single cause assumes that there is one, simple cause for something that may have several causes, none of which is sufficient by itself. The wrong direction fallacy reverses cause and effect.

Another fallacy that causes people to make false conclusions about causality is the regression fallacy. Regression refers to a feature of statistical probability. If you look at a bell curve, which describes a normal statistical distribution, you'll see that the most common values are clustered around the center. The extremely high or low values are rare. Thus, if a truly random process produces an extreme value—high or low—the next value that the process produces will probably be closer to average, just because the results that are closer to average are more common. This tendency of extremely high or low values to be followed by values that are closer to average is called regression toward the mean. If you don't take that fact into account when you are trying to figure out cause and effect, you commit the fallacy of regression.

One fallacy that seems to create a lot of trouble politically is the fallacy of reification. The word *reification* comes from the Latin word *re*, meaning thing. Reification therefore means "thingification." It's when you treat an abstraction as if it were a concrete thing. Many people reify political parties or the government. Instead of looking at a political party or a government as a group of human beings, they look upon it as a concrete thing that is somehow not answerable to anyone and is immune to influence from voters. The people who make this error in reasoning typically fail to develop workable political strategies.

The red-herring fallacies represent not only bad thinking but bad manners. A red herring is something that is used to mislead people. It came from the idea that a smelly fish could be used to lead bloodhounds or foxhounds off their intended trail. Perhaps the most obnoxious of the red-herring fallacies is the ad hominem argument. Ad hominem literally means "to the man." It means attacking the person rather than dealing with the argument that the person is making. When people say nasty things about someone for the purpose of discrediting everything they say, it's called poisoning the well. If the argument turns into simple name-calling, it's called the abusive fallacy. A straw-man argument is an argument based on a misrepresentation of what the other person thinks or says.

Other examples of red-herring fallacies include the appeal to emotion. This is closely related to the Aristotelian concept of pathos. You do need an appeal to emotion in ethics, which deals with questions of right and wrong. However, such concerns are not relevant to questions about whether something is true or false, or whether it is likely or not. Appeals to emotion include appeals to fear, flattery, pity, ridicule, spite, and wishful thinking.

Some red-herring fallacies exploit a person's prejudices or expectations. For example, the appeal to novelty claims that something is true because it is new, while the appeal to tradition claims that something is true because it has always been believed. An appeal to wealth suggests that someone is right because he's rich, while an appeal to poverty suggests that he's right because he's poor.

The genetic fallacy bases a conclusion on something's origin rather than on its current meaning or context. A typical example is a form of Nazi analogy that's often called *reductio ad Hitlerem*. If Hitler once said or did something, that thing must therefore be wrong. But Hitler quit smoking cigarettes. Does that mean it's bad to quit smoking?

The naturalistic fallacy claims that something ought to be a certain way simply because it is that way. In contrast, an appeal to nature encourages people to think that something is good because it is natural. This kind of thinking can be dangerous in medicine. On one hand, you want to work with the body's natural mechanisms for maintaining health. On the other hand, it's nice to be able to use something unnatural, such as a vaccine or an antibiotic, if it saves lives. Illness and death are natural. That doesn't mean that you want them to happen.

I've described just a few of the most common logical fallacies. There are many more. I think that the ability to recognize and avoid these errors in reasoning makes a person wiser. I also think that if these principles were more widely taught, then public discussions would become more pleasant and far more productive. More people would be able to recognize whether a deductive argument is valid or invalid. They'd be able to recognize whether an inductive argument is strong or weak. If a lot more people had this ability, and if people had more of a general education in history and the arts and sciences, then our political discussions in the United States would be far more pleasant and more productive.

CHAPTER IX

Logic and Persuasion

I think that the primary reason why political discussions in the United States are so pointless and ugly is that few of us have had any training in logic. The resulting lack of reasoning skills has implications for the individual and for the larger society.

People who have never had training in logic often make mistakes when sorting things into categories and using if-then statements and making generalizations and so on. As a result, they have trouble making sense of what they see and hear. It's hard for them to figure out whether a statement of fact is true or false. It's hard for them to draw reasonable conclusions from the facts that they do know. Worse yet, they are generally unaware that there is anything wrong with their thought processes. That's because you have to have a certain level of skill in reasoning even to realize that you can make mistakes in reasoning.

It's bad enough if one person out of a crowd has poor skills in logic. What's far worse is if such poor skills in logic are the norm, rather than the exception. Politics get ugly where ignorance and irrationality, rather than knowledge and civility, are the established norms.

All human beings have limited knowledge and can make errors in reasoning. One of the purposes of public discussions is to give people the opportunity to learn from each other, especially from people who have special training or a different point of view. Public discussions also give people the opportunity to evaluate opposing arguments. As I explained in Chapter 5, the process in which people reconcile conflicting points of view to develop a deeper understanding is called dialectic. Unfortunately, Americans are not taught about dialectic. Instead, all we learn about is debate, a competitive sport where there are winners and losers and nobody learns from anyone else. In ordinary life, political "debates" often turn into pointless pissing contests with no referee and no rules.

Sincere discussions in which people share knowledge and correct each other's mistakes are an essential part of modern science. That's one of the reasons why science has been advancing so rapidly, and why laymen should take the consensus of scientific opinion seriously, though not necessarily uncritically.

I worked for peer-reviewed scientific publications for many years. Before we accepted an article, we'd send a copy of the manuscript—minus the authors' identifying information—to people who were experts on that subject. Those experts would then give us an informed opinion about the quality of the work. Sometimes, reviewers would make useful suggestions. The editor of the publication would then decide whether to accept the work as is, to ask the author to make revisions, or to reject the work.

The peer-review process has its strengths and weaknesses. On the plus side, it weeds out a lot of nonsense that could pose a threat to public health. Also, the reviewers' suggestions often improve the quality of the work that does get published. On the minus side, the peer review process can suppress some important ideas that have not yet become popular. Reviewers are often good at spotting errors of fact or problems in methods or analysis; however, they're generally unable to detect deliberate fraud. As a result, there have been several high-profile cases of articles that were withdrawn after having been published in peer-reviewed journals.

The peer-review process is based on the idea that there are objective standards for establishing what is true or at least what is reasonable. Unfortunately, people who have not had a science education do not understand how to apply these standards. People who have not had a liberal arts education may have no idea that these standards even exist. The fact that most people don't seem to understand how science works should be a source of great shame for our educational establishment and for our scientific community. A scientist's work isn't just discovering things. It's also explaining those things to other people, including the general public.

People who have had no training in the liberal arts tend to base their opinions on their prejudices and their intuition, not on evidence or arguments. Thus, they base their opinions on something internal to themselves, not on the facts or on arguments. I think that's why some people get so offended if you try to reason with them. They tend to view any attempt at persuasion as a personal attack, and they generally respond defensively or even aggressively. That is the main reason why discussions of any serious topic often get pointlessly nasty and personal, and why so many Americans think that it's impolite to talk about any serious topic.

The liberal arts were developed specifically to help one learn to behave more like a human being—the rational animal—and less like a baboon or a sheep. The liberal arts were developed to help people respond rationally to what other people say, instead of mindlessly asserting social dominance or responding unthinkingly to fear or desire or conformity pressures. In other words, the liberal arts were developed to help people discuss sensitive topics rationally. This ability to discuss things rationally helps a person become more knowledgeable and wiser as time goes by. In contrast, people who stick to their preconceptions out of foolish pride never learn much of anything.

Many people seem to interpret any attempt to engage them in a serious conversation as a personal attack. Thus, if you try to reason with them about something, you could end up triggering a fight that could endanger your relationship. The only safe course of action is to avoid attempting any serious conversation. This solution is in line with the educational philosophy of John Dewey, who emphasized pleasant socializing and expressed contempt for the teaching of "facts and truths." Yet the social harmony that this approach seems to offer is an illusion. It's a bit like having a codependent relationship with an emotionally unstable person—you may avoid discussing important topics because you are afraid of triggering a tantrum. Unless people learn to have serious conversations about facts and truths, they cannot work together to solve real problems. Thus, they cannot have democracy.

I think that the suppression of the liberal arts and the humanities in our educational system has led to widespread dysfunction in the way people talk with one another. Many Americans seem to avoid talking about any serious topic at all. They think that it's weird or socially inappropriate to talk about any subject that is actually important. They act bored or condescending if you even try to engage them in a serious conversation. Although such persons view themselves as normal or even "cool," the autistic animal behaviorist Temple Grandin disparages them as "yak-yak social airheads." Grandin argues that if a society had nothing but yak-yak social airheads, there would be no science or art. I'm afraid that we wouldn't have democracy, either. In order to have public decision-making, we need for the members of the public to focus their minds on real problems and come up with real solutions.

Most American schoolchildren grow up with the idea that it's cool to be a yak-yak social airhead. Even if they go to college—especially at a "party school"—they may not learn anything different. The question that education reform activists must face is this: are young people learning this social norm despite or because of what's going on in our schools? In either case, what can we do to establish a norm that would better serve the needs of democracy?

Many progressive educators believe that children will learn about grammar and logic spontaneously while engaging in unstructured activities, just as they learned to speak their native language spontaneously through ordinary contact with other people. I disagree. Speech is a natural ability, but grammatical and logical analysis, like reading and writing, are disciplines that must be taught. To develop skill in grammar and logic, students must have their mistakes pointed out, so that they can learn to correct them. If children develop skills in reasoning and argumentation in school, they can go on to have serious discussions that produce some result other than hurt feelings or a decision to "agree to disagree." If they learn how to evaluate arguments, they could eventually come to consensus on matters of fact and even on matters of policy.

To become a reasonable person, one must develop disciplines in logical thinking. Simply knowing that logic exists—and even knowing the names of some of the logical fallacies—is not enough. I learned that lesson in the late 1990s, from discussions with a casual acquaintance of mine. This man had been a business major and had no training in the biological or social sciences. Although he had never taken any courses in logic, he was aware of some logic terminology from publications of the Skeptics movement.

My acquaintance tried to convince me to accept Peter Duesberg's theory that HIV does not cause AIDs. He didn't succeed. Back then, I was working at a veterinary journal and had read a lot about retroviruses, as well as about epidemiologic methods. In fact, I knew one of the veterinarians who had correctly predicted that the cause of AIDS would turn out to be a retrovirus, like the feline leukemia virus that causes immunosuppression in cats. So I tried to explain to my acquaintance what was wrong with Duesberg's theory.

My acquaintance turned a deaf ear to the technical explanations that I gave. But when I explained what Duesberg's critics were saying, he sneered at me for making an "argument from authority." I was stunned. An argument from authority is considered fallacious because authorities aren't always right. However, authorities are not always wrong, either. In fact, highly respected scientists are more likely than the average person to be right about scientific questions! It's not unreasonable to mention the scientific authorities who support a particular theory.

Science isn't a democracy. It is possible for a lone, dissenting scientist to be right and the rest of the scientific community to be wrong. It's also possible for everyone to be wrong. To decide whether to accept someone's idea, you have to look at the relevant evidence and arguments. However, it's unusual for a lone contrarian to be right while the rest of the scientific community is wrong. It's particularly unusual for one lone contrarian to be right about a subject that is not his particular field of expertise. Duesberg is an expert on molecular biology, not epidemiology. That's an important distinction.

I first became aware of Duesberg from his letter to the editor that was published in the July 29, 1988, issue of *Science*. I wasn't favorably impressed. In that letter, Duesberg made some mistakes that were obvious even to me. The people whose article Duesberg was criticizing pointed out Duesberg's misstatements of fact and errors in reasoning. That should have been the end of it. Unfortunately, Duesberg ended up getting the ear of policymakers in South Africa. Thus, Duesberg was partly responsible for policies that led to more than 330,000 excess deaths from AIDS as well as many preventable HIV infections, including infections in children, in South Africa. In other words, errors in reasoning can have life-or-death consequences in the real world.

I asked my acquaintance why he took Duesberg's opinions at face value but ignored the opinions of the overwhelming majority of the world's virologists and epidemiologists. He insisted that all those other scientists were "on the take"—that there was some grand conspiracy among scientists from all branches of medicine, biology, and public health to produce misleading results and biased interpretations to support the virus theory. The ironic thing is that my acquaintance was committing a far worse fallacy than the one he thought he detected in my thinking. He committed the fallacy of "argument from fallacy," which means to assume that a conclusion must be false if an argument that supports it contains a fallacy. He also violated Occam's razor: the principle that one should choose the simplest theory that accounts for all of the available evidence.

That conversation stands out in my memory because it was so surreal. Although my acquaintance was supposedly an atheist, he was following a catechism-evangelism approach to the sciences. He took Duesberg as his prophet, and he was zealously preaching Duesberg's opinions as if they were gospel. It was also illogical that someone who took his prophet's pronouncements at face value should criticize someone else for making an "argument by authority" by pointing out that his prophet wasn't well respected. The conversation was disorienting, like one of those drawings by M.C. Escher, in which up is also down.

A well-rounded education, including a solid grounding in the liberal arts as well as some basic studies in the sciences and the humanities, will give you the ability to decide whether to accept someone else's intellectual authority. You can approach the problem through a process of inductive reasoning. Look at what the person says. Check his or her facts, and evaluate his or her arguments. You can apply the same process to political figures.

I have heard many Americans claim that it's pointless to get involved in politics because it's impossible to tell whether you can trust a politician. I think that's just an excuse for laziness and political irresponsibility. It's surprisingly easy to tell whether you can trust someone who has been in public life for any length of time. Forget the crap that pundits say about a person. Just look at what that person has actually done. What legislation has a legislator actually supported? What has a mayor, a governor, or a President actually done or failed to do while in office? For example, what obviously innocent people are still in prison even though that governor or President could have freed them with the stroke of a pen on his or her first day in office? Nowadays, that kind of information is available in black and white to anyone with an Internet connection.

Fact-checking has been an important part of what I've done as an editor. The Internet has made it much easier to do fact-checking. I can do an extensive search of the world's medical literature for free without leaving my desk. I can confirm the who, what, where, when, and how of historical events. I can find and read historical documents, such as the Federalist papers. I can even search within some online textbooks. In short, the Internet has expanded my reach immensely. Unfortunately, it has also made it easier for people to spread all sorts of nonsense.

Nowadays, I meet a lot of people who have heard about alternative medical theories or political conspiracy theories over the radio or the Internet. I have found it to be pointless to try to engage in a real conversation about any of these topics. People start with their mind made up. They get angry or condescending if I disagree with them. One problem is that people are poorly equipped to critique what they read or hear. That problem is compounded by the fact that we have lots of pundits but few genuine public intellectuals.

By a public intellectual, I mean someone who has not only made important contributions to science or scholarship but who also takes a prominent role in educating the public and in helping to shape public policy and public education. The quintessential public intellectual was Benjamin Franklin, who was important not only as a scientist but as a statesman and educational theorist. Other important public intellectuals from days gone by include Albert Einstein, Bertrand Russell, and Steven Jay Gould. The most important public intellectual who is still alive today is Noam Chomsky. In contrast, most of the pundits whom people seem to take seriously are lowbrow celebrities—people who are famous merely because they are on television or the radio. They function more or less as cheerleaders, shaping public opinion in a mindless way. Some of the highbrow pundits serve as "fellows" or "scholars" at "think tanks" that serve as propaganda agencies rather than being centers for serious scholarship. Their work isn't necessarily taken seriously by real experts in their subjects.

As the Elizabethan composer Orlando Gibbons lamented, "More geese than swans now live, more fools than wise." How can we decide who is wise? The best way is by looking at what people say and do. How often do they tell the truth? How logical are the arguments they make? How often have their predictions turned out to be accurate? The problem is that you have to be well-informed and fairly wise yourself to answer those questions.

An argument from authority is a form of argument by analogy. It's based on the idea that if a person is right about some things, he or she is probably also right about other things. Like any other argument by analogy, an argument from authority can be strong or weak. Some people have such a track record of honesty and accuracy and brilliance that their opinions should be taken seriously. Other people have been wrong so many times that their opinions aren't worth much.

In deciding whether to trust what someone says, I apply the standards that journalists are supposed to use. Was that person an eyewitness to the events in question? Does the person's testimony make sense? Is it consistent with the other facts that I know? Has that person ever lied to me in the past? If the person is giving an expert opinion on some scientific subject, I apply the standards that a judge would use for allowing someone to testify as an expert witness.

Does that person have any real scientific training? Does that person have any published articles on that subject in the scientific literature? What do other scientists say about that person's work?

I think that it's important to be as dispassionate as possible when trying to figure out what is true and what is false. As I explained in Chapter 8, some of the red-herring fallacies represent ways in which emotion can cloud judgment. People can easily be fooled by someone they like, and they resist learning from someone they dislike. Also, they may like to believe what they want to be true, and they may refuse to accept unpleasant reality. The discipline of logic was developed specifically to help people avoid those pitfalls. Thus, it can help people to become more reasonable and to have more productive conversations.

CHAPTER X

Cause and Effect

Many political arguments hinge on questions of cause and effect. These questions can be extremely hard to answer, and the ancient Greeks gave us practically no help in answering them. In the 18th century, the philosophers David Hume and Immanuel Kant identified the basic underlying philosophical problem. However, we didn't get really useful methods for working out cause and effect until the 20th century.

Questions about cause and effect can be matters of life and death. That's because some effects are deadly. The study of the patterns, causes, and effects of diseases in a human population is called epidemiology. The founding event of the study of epidemiology took place during a deadly cholera epidemic in London in 1854. Dr. John Snow suspected that cholera was spread by water that had been contaminated by human feces. He put dots on a map to show where the cholera cases were occurring. After Snow realized that nearly everyone who had cholera had drunk water from a particular pump on Broad Street, he persuaded the local council to take the handle off the pump.

To be good at figuring out cause-and-effect relationships, you need some skills that can and should be taught in school. Some of these skills are best taught in language arts class. Others should be taught in science class, still others in math class. For example, I think that the basics of probability and statistics should be taught in high school. I haven't used calculus since I left school, but I need some knowledge of statistics to understand any modern research, or even to understand current events.

I have learned a lot about epidemiology and nutrition from having worked in various aspects of medical and veterinary publishing for more than 20 years. The most important lesson that I learned is that most medical doctors who were trained in the United States know far less about epidemiology and nutrition than the average veterinarian. As a result, few medical doctors realize how easily many of our major causes of death and disability in the United States could be prevented or even cured by a simple change in diet. Medical doctors won't start giving their patients this simple, life-saving advice until medical schools start doing a better job of teaching about nutrition and epidemiology. Of course, the study of epidemiology must start with a basic understanding of the nature of cause and effect.

Aristotle came up with a theory of causes that's useful for talking about things that are made on purpose, such as a bronze statue. He identified four kinds of causes:

- The material cause is the matter out of which something is made, such as the bronze from which a statue is made.
- The formal cause is the shape of the statue.
- The efficient cause is the artisan and the art of casting the statue. Aristotle also considered a person who gives advice and the father of a child to be efficient causes.
- The final cause would be the purpose of casting the statue.

Aristotle's four causes are useful for talking about things that were made on purpose by human beings, but what about things that happen by accident and things that happen in nature? For that, we need some lessons from philosophers David Hume and Immanuel Kant.

David Hume lived in Edinburgh, Scotland, and died in 1776. He is generally classified as one of the British Empiricist philosophers.

Empiricism is the theory that knowledge comes only or primarily from what human beings can observe: what we can see, hear, feel, taste, and smell. Hume argued that you can learn about cause and effect only through observation. However, he pointed out that you do not observe the causal relationship itself. For example, imagine that you are watching a game of billiards, which is similar to pool. You see a ball roll across the table and smack into a ball that is standing still. Then, the ball that was standing still starts to roll. As you watch the game, you see the same sort of thing happening over and over. Thus, you may develop the idea that a collision causes a ball that was sitting still to start moving. Yet as Hume explained, you don't really see the causal relationship itself. All you really see are the balls and how they move.

In his discussion of billiard balls, Hume pointed out a serious problem in science. If you want to find out whether A causes B, you must rely on observation. Yet you cannot observe the cause-and-effect relationship itself. All you can observe is whether A happens and whether B happens, and whether B happens after A. In other words, all you can directly observe is whether the events coincide.

Hume's discussion of the billiard balls stunned the German philosopher Immanuel Kant. He said that it shook him from his "dogmatic slumbers." Kant then set about trying to explain what kinds of things we can know without observation and the kinds of things that we can learn through observation.

As I explained in Chapter 6, Kant divided statements into two separate categories: analytic and synthetic. Statements about cause and effect are synthetic statements. Thus, you cannot figure out just from looking at the meanings of the words in the statement whether the statement is true or false. To figure out whether a statement about cause and effect is true, you must observe the things that the statement is talking about.

When you watch a game of pool, it makes sense to imagine that one ball causes another to move by banging into it. However, it's important to understand the difference between what's happening in your mind and what's happening on the pool table. Your mind creates an idealized model of how billiard balls move and interact.

To be a good pool player, you must have a good mental model of what happens on the pool table. Yet even a good and highly detailed model in your mind is still just a model. A theory is just a map; it's not the territory itself.

All theories of cause and effect are mental models that people create to explain what they can observe. Scientists consider a theory to be good if it lets them make precise, accurate predictions. A theory that leads to bad predictions gets rejected or modified. Sometimes, scientists have to pick between two theories that both provide equally good predictions. In that situation, they like to choose the one that is simpler and makes more sense in terms of other things that they know. This preference is called Occam's razor, after the medieval English monk William of Ockham. It's also called the law of parsimony, which means tight-fistedness. It's sort of like solving the puzzle on the television game show *Wheel of Fortune* without buying any vowels. Scientists want to answer questions without making unreasonable assumptions.

Of course, the basic idea expressed in Occam's razor had been understood for centuries before William of Ockham was born. In ancient Greece, Hippocrates applied it to medicine. He tried to explain disease in terms of ordinary causes, such as the effects of various foods, rather than the influence of the gods:

> Men think epilepsy divine, merely because they do not understand it. But if they called everything divine which they do not understand, why, there would be no end to divine things.

As scientists developed more understanding of such things as chemistry and microbiology, they became able to explain more and more things in terms of natural as opposed to supernatural causes. By the mid nineteenth century, some prominent German scientists went so far as to swear a solemn oath to assume that "no forces other than the ordinary physical and chemical ones are active within an organism." This attitude, along with advances in chemistry and microscopy, led to dramatic breakthroughs in medicine and physiology.

Today, many people want to reintroduce some supernatural concepts into medicine. Some of what are currently called alternative or complementary therapies are really based on old theories that were rejected as useless in the mid 19th century. Unfortunately, most laymen and even many doctors don't know that. As a result, some people end up promoting theories that became obsolete long before the invention of the light bulb.

There are two general reasons why people try to figure out cause-and-effect relationships: control and understanding. By control, I mean that they want to make things happen or prevent them from happening. Or maybe they want to be able to turn something on and off at will. Thus, they hope to find that the cause is something they can manipulate. By understanding, I mean that they want to find answers that satisfy their curiosity. Thus, they look for causes in terms of things that are already familiar. As a result, people tend to like simple theories that explain things in terms of causes that they understand and can control. Unfortunately, these are not necessarily the theories that hold water scientifically.

A scientific theory should be as simple as possible, but no simpler. The problem is that causality can be complicated because sometimes it takes a combination of causes to produce a particular effect. For example, if you want to build a campfire, you need to have fuel, oxygen, and some sort of ignition energy, such as a lit match. If you lack any of those three things, you cannot build a campfire. All three of those things are therefore necessary causes for a campfire: if you lack any of them, you cannot have the effect. Yet none of them is sufficient, by itself, to produce the campfire. Sometimes, you can solve a problem quickly and easily by removing a necessary cause. For example, you can smother a fire to remove its oxygen supply, or you can douse it with water to cool it down, thus preventing it from having enough ignition energy to keep burning, or you can simply stop adding fuel to the fire.

A cause could be sufficient but unnecessary. For example, an electrical short circuit in your house could be sufficient to cause your house to catch fire. So could spontaneous combustion from a pile of greasy rags in the basement. However, there are other things that could cause your house to catch fire, such as a lightning bolt.

Thus, either a short circuit or a pile of greasy rags could be sufficient but neither is necessary for causing a house fire.

Some kinds of causes are neither necessary nor sufficient but contribute in some way toward producing the effect. For example, heart disease is much more common in people with diabetes. However, not everyone with heart disease has diabetes, and not everyone with diabetes gets heart disease. Thus, we could say that diabetes contributes to heart disease but is neither a necessary nor a sufficient cause of heart disease.

Some kinds of cause-and-effect relationships are hit or miss. For example, if you run across the street without looking, you might get hit by a car. Not everyone who runs across the street without looking gets hit by a car. Also, you could get hit by a car even if you are standing on the sidewalk. Nevertheless, it's a bad idea to run across a street, especially a busy street, without looking.

Some kinds of events result from several contributing causes, and some causes can produce many different kinds of results. For example, many different factors can increase a person's risk of getting cancer, and a cancer can cause many different kinds of effects on the body. Likewise, there are many reasons why people end up poor, and poverty can affect many aspects of that person's life. In contrast, a cause is specific if it produces a particular kind of result. For example, exposure to the sap from a poison ivy plant causes a particular kind of skin rash.

In his essay Politics and the English Language, George Orwell described a situation in which the effects of a problem reinforce the cause of that problem: "A man may take to drink because he feels himself to be a failure, and then fail all the more completely because he drinks." That kind of situation is called a vicious circle. In contrast, a situation where a good effect reinforces its cause is called a virtuous circle. Both are examples of what is called a positive-feedback loop because the results intensify the cause. There is also such a thing as negative feedback, where the results of a process suppress its cause.

Scientists have worked out various methods for isolating a particular cause, to study its possible effects. They may alter one variable while holding everything else steady. The most familiar type of medical research study is the double-blind, randomized, controlled clinical trial. If you volunteer to take part in a study to test a new drug, you will probably be randomly assigned to one of two or more treatment groups. One group will get the new drug, often as a pill or an injection. The other subjects will get either a lookalike pill or shot that contains no active medication (a placebo) or a lookalike pill or shot that contains a conventional treatment for that disease (an active control). Neither you nor the doctor who is evaluating your treatment will know which treatment you got until after the study is over. The randomization is to make sure that the study drug doesn't get an unfair advantage or disadvantage. The purpose of keeping you and your doctor in the dark is to make sure that your judgments aren't unfairly distorted by your expectations.

The cause-and-effect relationships that are easiest to understand involve things that are easy to manipulate and that produce immediate and predictable results. For example, you can easily roll a billiard ball across a table so that it hits another billiard ball. The result of that collision is easy to predict because the table is smooth and level. Also, the balls are smooth and round and all have the same weight. In contrast, it's much harder to study causes that cannot be manipulated and problems that have too many variables. It's also hard to study effects that are delayed or that have to be expressed as a probability.

Most of the methods for applying statistical tests to scientific studies were developed in the 20th century. In the 1920s, a British statistician named Ronald Aylmer Fisher wrote a handbook to teach scientists how to use statistical methods, many of which Fisher himself had invented. Nowadays, these statistical tests are routinely used in nearly all research that involves counts or measurements. Statistical significance is a way of assessing whether any pattern that the research has revealed is due to random chance.

For example, if you are playing poker and one of your opponents gets a hand with four of a kind, it could be just luck. However, if that opponent keeps getting four of a kind, hand after hand, you quickly suspect that there's something more than luck going on. The problem is that you probably can't prove that your opponent is cheating, unless he accidentally gets five of a kind in one hand. What you can do is estimate how improbable his string of luck is. The chance that your opponent could have gotten at least that lucky on a particular night can be expressed as a probability, or P value.

Probability runs from 0 (never) to 1 (always). If the P value is .05, or 5%, then your opponent had a 1 in 20 chance of being at least that lucky. If the P value is .001, or 0.1%, he had a 1 in 1000 chance of being at least that lucky. You may decide that a P value of less than .001 represents cheating. In that situation, you are deciding that $P < .001$ is statistically significant. Yet even if your opponent isn't cheating, he should be expected to get that lucky on one night out of every thousand.

Most US-trained doctors understand how important it is to use the results of randomized, placebo-controlled clinical trials for evaluating the effects of a treatment. What they don't realize is that you can't use that method to figure out the cause of a disease. Nor can you use that method for evaluating the effects of a dietary change. As a result, they need to use information from other kinds of studies. Yet they often dismiss those studies out of hand.

Why can't you use a controlled experiment to figure out the cause of a disease? Because doing so would be not only immoral but illegal. You can't poison people just to see how sick they get. Also, the experiment itself would often be impractical. You simply can't randomly force some people to be smokers and others to be non-smokers for 20 years or more to show whether cigarette smoking causes lung cancer. Nor can you prevent people from knowing whether they smoke, or whether they drink alcohol, or whether they are vegetarians. Fortunately, we don't have to do double-blind, controlled experiments to find out whether lifestyle factors cause disease. We can use epidemiologic methods. These methods were refined in the 20th century to answer the question of whether smoking causes lung cancer.

At the beginning of the 20th century, lung cancer was rare. In the 1930s, it suddenly became common. Most of the cases were in men who had smoked cigarettes heavily for 20 years or more. By the mid 1930s, scientists in Germany had linked cigarette smoking to lung cancer, infertility, and heart disease. When British scientists finally started looking at the relationship between cigarette smoking and lung cancer after World War II, the tobacco industry responded by hiring Ronald Aylmer Fisher, who by then was Sir Ronald Aylmer Fisher, to set up a smokescreen.

To cast doubt on the relationship between smoking and lung cancer, Fisher made ridiculous criticisms of the design of the studies. He admitted that lung cancer is more common in heavy smokers. However, he claimed that it might have been because people started smoking to ease the symptoms of a precancerous condition. He also suggested that lung cancer is genetic, and that the genes that cause cancer might also cause people to smoke. Yet real genetic diseases run in families and affect practically the same percentage of the general population in each generation. They don't go from being rare to being common in one generation. As a geneticist and a statistician, Fisher knew that. Fisher also claimed (falsely) that the long-term data on cancer rates don't support a relationship to cigarette smoking and that people who don't inhale the smoke were more likely to get cancer.

To clear up the confusion that Fisher created, another famous British statistician, Sir Austin Bradford Hill, came up with some rules of thumb that are still widely used in epidemiology. The first is the obvious principle that a cause must happen before an effect. The lung cancer epidemic broke out about 20 years after large numbers of men started smoking cigarettes heavily. The epidemic among women broke out a few years later, about 20 years after large numbers of women started smoking heavily. The smoking started before the cancer happened.

Some of Hill's rules of thumb deal with statistics. Lung cancer is far more common in smokers than in nonsmokers. It is particularly common in people who have been heavy smokers for a long time (a dose-response effect). These statistical relationships between smoking history and the risk of lung cancer kept showing up in many different kinds of studies, in many different geographic areas, and in different time periods. Hill argued that all of these findings are important.

Statistical relationships aren't enough, by themselves, to prove that cigarette smoking causes lung cancer. Just because two things seem to happen together doesn't prove that one causes the other. As statisticians put it, "correlation does not prove causality." Two things that tend to happen together could both be the result of some third factor. For example, people with gum disease are more likely than people with healthy gums to have a heart attack. For years, many people suspected that curing gum disease might therefore protect the heart. Unfortunately, better dental care doesn't prevent heart attacks. Fortunately, changing to a low-fat, high-fiber, plant-based diet cleans up the arteries and reduces inflammation, thus solving the heart disease and the gum disease at the same time.

Doctors have been taught that correlation doesn't prove causality. Unfortunately, they often think that this means that they should dismiss correlation out of hand, rather than regarding it as a valuable clue. Finding a strong statistical correlation is like proving that a suspect was present at the scene of a crime. That, in itself, is not enough to prove that the suspect committed the crime. It just means that the suspect is a good suspect. To establish guilt or innocence, you have to look at other kinds of evidence. In contrast, if there is little or no statistical correlation, it's like finding out that the suspect has a good alibi.

I have had numerous frustrating conversations with medical doctors who get overly picky about the limitations of some epidemiologic study and then turn a deaf ear to my explanation about how that weakness has been addressed by different kinds of studies. Also, they often complain that no one has ruled out all of the possible alternative explanations. Yes, you should consider alternative explanations. However, you should stick to the reasonable alternatives. You shouldn't have to wait until every conceivable alternative theory is disproven before you accept the most reasonable explanation.

Sometimes, some epidemiologic studies compensate for other studies' weaknesses. For example, the early results from the Seven Countries study showed that heart disease was far more common in Finland and the United States than in Japan. In Finland and the United States, people ate a diet that included a lot of fatty animal-based foods. In Japan, however, people ate a low-fat diet based heavily on rice and vegetables. However, diet is not the only difference between the two societies. There are also genetic differences between the populations. To rule out genetic differences as an explanation, you need to look at other kinds of studies, such as studies of people who moved from one country to another and studies of populations whose diet is changing. When taken as a whole, all of these studies provide overwhelming support for a simple conclusion: it's the food. Yet American medical doctors still generally fail to give their patients good dietary advice.

Medical doctors often seem to get overly picky about what they think are methodological flaws in clinical trials of dietary interventions. Yet as Hill pointed out, if you can build up a strong-enough case from other kinds of evidence, including natural experiments and population studies, you might not even need to do any experiments. If you already have overwhelming evidence that a cause-and-effect relationship exists, then it doesn't matter if your experiments have weaknesses. In that context, the purpose of the experiment may be simply to confirm the direction of the cause-and-effect relationship and to rule out the possibility of unknown confounding variables. Another possible purpose is to show how much and how quickly a person's medical condition would improve if the cause of the person's illness were removed.

Hill also argued that ideally, a proposed cause-and-effect relationship should make sense in terms of what is known about the underlying biology and that the theory should not conflict too much with other well-established theories. Those aren't hard-and-fast rules. If we have enough evidence to support the cause-and-effect relationship, it may lead us to rethink our other theories. Hill felt that a theory should also be specific. The presumed cause should be associated specifically with a particular disease, although it could produce more than one disease.

The last of Hill's rules of thumb was analogy: do we have evidence that similar causes produce similar effects? The first known work-related cancer was cancer of the scrotum in chimney sweeps. If the products of combustion could cause scrotal cancer, we shouldn't be surprised that they could cause cancer of the lung as well.

Hill spelled out these rules of thumb in the 1960s. Unfortunately, few medical doctors and even fewer laymen understand them, even today. As a result, many debates go on and on, even after the evidence to support one side or the other becomes overwhelming. The debate about whether smoking causes lung cancer should have been solved in the 1930s. The debate about whether fatty diets cause high blood cholesterol, which in turn causes heart disease, should have been resolved by the 1950s, at the very latest. Similarly, the public is still debating about whether greenhouse gas emissions are causing climate change, long after the climate scientists have reached a consensus. Often, these debates are kept alive by propaganda efforts funded by industry.

When I look at the debates about health and environmental issues, I can't help but notice that the same "experts" keep cropping up in debates on widely different topics. In their book *Merchants of Doubt*, Naomi Oreskes and Erik M. Conway described how a small group of scientists with strong ties to industry and the media have cast unreasonable doubt on issues ranging from the hazards of tobacco smoke to the prospect of global climate change. Of course, it's unreasonable to expect that the same people could be experts in so many different scientific disciplines. It simply never happens in reality. On the other hand, it's quite reasonable to expect that a professional propagandist would be willing to work on more than one account.

As I mentioned above, people like to look for causes in terms of things that they understand and can control. Doctors control their prescription pads, and they can decide what kinds of surgical procedures to perform. In contrast, doctors have no control over what their patients eat. That, plus the fact that doctors learned almost nothing about nutrition in medical school, explains why doctors keep using drugs and surgery to manage the symptoms of chronic diseases that could be cured within a matter of weeks by a change to a healthy diet. Doctors think that their patients won't follow their dietary advice. However, many patients won't bother to change their diet unless their doctor tells them they must. The best thing that doctors can do in that situation is to send their patients to the best dietitian in town. That way, the doctor can use his or her authority and the dietitian can use his or her training in dietary counseling.

I wasn't the first person to notice that few American medical doctors know anything about nutrition. The American Medical Association published reports about the problem in the 1960s and 1970s. The National Research Council reported on the same problem in 1985, and the *American Journal of Clinical Nutrition* published its own report in 2006. Nor am I the first person to notice that many medical doctors have trouble with logic and critical thinking. The AMA Press published a book about the problem in 2005, *Evidence-Based Practice: Logic and Critical Thinking in Medicine*. Unfortunately, few healthcare reform advocates realize that the neglect of nutrition is largely the result of poor critical thinking.

Most of the cause-and-effect relationships I discussed in this chapter came from medicine. However, the same problems with figuring out cause and effect crop up in many other areas. Many people have no understanding of why wars happen, or why the economy collapsed, or why so many people were poor even when the economy was supposedly doing well, or why we're suddenly having so many extreme weather events. I think that Sam Cooke got it wrong in his song *Wonderful World*, which begins: "Don't know much about history, don't know much biology…" People *do* need to know facts from academic subjects, and they *do* need to learn how to think rationally about those facts, if they want to make the world wonderful.

CHAPTER XI

Rhetoric

In ancient Rome, rhetoric was one of the studies that were considered appropriate for free people, as opposed to slaves. Rhetoric is the art of persuasion. The art of persuasive speech, as opposed to writing, is called oratory.

The Founding Fathers of the United States knew how important persuasive speech and writing had been in the success of the American Revolution. Speeches such as Patrick Henry's "Give me liberty or give me death" and documents such as the Declaration of Independence and Thomas Paine's *Common Sense* helped persuade many colonists to rebel against their king, who supposedly ruled by divine right, and to establish instead an elected government that derived its authority from the consent of the governed. That change was truly revolutionary.

The liberal arts, including rhetoric, have always been valued in societies with a democratic or republican form of government. The Founding Fathers of the United States of America felt that public rhetoric was so important for the survival of their new republic that they guaranteed the right to freedom of speech, and of the press, in the Constitution. The First Amendment to the Constitution of the United States of America reads:

> Congress shall make no law respecting an establishment of religion, or prohibiting the free exercise thereof; or abridging the freedom of speech, or of the press; or the

right of the people peaceably to assemble, and to petition
the Government for a redress of grievances.

The First Amendment was perhaps the most revolutionary thing
that the Founding Fathers did. Although the Bill of Rights that the
British Parliament had passed in 1689 gave Britons the right to petition the monarch without fear of retribution, it guaranteed freedom
of speech only within Parliament. It did not grant ordinary people
the right to free speech.

The art of persuasion is valued wherever public opinion is valued. That included ancient Athens, the community that coined the
term *democracy*, which means rule by the people. The classic ancient
text on rhetoric was by the philosopher Aristotle, a Macedonian who
spent much of his career in Athens. Some philosophers argue that
everything written about rhetoric since then is just a series of responses to Aristotle.

Aristotle had been a student of Plato, who in turn had been a
student of Socrates. Socrates had a dim view of democracy, and his
pro-Spartan and antidemocratic political views probably explain
why the Athenians eventually sentenced him to death. Most of what
we know about Socrates comes from the writings of Plato. One of
Plato's early writings, the Socratic dialogue *Gorgias*, expressed a low
opinion of rhetoric and of the sophists, who were teachers of rhetoric
who often traveled from one city in the ancient Greek world to
another. Plato later expressed a more moderate view in the Socratic
dialogue *Phaedrus*, arguing that in the hands of a true philosopher,
rhetoric could serve as the "midwife of the soul," winning the soul
through discourse.

The ability to "win souls" through the power of speech can be a
source of great power. As Winston Churchill explained,

> Of all the talents bestowed upon men, none is so precious
> as the gift of oratory. He who enjoys it wields a power more
> durable than that of a great king. He is an independent
> force in the world. Abandoned by his party, betrayed by his
> friends, stripped of his offices, whoever can command this
> power is still formidable.

Tyrannical societies repress freedom of speech because they don't want just anybody to have that kind of power. In contrast, democratic societies often encourage the teaching of rhetoric as a means of strengthening democratic institutions, to prevent power from being concentrated in the hands of a few.

I look at rhetoric from two perspectives. One is the perspective of the person who attempts to persuade. The other is from the perspective of the audience. Training in rhetoric can help an individual learn to become more persuasive. As Churchill explained, "rhetorical power is neither wholly bestowed nor wholly acquired, but cultivated." At the same time, the audience can also become more sophisticated—less vulnerable to dishonest manipulation.

I believe that all young people should learn about the principles of rhetoric in high school, partly so that they can become more effective advocates on their own behalf and partly so that they can become a more critical audience. Training in rhetoric should not be reserved for pre-law students. If we want to "Secure the blessings of Liberty to ourselves and our Posterity," as the Preamble to the Constitution states, then everyone should learn how to think critically about what they are told.

In the classical liberal arts curriculum, rhetoric was the third of the verbal arts, after grammar and logic. The reason for this is simple. Grammar gives you skills that you need for the study of logic. In turn, logic gives you skills that you need for the study of rhetoric.

Aristotle said that there are three means of persuasion: logos, ethos, and pathos. By *logos*, Aristotle meant logic and reason. He meant the kinds of skills that you develop through studying grammar and logic. Logos includes the only arguments that really matter in a scientific debate. If you find a logical error or a false premise in a scientific argument, then you can cast doubt on the conclusion. In science, *ethos* and *pathos* don't matter.

By *ethos*, in contrast, Aristotle meant the character and reputation of the speaker. Aristotle meant that some people are more or less believable than others because they are known to be honest or dishonest, wise or foolish, well-informed or ignorant. That kind of reputation isn't supposed to be important in modern scientific debates. After all, even Albert Einstein was wrong about the expansion of the universe and about some aspects of quantum physics. Nevertheless, the opinions of an expert witness are still valued in a court of law.

By *pathos*, Aristotle meant an appeal to the emotions. Although modern scientists aren't supposed to be swayed by their emotions in making decisions about what is true or false, emotions are definitely important in making choices and in making decisions about moral issues. People who have lost their ability to have normal emotional reactions, because of disease or injury to the brain, also lose their ability to make simple decisions, even if they can still pass an IQ test.

The ideas of *logos*, *ethos*, and *pathos* are important if you are trying to persuade people and if you are in the audience. Logos (logic and reason) is important for persuading rational people, or for making decisions about matters of fact. Your own *ethos* (character and reputation) is important if you need to persuade people. If you are in the audience, you need to think about whether the reputation of the messenger matters, or whether you should judge the message on its own merits. *Pathos* (emotion), along with logos, is essential for making decisions about moral issues. However, one must also guard against being carried away by irrational biases, fears, and hatreds.

We learned in the 20th century that charismatic leaders who appeal to the population's irrational biases, fears, and hatreds can cause serious problems. As the Canadian sociologist Robert Altemeyer explained, "In a democracy, a wannabe tyrant is just a comical figure on a soapbox unless a huge wave of supporters lifts him to high office. That's how Adolf Hitler destroyed the Weimar Republic and became the Führer. So we need to understand the people out there doing the wave. Ultimately the problem lay in the followers."[1] Through his research, Altemeyer has found that the people who are most susceptible to fascist-style propaganda have poor skills in logic. That makes sense, because logic is one of the studies that are appropriate for free people, not slaves.

Aristotle argued that there are three branches of rhetoric, by which he meant that rhetoric is used for three different purposes. In the modern world, we can still find rhetoric being used for those same three purposes. The first branch is deliberative rhetoric, which is intended to persuade people to do (or not to do) something. Nearly anybody who lives, works, or plays with other people engages in deliberative rhetoric in daily life. It's how people bargain for what they want. Legislators use deliberative rhetoric when they ask for your vote in an election or try to persuade their fellow legislators to vote their way on a piece of legislation. The second branch of rhetoric is judicial or forensic rhetoric, which is the sort of rhetoric we see in modern courtrooms. The point of judicial rhetoric is to support or defend against a particular charge. The third form of rhetoric, called epideictic rhetoric, is ceremonial speech, the "praise and blame" rhetoric that you may hear at a funerals or in the nominating speech at a political convention.

According to the great Roman orator Cicero, there are five established principles (canons) of rhetoric: invention, arrangement, style, memory, and delivery. By invention, he meant that one should try to discover the available means of persuasion. For a speaker in the old days, that generally meant facts and arguments. Today, it could mean an entire "dog and pony show," with slide shows, videos, handouts, props, etc.

Arrangement means to select and assemble the arguments effectively. If you've ever had to make a sales pitch, you know how important it is to decide what to say and what not to say, and how to put together your entire presentation. Should you start off with a joke, or should you just get down to business? Should you try to make a logical argument, or should you just talk about feelings?

Style involves presenting the argument in an appealing way. It specifically meant word choice, sentence structures, and figures of speech. The style that you choose depends largely on your audience. Are you talking to scientists or to laymen? Are you talking to strangers, or to people who know you well?

Memory doesn't necessarily mean that you have memorized a particular speech. It means that you have done so much preparation that you can give a polished speech on the spur of the moment, without notes or text. It means that you can adjust your presentation to your audience, and respond to questions from the audience.

Delivery means the effective use of the voice, gestures, and exhibits. Can people hear you clearly? Is your voice pleasant, or does it grate on the ear? Do you move naturally and make gestures that reinforce your message, rather than distracting from it? Can you use your props and displays effectively?

I think that it's worthwhile for students to learn about these basic principles of rhetoric, and to study some of the speeches of great orators. Aristotle's treatise on rhetoric and the speeches and writings of great Roman orators have been used in modern times to teach rhetoric. To develop his powerful speaking skills, the anti-slavery activist Frederick Douglass memorized the speeches of the great Roman orators.

In the electronic age, it has become easier than ever to study rhetoric. Not only can we read some of the great speeches from throughout history, we can also hear sound recordings and even see video of some of the great speakers of the 20th century and today.

The classical authors' writings on rhetoric generally dealt with oratory—speech. The power of speech was a great leveler in the ancient world. Some men were far wealthier and more powerful than others; yet when a man spoke in a public assembly, he was, for at least that moment, on equal footing with everyone else. In contrast, modern communications are largely controlled by a handful of major corporations. Modern audiences are bombarded with a multimedia barrage of sound and visual and text messages. These messages are intended to reshape what we think is good or bad, what we think is possible, what we should want, and even what we are—all to serve the interests of the corporations rather than those of the audience.

Plato painted such an unsympathetic portrait of the rhetoricians (sophists) of his day that the term sophistry came to mean dishonest rhetoric. Yet I think that the modern public relations industry would have boggled his mind. In Part III, I'll deal with the methods of persuasion that were developed by the public relations and advertising industry in the 20th century and how democratic political activists responded to them.

Reference

1. Altemeyer R: *The Authoritarians*. Winnipeg, Manitoba: Robert Altemeyer. 2006. http://members.shaw.ca/jeanaltemeyer/drbob/TheAuthoritarians.pdf

PART III: *Propaganda and Politics*

The United States is the wealthiest and most powerful nation that has ever existed. It has a government that is supposedly based on the will of the people. The United States should therefore be the closest thing that there has ever been to a paradise on earth. Yet when you look at the statistics that describe human well-being, you make some disturbing discoveries.

The United States may have more Nobel laureates than any other country, but it lags behind many other countries—including other English-speaking countries—in literacy. The United States spends more per person on healthcare than the people of any other nation, yet the United States ranked 37th in terms of the performance of its healthcare system. The United States is often called the Land of the Free, yet we have more people in prison than any other country. The United States is called the Home of the Brave, yet the US population has been prone to bouts of paranoia about subversion by foreign agents, usually at a time when no other nation posed any imaginable military threat.

A wealthy country doesn't get outcomes like those through an open and democratic process. These problems reflect the fact that the United States has long been ruled by a self-described "invisible government"—a small but powerful wealthy elite who make the major policy decisions in their own interests and use the public relations industry to bring the rest of the population along, as a shepherd gently herds sheep.

Kurt Vonnegut Jr. explained this problem in his essay about the 1972 Republican Convention:

> The two real political parties in America are the *Winners* and the *Losers*. The people do not acknowledge this. They claim membership in two imaginary parties, the *Republicans* and the *Democrats*, instead.
>
> Both imaginary parties are bossed by Winners. When Republicans battle Democrats, this much is certain: Winners will win.

In the next few chapters, I'll explain how the public's ignorance of the liberal arts and the humanities has allowed the Winners to win and the rest of us to lose. These chapters will help you understand what's really at stake in debates about educational policy.

CHAPTER XII

Propaganda

B ack in the fourth century BC, Plato warned the Athenians that they could be misled by sophists—people who were skilled at debate. The word *sophist* originally just meant someone who was good at any skilled trade. Eventually, it came to mean people who were good at debating and at teaching debating tactics. As a result, the word *sophistry* came to mean subtly misleading arguments. By the mid 20th century, people in the United States had another term for misleading political communications: propaganda.

The term *propaganda* originally came from *Congregatio de Propaganda Fide*, or Congregation for Propagating the Faith, which was a missionary branch of the Roman Catholic Church. In some languages, *propaganda* simply means advertising. Yet in English, the word *propaganda* took on bad connotations because the Germans used it during World War I. To English-speaking people, the word *propaganda* suggests unfair manipulation for evil political purposes. Of course, dishonest rhetoric and unfair manipulation are as old as politics. In the 20th century, however, the development of mass communication techniques led to the birth of entire industries dedicated to shaping public opinion: public relations and advertising. These industries exist to serve whoever can pay their fees.

Rhetoric is one of the classical liberal arts, which meant the studies that are appropriate for free people, as opposed to slaves. The study of rhetoric helps an individual play a meaningful role in politics. Besides helping you learn to become more persuasive, it helps you sort out truth from lies. In the 21st century, the studies that are appropriate for free people would have to include not just Aristotelian rhetoric and Ciceronian oratory but the methods of persuasion that are being used by the public relations and advertising industries. In this chapter and in Chapter 13, I'll talk about how public relations and advertising have been used to manipulate the public. In Chapter 14, I'll talk about how various activists, writers, and scholars have tried to help the public resist being misled.

For centuries, the writings of Aristotle and the speeches of Cicero were the standard texts that were used for teaching rhetoric. It may seem odd for people in the 21st century to think so much about some ancient Greeks and Romans. Yet as I explained in Chapter 11, their ideas about the basic purposes and methods of persuasion are still important. To bring this curriculum up to date, it helps to study the careers of two pioneers in the field of public relations: Ivy Lee and Edward Bernays.

As you study the history of public relations, it's important to keep in mind a warning from Plato. Although Plato generally expressed a low opinion of the sophists, he pointed out that in the hands of a true philosopher, some of the techniques that the sophists used could be "midwife to the soul." In other words, some methods of persuasion aren't necessarily good or bad in themselves but can be used for either good or bad purposes. The best example is the press release, which is a message sent to journalists.

Ivy Lee is generally credited with inventing the press release. In 1906, while Lee was working for the Pennsylvania Railroad, a catastrophic train accident occurred in Atlantic City, New Jersey. Lee persuaded the railroad to hand out a printed statement to the journalists who were on the scene. The *New York Times* then printed the text of the statement word for word.

A press release is an efficient way to get your point across to journalists. If you put together a good press release, you will be more likely to get press coverage, and you will be far less likely to be misunderstood or misquoted. On the other hand, companies and organizations that put out lots of slick press releases may get more and better coverage than they deserve. Nowadays, many companies even send out video news releases that are sometimes run on news broadcasts as if they had been produced by the news outlet itself. These video news releases are a cheap way for news programs to fill up their airtime.

Lee understood how important it is for a company to get its side of the story out first, before rumors have a chance to spread. Lee also knew how important it is for a company to influence how the press will respond to a crisis. As a result, Lee became known as the father of modern crisis communications. One of those crises was one of the most violent labor strikes in US history, the 1913-1914 Colorado Coal Strike. That strike was a watershed event in US history, not only in labor relations but in the development of the field of public relations. Yet for some reason, children seldom learn about it in history class.

The Southern Coal Field of southern Colorado had large deposits of high-grade bituminous coal, which was used primarily as coking coal for the steel industry. Since this kind of coal was so important for making steel rails for the railroads, the Southern Coal Field became dominated by a few large companies. The largest was Colorado Fuel and Iron, which produced three quarters of Colorado's coal by 1892. In 1903, CF&I was bought by John D. Rockefeller Sr. and Jay Gould.

By 1906, roughly 10% of the population of Colorado depended on CF&I in some way for their livelihood. In the coalfields, the people who would ordinarily be independent professionals or public employees (doctors, clergy, teachers, and police) were all coal company employees. CF&I and other large coal operators also largely controlled the state government. When you have a situation where a few people control so much of what goes on in a society, you don't have democracy, even if the society goes through the motions of holding elections. What you have is oligarchy.

Mining is always a dangerous occupation, but the coal mines in Colorado were particularly dangerous. Mining was twice as deadly in Colorado as in the nation as a whole. Yet the hand-picked coroner's juries almost always decided that the coal companies weren't to blame for the deaths. Most of the miners in the southern Colorado coalfields were recent immigrants from Southern and Eastern Europe. Some had originally been brought in as strikebreakers in 1903. By September 1913, however, the United Mine Workers of America organized the workers in the Southern Coal Field. The union then issued a list of demands.

In addition to getting the company to recognize their union, the miners wanted the company to pay them 10% more per ton of coal. They also wanted the right to have a miner check the scales, to keep the company from cheating them. They also wanted to be paid for "dead work," such as laying track or shoring up the walls and ceilings of the mine. They wanted the right to trade in any store, instead of being ripped off by the company store. They also wanted the right to choose their own boarding places and to pick their own doctor. Finally, they wanted Colorado's mining laws to be enforced, and they wanted the company guard system to be abolished. When these reasonable demands were not met, about 90% of the miners struck. The strikers and their families moved into tent colonies established by the UMWA. The largest of these colonies was at Ludlow, Colorado. It consisted of about 200 tents and housed 1200 miners and their families.

In response, the coal operators brought in strikebreakers and launched a campaign of harassment and intimidation. The coal operators' men used high-powered searchlights to keep people in the tent camps awake at night. In addition to beating and sometimes murdering individual miners, the coal operators' men periodically sprayed the tent camps with bullets from a machine gun mounted on an armored car called the Death Special. To defend themselves and their wives and children from the bullets, the miners dug foxholes under the tents.

The coal operators wanted to provoke a violent response from the miners so that the governor of Colorado would call out the National Guard. Then, the taxpayers would get stuck with most of the bill for breaking the strike. After the Colorado National Guard was called out in October 1913, violence escalated still further. Its commander was an ophthalmologist named Gen. John Chase, who had been court-martialed for his brutality in putting down earlier coal strikes in Colorado.

On the evening of April 20, 1914, the National Guard sprayed the tent colony at Ludlow with bullets and set fire to some of the tents. At least 18 people died, including two women and 11 children who were asphyxiated in the cellar of one of the tents. In retaliation, miners attacked dozens of mines over the following 10 days, with the violence leading to 53 more deaths.

When news of the massacre at Ludlow was printed in the *New York Times*, it sparked public outrage, much of which was directed personally at John D. Rockefeller Jr., who had recently received controlling interest in CF&I from his father. The Ludlow Massacre became a public scandal, only partly because famous people like the novelist Upton Sinclair used it to highlight the harsh working conditions in the mines and the brutality of management. The scandal also provided an opportunity for anyone who resented the elder Rockefeller's sharp business practices—including some people who weren't exactly sympathetic to labor—to express their anger at the Rockefellers. The coal strike was also creating problems for the steel and railroad companies by causing the price of coal to go up. Something had to be done, and a lot of that something was done by Ivy Lee—a man who had already had experience in settling coal strikes.

Lee sent out information bulletins to opinion leaders, especially on the East Coast. Those bulletins contained lies about the strike, about the actions of the Colorado National Guard, and particularly about the Ludlow Massacre. After Ivy Lee spread the lie that the women and children had died because a stove fell over, Upton Sinclair dubbed him Poison Ivy. The poet Carl Sandburg referred to Ivy Lee as a "hired slanderer" and a "paid liar."

Lee's first chore was to help settle the coal strike. To defuse tensions, Lee had John D. Rockefeller Jr. make highly publicized personal visits to the coal camps. Then, Lee advised Rockefeller to set up company-controlled unions that were not part of the UMWA. To implement that plan, Rockefeller hired William Lyon Mackenzie

King, a former Canadian labor minister who later became the Prime Minister of Canada. In 1935, company unions were made illegal by the National Labor Relations Act (the Wagner Act).

Lee's second chore was to repair the Rockefeller family's reputation, which had been further damaged by the revelations that John D. Rockefeller Sr. had approved of what had been going on in Colorado. Lee made sure that the press was bombarded with positive images of the Rockefellers and their philanthropy. Lee even cultivated a new public persona for John D. Rockefeller Sr. As a result, the press began portraying the rapacious businessman as a kindly old gent who handed out dimes to strangers.

As one of the most prominent people in the newly established field of public relations, Lee argued that the field should establish some ethical standards. Some of these ethical standards were simply common sense. For example, Lee taught that companies shouldn't hesitate to tell people things that they are going to find out anyway. He also argued that companies should rethink policies that prove to be too unpopular. Lee even claimed to adhere to some ethical standards himself. Yet before his death in 1934 from a brain tumor, Lee did some consulting work for the government of Nazi Germany, specifically on "the disarmament question, the Jewish problem, and its handling of foreign debts."[1]

One of the most controversial and misunderstood events in Lee's career was his trip to the Soviet Union in 1927. Some people think that it meant that he was somehow in league with the Worldwide Communist Conspiracy. The truth is far simpler than that. It can be summed up in a single, three-letter word: oil.

Lee's main client was Standard Oil, which was in the oil business, not the ideology business. In 1901, the Russian tsar's empire accounted for 55% of world oil output. After the Bolsheviks took over, the Soviet Union continued to be a major producer of oil. To Standard Oil, commercial reality mattered far more than any political ideology. After all, the purpose of political ideology is to keep the public in line. No sensible captain of industry would use it as a guide for making business decisions. What mattered most to the Rockefellers was whether the Soviet Union's oil concessions would go to Standard Oil or to a British oil company, Royal Dutch-Shell. Lee's trip to the Soviet Union in 1927 was prompted by a temporary breakdown of relations between Britain and Russia. Note that John Dewey, who owed his career to Rockefeller philanthropy, made a grand tour of the Soviet Union in 1928.

Lee's main clients were big monopolistic companies like the Pennsylvania Railroad and Standard Oil. In fact, Lee felt that monopolies were natural and good and that competition was bad. He felt that all of a country's industries should eventually be brought under some sort of monopolistic centralized control. Back then, it was called being "Standardized"—a reference to the Standard Oil trust.

From the worker's perspective, there's not much difference between industries being controlled by the interlocking boards of directors of the trusts (as in the United States in the late 19th century) and industries being controlled by a Congress of Soviets (as in the Soviet Union). In either case, the productive assets within the society are under control of a small number of people who have little or no accountability to the public at large. Neither system can be considered government by the people. Therefore, neither could honestly be called a democracy. Also, both systems sometimes use deadly force to keep wages down.

Like Ivy Lee, Edward Bernays also had contempt for democracy. He preferred instead an "enlightened despotism." Bernays, who is often called the father of public relations, wrote several books about the subject. In his book *Propaganda*, he wrote, "The conscious and intelligent manipulation of the organized habits and opinions of the masses is an important element in democratic society. Those who manipulate this unseen mechanism of society constitute an invisible government which is the true ruling power of our country." Yet the manipulation of the masses by elites is not "an important element in democratic society." It's the exact opposite of democracy, if the word *democracy* has any real meaning.

Bernays saw public relations as an applied social science that uses insights from psychology, sociology, and other disciplines to scientifically manage and manipulate the thinking and behavior of the public, which in his view was irrational and herdlike. He felt that the American public could not be trusted to vote for the right men. Thus, they had to be "guided from above." He also felt that Guatemalans, in particular, voted for the wrong men and needed to be guided from the United States. Bernays engineered the propaganda campaign that supported the CIA's overthrow of a democratically elected government in Guatemala, launching a 36-year civil war in which roughly 250,000 people were killed.

In addition to popularizing the works of his uncle Sigmund Freud in the United States, Bernays helped to get American women hooked on cigarettes. He staged a demonstration at the 1929 Easter Parade in New York City, hiring models to hold lit Lucky Strike cigarettes, sold by the American Tobacco Company, as "Torches of Freedom." Thus, Bernays exploited the positive feelings that women had about the women's suffrage movement and used them to sell cigarettes. In the 1970s, the Phillip Morris Company used imagery from the Women's Liberation movement ("You've come a long way, baby!") to sell Virginia Slims cigarettes.

To boost the sales of Lucky Strike cigarettes, which came in a dark green package, Bernays persuaded the fashion industry to make dark green the hot color for the 1934 season. When the chromium used in Lucky Strike's green ink was in short supply during World War II, American Tobacco made a big fuss about a change to a white package: "Lucky Strike green has gone to war!" American Tobacco and its ad agency got a lot of hate mail because of that campaign, but sales of Lucky Strike cigarettes soared.

Students can learn several important lessons from studying Bernays' career. One is that many events that appear to be spontaneous are actually being stage-managed for political or commercial purposes. Although the staged events themselves may be extensively covered in the news (like the Torches of Freedom demonstration and the hot color for 1934), the role of the public relations firms in creating and publicizing these events is rarely revealed.

One telling exception occurred in 1990 during the lead-up to Operation Desert Storm, which was the first US war against Iraq. A 15-year-old Kuwaiti girl known only as "Nayirah"—supposedly to protect her family back in Kuwait—testified before the US Congressional Human Rights Caucus. She claimed that Iraqi soldiers had taken babies out of incubators at the al-Addan Hospital, leaving the babies on the cold floor to die. Thus, *pathos*, meaning an appeal to the emotions, was used to stir up war fever against Iraq. However, I could tell from the beginning that Nayirah's story was a load of crap. I relied on a combination of *ethos* and *logos*.

By *ethos*, I mean that I didn't trust Nayirah personally. I had no way of knowing who she was, and nobody bothered to explain how she had miraculously escaped from an occupied country and made her way back to the United States. She sounded Americanized to me. Thus, I thought it was much more likely that she'd been in the United States all along. Also, she didn't look or sound like someone who was talking about horrors she'd seen personally. To me, she looked and sounded like a high school drama student reading from a script. Why would she need to read from a script to tell us about horrifying things that she had seen in person? By *logos*, I mean that her story made no sense. Why would soldiers waste time with incubators, which have no military value and would not bring a high price on the black market? Besides, how cold is the floor in Kuwait in August and September? If soldiers did come in and take the incubators, leaving babies on a cold floor, wouldn't Nayirah or somebody else have simply picked the babies up and put them someplace warm?

Reporters and editors seemed to take the story at face value. However, the newspaper accounts included details that made it even more obvious to me that Nayirah's testimony was a hoax. According to the news reports, 312 babies had been taken from incubators and left on the floor in Kuwait. That number seemed suspiciously large, not to mention suspiciously precise. Only after the war was it publically revealed that the whole story was cooked up by the public relations firm Hill and Knowlton, which received about $11 million for its services. Hill and Knowlton was run by men with political connections to former President Reagan and then-President George H. W. Bush. "Nayirah" was actually Nijirah al-Sabah, the daughter of the Kuwaiti ambassador to the United States. As I suspected, she was not in Kuwait during the invasion.

The false stories about the babies being taken from their incubators and left on the cold floor to die were an attempt to persuade the people of the United States to support the President's decision to go to war with Iraq. Thus, these lies were an attempt at deliberative rhetoric—rhetoric intended to persuade people to adopt a particular course of action. These stories used *pathos* as a method of persuasion.

I wasn't taken in by the propaganda because I knew too many facts about the politics of the Middle East—partly because of what I'd learned in school and partly because of what I had learned from acquaintances who had lived in the Middle East and from library books I had read. Yet even if I didn't know those facts, I would have been suspicious just because of the nature of the rhetoric that was being used. In Chapter 13, I'll explain in more detail how a propaganda campaign led the American people to support World War I. In Chapter 14, I'll explain how other Americans learned to resist such propaganda campaigns.

Reference

1. Ivy Lee down for $25,000 on Nazi Payroll. P.R.R. Rockefeller press aid cited in inquiry. Paid by dye trust; Counseled German on arms, Jews, debt questions. *Pittsburgh Post-Gazette.* July 12, 1934.

CHAPTER XIII

Naturally, the Common People Don't Want War

W hen people in the United States talk about problems in education, they generally talk about the problems that young people will face in the job market. Children who do well in school can go on to become doctors, lawyers, and business executives. Children who don't do well in school will end up in McJobs that pay less than a living wage and that provide no pension or healthcare benefits—if they don't end up unemployed or in prison. But I think that we, the people of the United States, should be talking about far more than that.

We should be talking about why we tolerate bad public schools in poor neighborhoods. Why do we tolerate no-benefits McJobs, high unemployment rates, and a growing prison-industrial complex? Why aren't we demanding universal not-for-profit national health insurance? Why do we tolerate endless war? These problems are actually symptoms of a lack of democracy. Other societies have avoided or solved these problems through democratic means. We could, too.

Many people are shocked by the suggestion that the United States doesn't have the world's highest standard of living and the world's best human rights record. They are positively stunned by the suggestion that there might be a shortage of democracy in the United States. Isn't the United States the "City on a Hill" that the rest of the world is supposed to imitate? Isn't democracy supposed to be one of our major exports? Besides, don't we have regular elections? Doesn't that prove that our country is a democracy?

Unfortunately, surprisingly few people in the United States have given serious thought to the Socratic question "What is democracy?" Those who do ask the question often get sidetracked into technical questions, such as whether a particular society has direct democracy or representative democracy, or whether a particular government should be classified as a democracy or a republic. As a result, people have lost sight of the idea that democracy is supposed to mean government "of the people, by the people, and for the people." Elections and so on are merely a means to an end. The real question is not whether decisions are made through public referendum or by elected representatives. The real question is whether government policy represents the will of the people, or whether it represents the will of a small ruling class and is merely being imposed on everybody else.

If you want to understand what democracy is and what happens when rule by the people is subverted, you need to study some history. In 1916, President Woodrow Wilson was re-elected, partly on the strength of the slogan "He kept us out of war." Yet within a few weeks of starting his second term as President of the United States, he asked Congress to declare war on Germany. Thus, the United States entered World War I.

Why did Wilson think that the United States needed to get tangled up in a pointless, mechanized slaughter that had already been going on for more than two years? Wilson said that it was "to make the world safe for democracy." Yet hadn't his own people re-elected him because they didn't want war? What about democracy at home? How could anyone believe that the war was a struggle for democracy if the Russian Tsar was one of our allies?

A naïve person might think that the re-election of the President who "kept us out of war" would be a mandate for peace. Yet the United States entered the war just a month after the start of Wilson's second term. In other words, the decision to enter the war was undemocratic, which is hardly surprising. The decision to enter a modern war is never made democratically. Besides, the idea that Wilson had kept the United States out of war was ludicrous. Wilson had invaded Nicaragua in 1914, Haiti in 1915, and the Dominican

Republic in 1916. He'd sent an expeditionary force into Mexico in 1916 and had stationed 100,000 troops along the Mexican border to prepare for aggressive war against Mexico. Only the prospect of war in Europe prevented a major war with Mexico in 1916.

When I look at Web sites that try to explain why the United States entered World War I, I find a lot of sentences that say "The United States wanted this" or "The United States didn't want that." These sentences make no sense. This is one of those situations where one must carefully study the noun-verb transactions in a sentence. What does it mean for the United States to *want* something? The United States of America is not a person but a mental construct—an abstraction. Unlike a human being, an abstraction cannot want things. All this talk about what the United States "wanted" obscures the real question, which is *who* in the United States wanted the war, and who did not.

The pressure to enter the war came from bankers and industrialists, who were mainly affiliated with the Republican Party. They wanted profits. The war started in August of 1914. At that point, the Central Powers (the German Empire, the Austro-Hungarian Empire, and the Ottoman Empire) were at war with the Allies (Britain, France, Russia, and Serbia). Italy had originally been allied with Germany but entered the war on the Allied side in 1915. Although the United States was officially neutral until April of 1917, President Wilson was sympathetic to the Allies from the beginning. He lifted the ban on private bank loans to the Allies in 1915. From then on, American banks lent vast amounts of money to the Allies, mainly to Britain. Most of this money went through the "House of Morgan" —J.P. Morgan and Company, which served as the agent for the Allies.

The Allies used that borrowed money to buy enormous amounts of goods—including weapons and ammunition—from manufacturers in the United States. The bankers profited because the loans yielded interest, and the steelmakers and the weapons and ammunition manufacturers profited because they sold lots of merchandise. The wealthiest people in the United States were making money hand over fist as millions of men were dying in Europe. The challenge for American businessmen was how to keep the war going.

From the very beginning, prominent Republicans such as former President Theodore Roosevelt and former President William
Howard Taft wanted the United States to enter the war. Meanwhile,
President Wilson, who was a Democrat, maintained the fiction that
the United States was officially neutral, even as he allowed US banks
and industry to profit from selling weapons and other supplies to
the Allies. That kind of fake neutrality could not last forever, and
German submarines eventually started sinking US-flagged mer-
chant ships without warning. This unrestricted submarine warfare
was supposedly the casus belli—or justification for the United States
to declare war against Germany.

Another casus belli was the Zimmermann telegram. Arthur
Zimmermann was the Foreign Secretary of the German Empire. On
January 16, 1917, he sent a telegram to the German Ambassador to
Mexico, asking him to try to persuade Mexico to enter a military
alliance with Germany. Then, if the United States declared war on
Germany, Germany would provide financial and military support to
help Mexico reconquer Texas, New Mexico, and Arizona. The
British intercepted and decoded the telegram and informed the US
government.

Historians like to say that the Zimmermann telegram "inflamed
tensions" between the United States and Mexico. Hardly. No sane
person would have taken Zimmermann's suggestion seriously. Nor
would any sane person be angry at Mexico for something that the
German foreign secretary said in a telegram. Nobody in the US
State Department or War Department had any fear of Mexico. In
fact, President Wilson had been pointlessly belligerent toward
Mexico. He'd used a misunderstanding between US Navy sailors
and Mexican federal soldiers at Tampico, Tamaulipas, as an excuse
to launch a military occupation of the port of Veracruz. Shortly
thereafter, the counterrevolutionary General Victoriano Huerta
ceded power to Venustiano Carranza, whom Wilson immediately
recognized as the de facto president of Mexico.

After Carranza's rival Pancho Villa made some cross-border
raids, in the hopes of provoking a war between Carranza and the
United States, Wilson sent a military expedition into northern

Mexico to pursue Villa. The US expedition failed to capture Villa but did provoke a confrontation with Carranza's forces. Carranza, of course, did not want war with the United States. In fact, he'd called for mediation in 1916, to prevent a major invasion from the United States. Carranza knew that he'd never win a war against the Giant of the North, and he'd never be able to pacify the English-speaking population of those three states even if he did manage to occupy them militarily. Carranza also knew that Germany wouldn't have been able to give him any meaningful support in any event.

I initially suspected that what triggered the US entry into World War I was the breakdown of military discipline in the French army in the spring of 1917. By that time, France had already lost a million men (out of a total population of 20 million males of all ages). If the French refused to continue fighting, the war would have to end, along with the war industries' profits. However, my friend Peter Geidel argues persuasively that Wilson and his advisors were far too stupid to have realized that the French army was on the point of collapse when the US entered the war. Dr. Geidel feels that Wilson wanted to enter the war after the sinking of the British passenger liner *RMS Lusitania* in May of 1915. Only the strong antiwar public sentiment, and in particular the opposition of his Secretary of State William Jennings Bryan, thwarted those desires, delaying US entry into the war.

World War I started in August 1914. Within a few months, some wealthy and prominent Americans had set up organizations to promote the idea that the United States should prepare to enter the war. The so-called Preparedness movement was led by such organizations as the National Security League, which was founded by Gen. Leonard Wood, a close friend of Theodore Roosevelt. The National Security League then gave rise to the American Defense Society. Another organization that helped to promote the war effort was the League to Enforce Peace, whose first president was William Howard Taft. Theodore Roosevelt wrote two books to promote the Preparedness movement. Roosevelt and Gen. Wood also wanted to set up a training camp in Plattsburgh, New York, to prepare businessmen and professional men to serve as military officers.

There was a lot of pro-war sentiment among wealthy Republicans. However, the idea of war—and especially the prospect of a draft—was extremely unpopular among the general population. The Wilson administration was worried about the possibility of draft riots, like those that shook New York City during the Civil War.

The idea of war was particularly unpopular among farmers and members of the urban working class. German and Scandinavian immigrants tended to favor neutrality. All of Ireland was still under British rule, and few Irish-Americans wanted to risk their lives to help Britain. Many trade unionists, socialists, and anarchists actively opposed the war. The war was also unpopular with the antimilitarists and pacifists who were strong in Protestant churches and in women's groups.

There were two basic ways in which the people of the United States were brought to do the bidding of their leaders in World War I. One approach was an onslaught of pro-war propaganda organized by the Committee on Public Information, which was established as an independent agency of the US government in April of 1917. It is more widely known by the name of its chairman, George Creel. The other approach was to crush dissent, often through unconstitutional means.

The Creel Committee used a multimedia approach to propaganda. It published a daily newsletter that went to all of the nation's newspapers. It also hired some of the nation's most famous illustrators to work on war posters. The Creel Committee also used telegraph, cable, and radio to coordinate its efforts (there were no commercial radio stations back then). It also recruited 75,000 "Four Minute Men"—volunteers who were asked to give short, up-beat, pro-war speeches at social events and during reel changes at movie theaters. The Creel Committee even recruited high school students to give Four Minute speeches at their schools.

Of course, some people were resistant to the Creel Commission's message. However, anyone who did or said anything that was deemed to obstruct the military draft or military recruitment could be punished under the newly passed Espionage Act. Foreign-born people who criticized the war in any way could be deported. Wilson had wanted the Espionage Act to give him censorship power over the press. Congress refused to pass something that so blatantly violated the First Amendment, but it did block the distribution of antiwar literature through the Post Office.

The propaganda efforts did more than build public support for the war. They also promoted narrow-mindedness and inflamed ethnic hatred. Sauerkraut was renamed "liberty cabbage," and the use of foreign languages such as German and Russian was banned in many cities. Immigrants such as Irish-Americans or German-Americans were disparaged as "hyphenated Americans" and presumed to have divided loyalties. In a speech in September 1919, Woodrow Wilson said, "Any man who carries a hyphen about with him carries a dagger that he is ready to plunge into the vitals of this Republic whenever he gets ready." In April of 1918, a naturalized US citizen named Robert Prager was lynched because he was a German immigrant and had socialist political views. Twelve men were tried for his murder but were acquitted by a sympathetic jury.

More than 100,000 American servicemen and –women died in World War I, and 200,000 more were injured. Yet the first American casualty of the United States' "war to make the world safe for democracy" was democracy itself. The propaganda efforts that were developed to get the people of the United States to support the war were then used to undermine democracy in other ways after the war, as I'll explain in Chapter 15.

The Creel Commission's success in building support for war in the United States made a deep impression on influential members of the Nazi Party, which developed in Germany in the aftermath of World War I. In the campaign to stir up hatred against the Jews, Nazi Propaganda Minister Joseph Goebbels used methods described in the book *Crystallizing Public Opinion*, which was written by Edward Bernays, who had been a member of the Creel Committee.

After World War II, an American psychiatrist named Gustave Gilbert had the opportunity to interview former Reichsmarshall Hermann Göring, who was in prison awaiting trial for war crimes. Göring clearly explained how war represents a subversion of democracy:

Göring: Why, of course, the people don't want war. Why would some poor slob on a farm want to risk his life in a war when the best that he can get out of it is to come back to his farm in one piece? Naturally, the common people don't want war; neither in Russia nor in England nor in America, nor for that matter in Germany. That is understood. But, after all, it is the leaders of the country who determine the policy and it is always a simple matter to drag the people along, whether it is a democracy or a fascist dictatorship or a parliament or a Communist dictatorship.

Gilbert: There is one difference. In a democracy, the people have some say in the matter through their elected representatives, and in the United States only Congress can declare wars.

Göring: Oh, that is all well and good, but, voice or no voice, the people can always be brought to do the bidding of the leaders. That is easy. All you have to do is tell them they are being attacked and denounce the pacifists for lack of patriotism and exposing the country to danger. It works the same way in any country.

Göring had a point. World War I and World War II provide strong evidence of the fact that ordinary people have been brought along to do the bidding of their leaders, often with disastrous effects. According to Göring, the leaders of a country determine policy. It's obvious to anyone who has ever studied history, psychology, or economics that the leaders can be depended upon to design policies that serve their own interests. Unfortunately, those policies often serve the powerful at the expense of ordinary people. In the early 20th century, socialists were quick to point out that it made no sense for the working class men in the trenches to be fighting each other when their real enemies were the wealthy people who sent them all to war.

War is not the only thing that people have been dragged along to accept. Unlike the people of other industrialized countries, we the people of the United States have also been dragged along to ac-

cept lousy public schools and outrageously expensive higher education. We have been dragged along to accept a healthcare system that
is designed to maximize corporate profits, rather than the health of
the people. The United States is the only major industrialized country where medical bills are the major cause of personal bankruptcy
and lack of medical insurance is a major cause of death. We think of
the United States as the land of the free, yet we have the world's largest prison population—not just in terms of the percentage of our
population but in terms of total numbers. We really don't have to
tolerate any of this.

The idea that the people should be dragged along to support or
at least accept whatever their rulers want is based on the idea that
ordinary people are not fully human or at least not fully adult—that
they are not capable or worthy of having any real voice in shaping
public policy. Especially after the rise of the public relations industry,
many in the ruling elite in the United States came to regard the
ordinary people of the United States as subhumans whose decisions
were unwitting responses to the primitive drives in their subconscious
minds. Others sided with psychologist B. F. Skinner, who wanted to
use the scientific application of rewards and punishments to
"modify" other people's behavior, as one might train a dog. Both of
those approaches seem to me to be a violation of the moral principle
of mutual respect.

I wrote this book because I hope that humanity can ultimately
prove Herman Göring wrong. I think that the solution is in education. As the Austrian musician and composer Gerhard Bronner explained,

> There are three things that cannot coexist: intelligence,
> decency, and National Socialism. A person can be
> intelligent and a Nazi, but then he is not decent. A man can
> be decent and a Nazi, but then he is not intelligent. And a
> man can be decent and intelligent, but then he is no Nazi.

I think that both intelligence and decency can be cultivated, and the
traditional approach to doing that has been education in the liberal

arts and humanities. The question is who should get that kind of
education. Woodrow Wilson felt that it should be reserved for a privileged few. In 1909, he told the New York City High School Teachers
Association,

> We want one class of persons to have a liberal education
> and we want another class of persons, a very much larger
> class of necessity, to forgo the privileges of a liberal
> education and fit themselves to perform specific difficult
> manual tasks.

In other words, people who disapprove of democracy in principle
think that a liberal education should be reserved for a privileged
few. They think that everyone else should remain ignorant—and
vulnerable to manipulation. In contrast, I think that the only way to
have real democracy is to provide training in the liberal arts, the
humanities, and the sciences to everyone, especially to the people
who are suffering from injustice. I base that conclusion on the
obvious fact that remarkably few members of the educated upper
and middle classes get involved in the struggles for peace and social
justice. The British Royal Navy summed up this problem in its
traditional toast for Wednesdays, "To ourselves! (As no-one else is
likely to concern themselves with our welfare!)"

CHAPTER XIV

Resisting Propaganda

E ven in the days of ancient Athens, people were concerned about dishonest methods of persuasion. By the mid 20th century, however, the available methods of communication had grown dramatically and an entire industry had developed to help wealthy people and corporations shape public opinion. As I explained in Chapter 13, the pioneers of the public relations industry had contempt for democracy. They thought of the people of the United States as a herd of animals, whereas they thought of themselves as the nation's invisible government.

Propaganda can have profound effects on a population. By the 1930s, many Americans became concerned about the power of propaganda to undermine democracy. They remembered the Creel Commission and the campaigns of political repression that occurred in the United States during and after the war. They were also disturbed by undemocratic political developments in fascist Italy, Nazi Germany, and the Soviet Union. They feared that anything that undermined democracy represented a threat to world peace and human rights. The question was how to respond to propaganda.

In George Orwell's novel *Nineteen Eighty-Four*, the totalitarian ruling Party used the slogan "Ignorance is strength." The novel's protagonist, Winston Smith, eventually discovers the slogan's real meaning: that the strength of a tyrannical government is based on the people's ignorance. Not only did the Party provide only restricted, distorted information to the public, but it made sure that the members of the general public had no skills in reasoning. Even the language that they used was deliberately distorted and debased so that logical thought became impossible. In contrast, democracy is based on respect for the dignity and equality of the individual members of the public. Democracy can function only when the members of the general public have access to vital information and have the ability to think critically about what they see and hear. The liberal arts are the studies that help people develop those abilities.

If the populace is to remain ignorant, then education can be nothing more than indoctrination. To achieve a well-informed populace, in contrast, education must include the classical liberal arts of grammar, logic, and rhetoric plus training in the arts and sciences and the humanities. That kind of well-rounded education gives people the facts they would need in order to see through propaganda.

Nowadays, the public is continually bombarded by public relations and advertising messages. Thus, it is important for everyone to learn the techniques that propagandists use to mislead. Since so many of those messages come to us through the commercial media, it's important for people to understand how the media work, and whom they serve. One easy way to study propaganda is to review the principles that the Institute for Propaganda Analysis developed in the 1930s. A useful model of media bias was developed by Noam Chomsky and Edward S. Herman in the 1980s.

By the mid 1930s, there was growing concern about the threat that propaganda posed to democracy in the United States. In 1935, the novelist Sinclair Lewis published a novel *It Can't Happen Here*, which described how easy it would be for a fascist movement to gain control in the United States, as similar movements had gained control in Italy and Germany. Lewis's novel wasn't pure fantasy.

In 1934, the retired Commandant of the Marine Corps, Major General Smedley Butler, told the House of Representatives' Special Committee on Un-American Activities (McCormack-Dickstein Committee) that a group of wealthy businessmen had tried to recruit him to lead a private army of veterans to overthrow the Roosevelt administration. The committee concluded that Gen. Butler was telling the truth. However, no further investigations were undertaken, and nobody was convicted or even indicted. The *New York Times* dismissed General Butler's testimony as "a gigantic hoax," which I guess is *Times*-speak for "These are not the droids you are looking for."

To help Americans resist being misled by propaganda, the businessman and philanthropist Edward Filene founded the Institute for Propaganda Analysis. Filene was one of the sons of William Filene, the founder of Filene's Department Store in Boston. Since Edward Filene never married and had no children, he wanted to use his wealth to create a different kind of legacy. He helped to get the nation's first workers' compensation law passed, and he played an important role in the creation of the first credit unions. Alarmed by the rise of Nazism in Germany, Filene organized the Institute for Propaganda Analysis in 1937.

The Institute for Propaganda Analysis was an organization of social scientists, journalists, historians, educators, and other opinion leaders. The institute's goal was to spark rational thinking and help the public have well-informed political discussions:

> It is essential in a democratic society that young people
> and adults learn how to think, learn how to make up their
> minds. They must learn how to think independently, and
> they must learn how to think together. They must come to
> conclusions, but at the same time they must recognize the
> right of other men to come to opposite conclusions. So far
> as individuals are concerned, the art of democracy is the
> art of thinking and discussing independently together.[1]

In an attempt to teach the public how to recognize propaganda, the Institute for Propaganda Analysis identified seven techniques that propagandists often use. The first is name-calling, which links a person or idea to a negative symbol. One particularly common form of name-calling in the mid 20th century was red-baiting, which meant accusing a person or idea of being communist, socialist, or anarchist.

Most people in the United States associate red-baiting with McCarthyism, in reference to Sen. Joseph McCarthy's wild accusations that the State Department and even the US Army had been infiltrated by "communists." Stanley Kubrick lampooned this anti-Communist hysteria in his classic 1964 movie *Dr. Strangelove, or How I Learned to Stop Worrying and Love the Bomb*. In the movie, General Jack D. Ripper of the US Air Force's Strategic Air Command went "a little funny in the head" and launched a thermonuclear war against the Soviet Union because he was convinced that fluoridation of the water was a Communist plot:

> I can no longer sit back and allow Communist infiltration, Communist indoctrination, Communist subversion, and the international Communist conspiracy to sap and impurify all of our precious bodily fluids!

That kind of red-baiting may sound crazy today; but during the Cold War, Americans had become so accustomed to that sort of rhetoric that it might not have struck some of them as peculiar. Kubrick had two of the movie's other characters, both played by Peter Sellers, explain that General Ripper was "psychotic" and "mad as a bloody March hare." Otherwise, I'm afraid that a lot of Americans might not have realized that General Jack D. Ripper ("Jack the Ripper") was a paranoid homicidal maniac.

Another propaganda technique involved the use of "glittering generalities," which are words that have a vague meaning but have positive connotations. Examples include *reform, hope,* and *freedom*. This concept is similar to the idea of "purr" words and "snarl" words, as later described by the late Senator S.I. Hayakawa (R, California). These words say little but convey strong emotions. For example, a politician who has changed his mind about some matter of policy could be called either a wishy-washy flip-flopper or a practical realist. Thus, glittering generalities and purr and snarl words are used to shape feelings, without stimulating any logical thought.

The third propaganda technique that the Institute for Propaganda Analysis described is called transfer. It refers to the propagandist's attempt to get people to transfer the feelings that they have for one thing to something else. For example, people may use patriotic imagery to get people to associate their cause with patriotism. They may also invoke religion for some political purpose. The techniques used are often highly visual. A red, white, and blue color scheme and the American flag are often used to evoke feelings of patriotism. White coats and laboratory equipment are often used to give an impression that something is based on science. The color green is used to give the impression that something is good for the environment. Yet not everyone who wraps himself or herself in the flag has the nation's best interest at heart. Nor is everything that's in a green package necessarily good for the environment.

The fourth technique is testimonial, such as a celebrity endorsement. Testimonial is based on the Aristotelian concept of ethos, or character. It may be reasonable to trust the testimonial of a person who has genuine expertise and a track record of honest dealing. However, many celebrity endorsements come from people who have no particular expertise and have never even used the product they endorse. When you see someone promoting a particular product or idea, ask yourself whether the person is not only trustworthy but knowledgeable about that subject.

The "plain folks" technique attempts to portray someone and his or her ideas as "of the people." Thus, we have the spectacle of highly educated, millionaire politicians pretending to have something in common with working-class Americans. This technique exploits people's prejudices. Personally, I don't care about a politician's family or social background one way or another. Both the appeal to wealth and the appeal to poverty are red-herring fallacies. What I care about is the political platform that person is supporting.

Card-stacking means presenting only the information that supports an idea, while leaving out the information that undermines it. Good liars never hesitate to tell the truth when it suits their purposes. To prevent drug companies from using this technique for promoting prescription drugs, the US Food and Drug Administration requires the advertisements for prescription drugs to contain "fair balance" information about risks and side effects.

The bandwagon appeal attempts to persuade people that a large number of people like themselves are already supporting the cause. A bandwagon was once literally a wagon with a band of musicians on it. Politicians used bandwagons in parades to promote their campaigns. People who were running for a lower office would generally want to ride on the bandwagon of a popular politician from their party. The bandwagon appeal works because people like to ally themselves with winners. Many people would rather follow the crowd than think things through for themselves, especially if they don't have the reasoning skills or the knowledge base that they would need to think for themselves. The solution to that problem is obvious: proper education.

The Institute for Propaganda Analysis did some important work. As one might imagine, however, it had some powerful enemies and faced some strong criticism. The United States' entry into World War II in December of 1941 posed a particular problem. How could the organization credibly address enemy propaganda without at the same time undermining the propaganda that served the war effort? Thus, it's not surprising that the Institute for Propaganda Analysis suspended operations in 1942.

Awareness of propaganda techniques can go far toward helping people recognize when they are being misled. A clear understanding of the nature of the propaganda system is also helpful. One useful model can be found in the book *Manufacturing Consent: The Political Economy of the Mass Media*. In that book, Edward S. Herman and Noam Chomsky describe five filters that distort the news reporting in the mass media.

The first of these filters results from the fact that the news media are for-profit businesses that are owned by large, diversified corporations. The media serve the interests of their owners, not the interests of the general public. As A. J. Liebling once quipped, "Freedom of the press belongs to the man who owns one." The owners of the press are far more sympathetic to business owners than to workers. Corporations may also pressure their news and entertainment divisions to promote the corporation's other products, such as movies.

The second filter is the fact that the money that supports the media comes from advertisements. The news media cannot survive without the support of advertisers. Thus, the news media must cater to their advertisers' political and economic needs. Sometimes, there's a direct quid pro quo (which means "this for that" in Latin). An advertiser may buy more ad space from a media company that provides news coverage and other content that suits that advertiser's political and economic needs. Advertisers can also decide not to support a particular program or publication with its advertising dollars. The threat of an advertiser boycott is serious because one company or agency can control a lot of ad revenue.

A third filter results from the fact that large corporations and large bureaucracies subsidize the mass media by reducing the cost of producing the news. These corporations' public relations agencies can do a lot of the work that would ordinarily be done by reporters. Besides issuing ordinary press releases, public relations agencies can also issue video news releases. News programs and other programs often run such footage without revealing its source. Thus, these large entities become routine sources. Other potential sources, such as labor unions or grass-roots activists, have to struggle to get any coverage at all.

The fourth filter results from fear of flak. The word *flak* originally meant antiaircraft guns, or the exploding shells that those guns fired at aircraft. It is used to mean criticism or opposition. Editors know that if they cover certain kinds of topics or cover them a certain way, they could suffer serious consequences. In some countries, editors fear for their lives. In the United States, they are mainly worried about keeping their jobs. They know that their publications can be punished by lawsuits, loss of advertising revenue, and boycotts. Flak can be organized by powerful private groups, including think tanks. For example, the mainstream media are continually being criticized by right-wing organizations for being "leftist," even though the mainstream media are for-profit businesses that are owned and controlled by the rich and powerful and predictably serve their interests.

In the original edition of *Manufacturing Consent*, Herman and Chomsky noted that anticommunist ideology was the fifth filter. In subsequent editions, after the fall of the Soviet Union, they added "the miracle of the market" to the fifth filter. Since the September 11, 2001, attacks on the World Trade Center, the "War on Terror" has also served as an important filter.

It's important for young people to learn about rhetoric and the propaganda techniques used in the advertising and public relations industry. It's also important for them to develop an understanding of the political economy of the communications media. In the end, however, they will still have to depend on logos (logic and reason) for deciding matters of fact and on a combination of logos and pathos (emotion) for making moral decisions.

If young people develop skills in grammar and logic in English class, they will be able to use those skills to parse sentences and evaluate the validity of arguments. However, logical arguments are based on statements of fact. To evaluate the truth or falsity of statements of fact, students need to learn a lot in their other classes as well, especially history and the sciences. The classical trivium (grammar, logic, and rhetoric) represents skills that are necessary for developing skills in critical reasoning. Although these skills are necessary, they are not sufficient by themselves. One also needs enough background knowledge to decide whether the statements of fact that make up the premises of the arguments are true. For that, one also needs training in history and the sciences.

It has never been more important for young people to study the techniques of persuasion. Not only are they facing serious political problems that threaten their future, but they also have the power through the Internet and social media to challenge the control that large corporations have over communication. To make use of these new communications technologies, young people will need to learn various kinds of computer skills. Yet to understand what is going on in the world, and to develop political movements to address those problems, they will need to develop the basic reasoning and communication skills that Aristotle talked about, as well as developing a strong background in history and the sciences.

Reference

1. Lee AM, Lee EB. *The Fine Art of Propaganda.* Institute for Propaganda Analysis. New York, NY: Harcourt Brace & Co, 1939.

CHAPTER XV

Right and Left

Much of the political rhetoric that I hear deals with assigning people and ideas to some point along a political spectrum. I hear people talking about "the far right" or the "radical left." Yet hardly anyone spells out what the words *right* and *left* really mean. For example, many Christians identify with the right wing; yet Sermon on the Mount, in which Jesus blessed the peacemakers and asserted that the meek shall inherit the earth, was strongly leftist.

The word *politics* can be defined narrowly as the art and science of government. Yet it can also be defined more broadly as the total complex of all relations among the people living in a society. The only way to avoid politics is to live by yourself on a desert island. As soon as there is at least one other person in the picture, there will be politics. The methods used in politics can be classified along a spectrum. On the right-hand end of the spectrum, the strong rule the weak by force—or at least by threats of force. At the left-hand side of the spectrum, people work out mutually acceptable solutions through discussion. Note that according to this definition of *right* and *left*, Lenin and Stalin were rightists, not leftists!

This political meaning of *right* and *left* came originally from the French legislature. The aristocrats sat on the right, which was traditionally a position of honor. The common people sat on the left. Thus, people who supported the interests of the rich and powerful came to be known as rightists or right-wing. The people who stood up for the common people became known as leftist or left-wing. The idea that a king rules by divine right is a right-wing idea. The idea that a government's legitimacy derives from the consent of the governed is a left-wing idea.

Religion could be used for rightist or leftist purposes. During the 18th and 19th century, both the people who wanted to perpetuate slavery (a rightist purpose) and those who wanted to abolish it (a leftist purpose) quoted Bible verses to support their positions. In the 20th century, the Social Gospel movement in Protestant Churches urged Christians to apply the lessons of the Sermon on the Mount to modern social problems. Thus, the Social Gospel movement encouraged people to oppose child labor, to support labor unions, and to oppose racism and war. In the 1960s, Pope John XXIII launched a similar movement called Liberation Theology within the Roman Catholic Church. Both the Social Gospel movement and Liberation Theology belong to the political left.

The Social Gospel movement peaked in the early 20th century. Scholars argue about why it declined after that. Personally, I suspect that money—especially oil money—had a lot to do with it. The Fundamentalist-Modernist controversy that raged in the Protestant churches in the United States in the early 20th century was largely a proxy war between the theologians being paid by Lyman Stewart of Union Oil versus those being paid by the Rockefellers of Standard Oil.

The Social Gospel went into decline because it tended to afflict the comfortable while comforting the afflicted. The captains of industry wanted to be the ones who made the decisions about labor policy and foreign policy and so on. The captains of industry did not want church people to support strikers or oppose war, etc. Not only do the rich and powerful generally want religion to serve right-wing purposes, they can use their money and power to influence church teachings.

At the time of the founding of the United States, there were two basic ideas about who should make the decisions that affect everyone. On the left, there was the New England town hall tradition of direct democracy, where those decisions are made directly by the people. On the right was John Jay's idea that the country ought to be governed by those who own it. The Constitution was actually a compromise between those two extremes. The members of the House of Representatives were elected every two years by the people (or at least by the white, male property owners). Senators, in contrast, were elected once every six years by the state legislatures and thus were hand-picked by a political elite. The President was chosen not by direct vote of the people but by the Electoral College. This setup gave the wealthy and connected people additional influence over public decision-making.

World War I provides an example of a situation where the US government served the interests of a handful of wealthy people instead of the wishes of the majority of the population. As I explained in Chapter 13, the Wilson administration's success in mobilizing the country for war was due in large part to the propaganda campaign coordinated by the Creel Committee. However, that propaganda campaign was backed up by a campaign of vicious political repression that culminated in the so-called Red Scare of 1919 through 1921.

Before August of 1914, there were several prominent peace organizations in the United States. One was founded and supported by steel magnate Andrew Carnegie, another by carmaker Henry Ford. By 1917, however, their antiwar initiatives had collapsed. Once the United States entered the war, the Ford Motor Company became a major producer of airplanes, tanks, and ammunition for the war, and Ford profited handsomely.

The real opposition to the war came from working-class people. In April of 1917, the Socialist Party of America called an Emergency National Convention in St. Louis, Missouri. There they declared that Wilson's decision to enter World War I was "a crime against the people of the United States and against the nations of the world." Their St. Louis Resolution explained,

> Wars bring wealth and power to the ruling classes, and suffering, death, and demoralization to the workers. They breed a sinister spirit of passion, unreason, race hatred, and false patriotism. They obscure the struggles of the workers for life, liberty, and social justice. They tend to

> sever the vital bonds of solidarity between them and their
> brothers in other countries, to destroy their organizations
> and to curtail their civic and political rights and liberties.

They were absolutely correct. The war did breed a sinister spirit of passion, unreason, race hatred, and false patriotism. It did cause civil and political rights and liberties to be curtailed. Although Socialist Party member Eugene Debs had worded his speeches carefully, he was still arrested and convicted under the Espionage Act because his speeches had the intention and effect of obstructing the draft and military recruitment. When a parade and assembly of 20,000 to 30,000 people was held in Cleveland to protest Debs' conviction, the marchers were clubbed by mounted police, backed up by tanks. Two marchers died, hundreds were injured, and 150 were arrested in what has been called the 1919 Cleveland May Day Riot. When Debs ran on the Socialist Party ticket for President in 1920, he got 900,000 votes—even though he could not campaign because he was still in federal prison.

Another key peace organization was the People's Council of America for Democracy and the Terms of Peace, which was founded in May, 1917. Its purpose was to unite workers and intellectuals in opposition to the war. Its membership included socialists, liberals, civil libertarians, trade unionists, and religious pacifists. The People's Council rapidly became a nationwide movement that had as many as two million participants. Of course, it was rapidly targeted by federal, state, and local authorities, who banned or disrupted its meetings and arrested many of its participants, some of whom were charged under the Espionage Act.

The assaults on civil and political rights and liberties got so bad that Crystal Eastman and Roger Baldwin formed a Civil Liberties Bureau to provide a legal defense for pacifists and conscientious objectors. In 1920, the organization became the American Civil Liberties Union.

Many labor leaders were against the war. One exception was Samuel Gompers, who was President of the American Federation of Labor. In March of 1917, Gompers called a special labor assembly of the leaders of the AFL's constituent unions. He got them to pledge to support any US war effort. Gompers then created an organization called the American Alliance for Labor and Democracy, which worked hand in glove with the Creel Committee to spread pro-war propaganda.

Gompers hoped to use his support for the war as a bargaining chip to help his union's members. However, this move was widely criticized by many within and outside the AFL because Gompers refused to ask the rank-and-file members to vote on whether they actually favored war with Germany.

Although many labor organizations were against the war, the economic boom that resulted from the war strengthened the bargaining position of labor. So did the labor shortages that resulted from so many men entering military service. For African-Americans, the war provided opportunities that undermined racial segregation. The labor movement grew larger and more radicalized. Inspired by the revolution in Russia, many American workers were talking about using "workers' power" to improve their own society. In the autumn of 1919, longshoremen in Seattle refused to load weapons that were intended for the counterrevolutionary White Army in Russia, and they attacked those who tried to load the weapons.

The end of the war caused further unrest in the labor market. Most of the 4 million men in the US armed forces were about to be discharged, and many of the 9 million people employed in war industries were about to lose their jobs. Also, many workers started demanding an end to the wage controls that had been imposed during the war. In February of 1919, a general strike involving 110 locals and 65,000 workers shut down business in Seattle for five days. In September of 1919, the police in Boston went on strike. These strikes created a sense of paranoia among the ruling class in the United States. The paranoia deepened in 1919 because of a wave of bombings that targeted politicians, law enforcement officials, and businessmen, including John D. Rockefeller Sr.

The result of all this paranoia was a "Red Scare"—a wave of political oppression directed at anything that seemed to threaten the existing order in society. US Attorney General A. Mitchell Palmer

ordered the arrest and deportation of radical leftists, especially anarchists. Roughly 10,000 people were arrested, and many were im-
prisoned incommunicado and without charge for long periods. Fortunately, cooler heads and the rule of law eventually prevailed. Most
of the people who were arrested were eventually released because
there was no evidence that they had committed any crimes. The
raids finally ended after a federal judge in Massachusetts denounced
them, comparing them to mob rule. Ultimately, only a few hundred
persons were eventually deported.

Palmer had claimed that his raids would destroy a widespread
revolutionary conspiracy. In reality, there was no widespread conspiracy, and his main target was peaceful political activity that is
specifically protected by the First Amendment. Although many
American workers had been inspired by the success of the Russian
Revolution, it was ridiculous to imagine that the newly established
Soviet Union posed any threat to the United States in 1919. In contrast, the United States did pose some threat to the Soviet Union,
having landed more than 5000 troops to intervene in the Russian
Civil War.

In the 19th century, it was common for just about any opposition
party in Europe to be labeled communist. When Karl Marx and
Friedrich Engels issued the Communist Manifesto in 1848, their
main objective was to explain what the word *communist* actually
meant, so that people could figure out which political parties were
really communist and which ones were not. Of course, after the
Russian Revolution, people in the United States tended to label any
popular political movement, and even some mild reforms advocated
by upper-class liberals, as communist or socialist.

In his novel *The Grapes of Wrath*, John Steinbeck explained the
underlying problem of defining who is or is not a communist—or in
the vernacular, a "red." The novel was about people who went to
California to work in the orchards after having been displaced from
Oklahoma by the Dust Bowl:

> Fella named Hines—got 'bout thirty thousan' acres,
> peaches and grapes—got a cannery an' a winery. Well,

he's all a time talkin' about "them goddamn reds." "God-damn reds is drivin' the country to ruin," he says, an' "We got to drive these here red bastards out." Well, they were a young fella jus' come out west here, an' he's listenin' one day. He kinda scratched his head an' he says, "Mr. Hines, I ain't been here long. What is these goddamn reds?" "Well, sir", Hines says, "A red is any son-of-a-bitch that wants thirty cents an hour when we're payin' twenty-five!" Well, this young fella he thinks about her, an' he scratches his head, an' he says, "Well, Jesus, Mr. Hines. I ain't a son-of-a-bitch, but if that's what a red is—why, I want thirty cents an hour. Ever'body does. Hell, Mr. Hines, we're all reds."

The economic system that Lenin and the Bolsheviks imposed on the Soviet Union was not at all leftist. Even at the time, Lenin was round-ly criticized by "left communists" because he wanted a small ruling elite—although he did not call it that—to exert control over the population. A dictatorship is rightist by definition, even if it pro-claims that it is Marxist.

Marx and Engels' Communist Manifesto, which urged the work-ers of the world to unite and lose their chains, was leftist. Socialism, which means that the workers get to control the means of produc-tion, is also a leftist concept. Yet as soon as Lenin took power in the Soviet Union, he set about destroying the workers' councils and so on that the workers had developed through a long political struggle to exert some sort of democratic control over their workplaces. Thus, Lenin set out to destroy socialism in the Soviet Union, and he recon-structed the tsarist institutions of control and oppression. Trotsky supported him in this attempt. Lenin and Trotsky advocated the development of a "labor army" that was submissive to a single leader. At the time, this concept was criticized as leading back to tsarism and serfdom.

From a worker's perspective, the model supported by Lenin and Trotsky and Stalin wasn't much different from pure capitalism. The decisions that affected workers' lives were made by a tiny minority of people who were in no way accountable to anyone but themselves.

Both Leninism and capitalism are the opposite of socialism. The odd thing is that the apologists for the Soviet Union and apologists for Western capitalists agreed that the Soviet Union was a socialist society. Thus, propaganda coming from both the Soviet Union and the right wing in the United States reinforced the myth that the only alternative to the capitalist model was an even worse form of oppression.

Note that what limited the political oppression in the United States during World War I and its aftermath were the social and political institutions that the right wing in the United States despises to this day—the Department of Labor, the American Civil Liberties Union, the First Amendment, and federal judges. The Russian tsars had prevented such institutions from developing. Thus, Russian society had no civil institutions to put a brake on tyranny or civil rights abuses when the tsarist autocracy collapsed.

Political repression in the United States did not end when the Palmer Raids ended. They continued for decades under the direction of Palmer's assistant, J. Edgar Hoover, who then served as director of the Federal Bureau of Investigation until his death in 1972. As head of the FBI, Hoover was responsible for many illegal activities against popular political movements, such as the civil rights and antiwar movements. It's bad enough that American Communists often gave uncritical support to the Party Line coming out of Moscow. What was far worse was that many popular political organizations were infiltrated, discredited, and disrupted by FBI agents. During the period of 1966 to 1971, these activities fell under a heading called the counter-intelligence program, or COINTELPRO.

In 1971, an unidentified group of people who called themselves the Citizens' Commission to Investigate the FBI broke into an FBI field office in Media, Pennsylvania, and stole more than 1000 documents, which they then mailed anonymously to American newspapers, as well as to Senator George McGovern and Representative Parren J. Mitchell. About 40% of the documents described the FBI's illegal surveillance and other activities against peaceful political organizations. Another 14% dealt with draft resistance and military desertion. Less than 20% of the total documents dealt with investigation of actual crimes, and only 1% dealt with organized crime, mainly gambling. In short, the agency that was responsible for investigating federal crimes evidently spent more of its resources to violate the Constitution than to investigate federal crimes.

Hoover was notorious for the secret files he kept on political figures. Shortly after Hoover's death, a senior federal judge named Laurence H. Silberman who was serving as Acting Attorney General read through all of Hoover's secret files. In 2005, Silberman explained in a *Wall Street Journal* op-ed that reading those files was "the single worst experience of my long governmental service." He thought that the collection of "nasty bits of information on various political figures" was bad enough. What was worse was that Hoover allowed and even offered the FBI to be used by presidents for nakedly political purposes. "[T]he most heinous act in which a democratic government can engage is to use its law enforcement machinery for political ends."

The first casualty in the war to "make the world safe for democracy" was democracy itself. The political elite in the United States used Red Scare tactics and their ownership of the media to squash any threat to their power, whether that threat came from labor unions or the civil rights movement or other popular organizations. During Wilson's Red Scare, and during the Red Scare that arose in the late 1940s, the image of the Bolsheviks of the Soviet Union was used to frighten people. Yet the real threat to freedom in the United States came not from the Soviet Union but from our own willingness to abandon the principles of democracy. The real threats we face come not from foreigners but from our own inability to think logically about words like *left* and *right*.

CHAPTER XVI

Conspiracy Theories
and Real-Life Conspiracies

In 1917, President Woodrow Wilson told us that the United States had to go to war against Germany to "make the world safe for democracy." Millions of Americans fell for it, and then more than 100,000 Americans died in the war. In 1999, President Bill Clinton said that NATO (but mainly the United States) had to bomb Yugoslavia to smithereens in order to put an end to "ethnic cleansing" in Kosovo. Millions of Americans fell for it, but I didn't. I figured that the bombing would actually make the "ethnic cleansing" worse—and it did.

From looking at a relief map of Europe, I could tell that the best route for an oil pipeline to bypass the Bosporus and the Dardanelles ran right through Kosovo. I guessed—correctly, as it turned out— that Western interests wanted to control this region by separating Kosovo from the rest of Yugoslavia. Similarly, the United States had severed Panama from Colombia in 1903 in preparation for building the Panama Canal.

What happened when I tried to explain these simple concepts to my fellow Americans? Hardly anyone took me seriously. Several people told me that I was a "conspiracy theorist." In other words, they thought I was nuts. Long after the bombing, I found out that there were indeed plans for a major pipeline through Kosovo. But when I tried to say "I told you so," most of the people who had sneered that I was a conspiracy theorist acted as if they had never heard of Kosovo. I was mystified. These were people who could play strategy games and remember decades-old sports trivia. Yet when it came to matters of war and peace, they seemed to have the reasoning capacity and memory span of a goldfish.

What is a conspiracy? How does a conspiracy differ from a conspiracy *theory*? According to the dictionary, a conspiracy is a secret agreement to do something that is wrong or illegal—or to do something that becomes wrong or illegal if it is done secretly, such as bid-rigging. Conspiracies happen all the time. Lots of people get convicted in a court of law for conspiracy. Yet the term *conspiracy theory* means something else.

The dictionary defines *conspiracy theory* as a theory that explains an event or set of circumstances as the result of a secret plot by usually powerful conspirators. Often, the term *conspiracy theory* is used in a derogatory sense. It suggests that the theory makes little or no sense and has no basis in fact. One common conspiracy theory is that the United Nations has taken control of the US government. In reality, the United States is one of the permanent members of the UN Security Council. Thus, the United States has veto power over the United Nations. In the real world, the United Nations has no power whatsoever over the United States, but the United States can thwart anything that the United Nations wants to do. Some conspiracy theories are even more bizarre, involving nonexistent secret organizations or lizard people from outer space.

In real life, conspiracies are common. In the United States today, thousands upon thousands of people are serving prison sentences for criminal conspiracy. Most cases involved conspiracy to sell illegal drugs. In the Nuremberg Trials that followed World War II, some prominent Nazis were convicted of "participation in a common plan or conspiracy for the accomplishment of a crime against peace." They were sentenced to life in prison or death by hanging.

In 1935, Major General Smedley D. Butler, the retired Commandant of the US Marine Corps, explained that war is a criminal conspiracy—or in his words, a "racket":

> War is a racket always has been. It is possibly the oldest,
> easily the most profitable, surely the most vicious. It is the

only one international in scope. It is the only one in which the profits are reckoned in dollars and the losses in lives.

A racket is best described, I believe, as something that is not what it seems to the majority of people. Only a small 'inside' group knows what it is about. It is conducted for the benefit of the very few, at the expense of the very many. Out of war a few people make huge fortunes.

In the World War [World War I] a mere handful garnered the profits of the conflict. At least 21,000 new millionaires and billionaires were made in the United States during the World War. That many admitted their huge blood gains in their income tax returns. How many other war millionaires falsified their income tax returns no one knows.

How many of these war millionaires shouldered a rifle? How many of them dug a trench? How many of them knew what it meant to go hungry in a rat-infested dugout? How many of them spent sleepless, frightened nights, ducking shells and shrapnel and machine gun bullets? How many of them parried the bayonet thrust of an enemy? How many of them were wounded or killed in battle?

Clearly, there is such a thing as criminal conspiracy. Furthermore, some major events in world history really have resulted from criminal conspiracies. The challenge for the ordinary person is to sort out fact from fantasy. Which theories about conspiracies provide an accurate picture of reality, and which ones are fever dreams?

Psychologist Michael Shermer, who is a prominent member of the self-styled Skeptics movement, has pointed out that many people believe in kooky conspiracy theories. He noted that people who believe in one kooky conspiracy theory are likely to believe in others as well. For example, the people who believe that the US government faked the moon landings are also likely to believe that the US government is hiding evidence of visitors from outer space. Some people even manage to believe two contradictory theories at the same time. For example, some people believe that Princess Diana faked her own death *and* that she was murdered—as if she could be both alive and dead at the same time, sort of like Schrödinger's cat.

As a psychologist, Shermer looks for personal, psychological explanations for people's willingness to believe kooky conspiracy theories. In contrast, I look at the problem from a political perspective. The problem involves something that George Orwell called doublethink:

> To know and not to know, to be conscious of complete truthfulness while telling carefully constructed lies, to hold simultaneously two opinions which cancelled out, knowing them to be contradictory and believing in both of them, to use logic against logic, to repudiate morality while laying claim to it, to believe that democracy was impossible and that the Party was the guardian of democracy, to forget, whatever it was necessary to forget, then to draw it back into memory again at the moment when it was needed, and then promptly to forget it again, and above all, to apply the same process to the process itself—that was the ultimate subtlety; consciously to induce unconsciousness, and then, once again, to become unconscious of the act of hypnosis you had just performed. Even to understand the word 'doublethink' involved the use of doublethink.

In the fictional Oceania in Orwell's novel *Nineteen Eighty-Four*, to remember the past and to think logically about it was a crime—thoughtcrime. Party members were supposed to think exactly what the Party wanted them to think at any given moment. The working-class people (the proles) weren't supposed to think at all. The protagonist, Winston Smith, wrote in his diary, "Freedom is the freedom to say that two plus two make four. If that is granted, all else follows." According to the Party, this meant that Smith was insane. To become sane, he had to believe that two plus two sometimes make five, sometimes three, or sometimes all of them at once.

It wasn't enough for Smith to mouth the Party line. He had to reshape his mental processes so that he could not think anything but what the Party wanted him to think. This goal was identical to the stated goal of the Prussian educational system, as explained by Johann Gottlieb Fichte in 1807: The schools must fashion the person "in such a way that he simply cannot will otherwise than what you wish him to will." In short, the kind of education that the Party was promoting in *Nineteen Eighty-Four* was exactly the opposite of the liberal arts. The Party also undermined the humanities, which include history:

> And if all others accepted the lie which the Party imposed—if all records told the same tale—then the lie passed into history and became truth. "Who controls the past," ran the Party slogan, "controls the future: who controls the present controls the past." And yet the past, though of its nature alterable, never had been altered. Whatever was true now was true from everlasting to everlasting. It was quite simple. All that was needed was an unending series of victories over your own memory. "Reality control," they called it: in Newspeak, "doublethink".

Why could I figure out, just from looking at a map, what the war in Kosovo was really about, while most American citizens—and worse yet, most American journalists—accepted the official story uncritically? It's partly because I studied economics and geography in school and because I have read so many library books about history. However, I think that it's mainly because I'm willing to use the knowledge and skills that I got from that grounding in the liberal arts and the humanities and the sciences to evaluate the truth or falsity of what politicians say.

I knew that Clinton did nothing to intervene in the genocide in Rwanda in 1994. I also knew that the brutalizing effects of war have always tended to make the human rights situation worse, not better. The Armenian genocide happened during World War I and the Holocaust during World War II. The British and the Americans bombed Germany to bits during World War II, but the bombing did nothing to stop the Holocaust. Thus, the claim that Yugoslavia was being bombed for humanitarian reasons struck me as hypocritical and absurd. Unfortunately, any mainstream journalist who expressed that kind of independent thought would not remain a mainstream journalist for long.

I knew that there were two basic reasons why the United States had gone to war in the past. One reason is to gain control of resources, markets, or trade routes for US-based transnational businesses. The other is to suppress any alternative to the capitalist model. Yugoslavia was in the crosshairs for both reasons. Not only was Yugoslavia straddling the route by which all that oil in the Caspian Sea region would eventually reach Western Europe, but Yugoslavia was a thriving socialist country with many state-owned industries. Because Yugoslavia was more prosperous than many other second- and third-world nations, it provided an attractive alternative to the capitalist model—an alternative that US business interests wanted to suppress. That's why the members of NATO fomented ethnic conflicts to tear Yugoslavia into pieces and then pounded the remnants of it so heavily with high explosives for 78 days in early 1999.

When Michael Shermer or other members of the Skeptics movement complain about conspiracy theories, they focus on relatively harmless theories, especially the ones that unfairly cast the US government in a bad light, such as the idea that the government faked the moon landings or is hiding the remains of dead space aliens at Area 51 in Nevada. Yet the Skeptics movement, as such, never seems to criticize the kooky theories that Presidents put forth as justification for military adventures. In other words, the Skeptics are quick to point out the irrationality of what they call "fringe beliefs." However, they seem unwilling to point out the irrationality of some far more dangerous "core beliefs." They seem to be, in Orwellian terms, "goodthinkful." Thus, I wasn't surprised to discover that some of the founders of the Skeptics movement were great admirers of John Dewey's acolyte Sidney Hook.

Sidney Hook was originally a Marxist academic who then became a fierce anti-Communist. Thus, Hook's career was like that of Saul/Paul as described in the Book of Acts, except played in reverse. Saul was a zealous persecutor of Christians. After a religious

conversion, Saul the persecutor of Christianity became Paul the pro-
ponent of Christianity.

Hook had supposedly become disenchanted with communism
because of Stalin's brutal purges in the Soviet Union in the 1930s.
But then, Hook promoted kinder, gentler purges in academia in the
United States during the Red Scare after World War II. Professors
who had the wrong sort of political affiliations weren't killed or sent
to prison camps, but they often lost their teaching jobs, even if they
had never done anything wrong. Tens of thousands of schoolteachers were investigated and hundreds were fired during the Red Scare
—supposedly for disloyalty but usually just for being Jewish in a society dominated by Protestants. (The Catholic Church had its own
educational system, from kindergarten through university.)

Hook was also involved in the founding of several organizations, including the Congress for Cultural Freedom, that were later
found to be fronts for the US Central Intelligence Agency. He became a major apologist for US military actions in Vietnam, although
he did acknowledge that the saturation bombing of heavily popu-
lated areas did lead to "unfortunate accidental loss of life." In other
words, Hook really was involved with a conspiracy that worked to
overthrow democratically elected governments, often by violence,
all over the world. In comparison, most of the people whose careers
and lives were ruined by anti-Communist witch hunts had never
done anything wrong.

Some historians criticize the anti-Communist purges of academia and Hollywood during the Red Scare after World War II as a
disproportionate response—like using a sledgehammer against a
swarm of gnats. Such analysis bothers me for two reasons. One is
that it's always a bad sign when someone refers to some group of
people—whether it be Jews, Hutu, or communists—as insects or
other vermin. That kind of dehumanization has often been a
prelude to mass murder. The second reason is that the analysis
suggests that those historians entirely misunderstood the purpose
of the anti-Communist purges.

The purpose of the anti-Communist witch hunts after World
War II was not to prevent a handful of leftist screenwriters and

actors and college professors from overthrowing the US government by violence. The purpose was to silence anyone who would undermine the efforts of the public relations industry to "engineer consent." The purpose was to eliminate any voice that would encourage Americans to think and want anything other than what the clients of the public relations industry and advertising industry want them to think and want. These purposes were achieved not only by silencing critics but by promoting xenophobia, narrow-mindedness, and a worshipful attitude toward the rich (as if material wealth demonstrated God's blessings). The goal was to ensure that most people would mindlessly shun any challenge to the status quo—especially from the Civil Rights Movement, which was a major target of anti-Communist hysteria.

The purpose of the anti-Communist hysteria that was whipped up by US politicians and the media after World War II was to get Americans to view capitalism as the defender of democracy and Christianity. In short, the problem was how to get the American Christians to worship the rich, even though Jesus had been quoted as saying that it was harder for a rich man to enter the kingdom of God than it would be for a camel to pass through the eye of a needle. The challenge was to get Americans to support plutocracy in the name of democracy—something that they would do only if they could not or would not think logically.

Many of the prominent members of the Skeptics movement are also atheists, and some of them have taken pains to point out that not all atheists are communists. What many atheists don't understand is that many Americans during the Red Scare had no particular problem with "from each according to his ability, to each according to his needs." Many Christians mistakenly believe that those are the words of Jesus Christ, not Karl Marx. In other words, many Americans had no real problem with communism, per se. They hated communists because they thought that communism meant atheism.

To promote the interests of the wealthy few over those of the general public, it was essential to keep the American public from thinking logically about democracy and economics. Two basic strategies were used. One was to keep the people ignorant by undermining public education. The other was to keep people fearful through propaganda campaigns about Communist spies and subversion and the threat of bomber gaps and missile gaps and so on.

Fear is a primitive emotion, and it arises in a primitive part of the brain. Although nonhuman animals cannot use words to describe their emotional states, they respond to threatening situations in many of the same ways that human beings do. Even the brain structures that are involved in fear responses in human beings look remarkably similar to the corresponding structures in the brains of lower animals. To me, that helps to explain why frightened people are often irrational. They behave a lot like animals because they are experiencing a powerful, primitive emotion.

Unlike other animals, human beings have a huge forebrain on top of the primitive brain structures that are involved in fear. That huge forebrain enables us to think about our fears and often to overcome them. Part of the purpose of a liberal arts education is to develop virtues such as courage, which means using our forebrain to overcome our irrational fears.

Fear is one of the basic emotions that help to regulate behavior. People who have lost the connection between the logical and emotional circuitry in the brain become unable to make the simplest decisions, even if their IQ remains intact.

Psychiatrists have found that people can suffer from having either too little or too much fear. Abnormally fearless people can be reckless and are thus a danger to themselves and others. In contrast, people with phobias, anxiety, and paranoia are suffering from abnormally high levels of fear.

When people are fearful, they tend to become submissive to authority figures. That's why so many people were willing to accept an erosion of civil liberties after the terrorist attacks on the World Trade Center. It also explains why so many people are swayed by ridiculous fear-mongering, such as Ronald Reagan's claims that the Sandinista revolution in Nicaragua posed some sort of threat to US national security because Nicaragua was "two days' driving time from Harlingen, Texas!"

Even in the 1940s and 1950s, the anti-Communist witch hunts seemed to many people to be an outbreak of mass hysteria. Yet Richard Hofstadter pointed out in the 1960s that what he called the paranoid style was a longstanding feature of American politics. Hofstadter was apologetic about borrowing the medical term *paranoia*. He wasn't talking about people who were clinically mentally ill. He was talking about paranoid modes of expression by more or less normal people. Hofstadter then went on to describe the kinds of things that Americans have traditionally been paranoid about. They include intellectuals (the Illuminati), organizations (Masonry), and religion (Catholicism).

Hofstadter was right to emphasize the difference between clinical paranoia and the paranoid style in politics. In psychiatry, diagnostic labels such as *paranoia* are used to describe not just *what* a person thinks but *why* the person thinks that way. Diagnoses such as psychosis, delusions, and paranoia are used to describe kooky ideas that an individual came up with all by him- or herself. In contrast, people who merely believe the kooky things that they have been told by authority figures are considered to be sane.

People whose thinking fits the paranoid style, as described by Hofstadter, tend to imagine that events are being engineered behind the scenes. However, the supposed conspirators are not imagined to be ordinary human beings, each of whom has an individual, more or less rational political agenda. Instead, the imagined conspirators are viewed as selflessly dedicated to some larger organization, like members of the Borg collective from *Star Trek*. Nor is the theory about the conspiracy tested against evidence. In fact, the very lack of supporting evidence is interpreted as proof of the power of the conspiracy to cover its tracks. As a result, belief in the conspiracy theory is supported by a watertight process of circular reasoning.

Although the paranoid style of thinking is sometimes directed at the US government, which may be characterized as mere puppets of the secret conspiracy, this kind of thinking is often pro-Establishment. It criticizes the wrong things, and it leads people either to quixotic misadventures or to defeatism.

A conspiracy theory gives people an opportunity to express their anger about injustice. However, conspiracy theorists usually don't feel that the existing economic system, which inevitably gives a few people power over many others, is inherently unfair. Rather than worrying about the concentration of power per se, conspiracy theorists seem to be worried that power has simply fallen into the wrong hands. They suspect that power has been usurped by some secret, often nonexistent organization, such as the Illuminati, the Elders of Zion, or a race of lizard people from outer space. Such conspiracy theories provide a false picture of the existing power relationships within a society and thus provide no real guidance for constructive change.

Sometimes, the government itself is viewed as the evil conspiracy. For example, many people are convinced that the buildings at the World Trade Center were brought down by explosives that had been planted in the buildings before the morning of September 11, 2001. In contrast, structural engineers insist that the buildings collapsed under their own weight after the massive, uncontrolled fires weakened and distorted the steel support beams. The conspiracy theorists cannot explain why nobody who worked at the World Trade Center noticed anybody planting any of the thousands of pounds of explosives that would have been required, why the explosives wouldn't have been set off prematurely by the aircraft collision and the fires, and why none of the hundreds of people who would have to have known about the supposed plot have confessed. Real conspiracies tend to be simple, easily discovered, and easily proved. Three people can keep a secret only if two of them are dead.

How can antigovernment paranoia be viewed as pro-Establishment? Simple. By "the Establishment" I mean the people who hold the real power in a society: the people who own the controlling interest in the major corporations and who sit on the corporations' boards of directors. These people have direct control over a huge portion of the society's productive assets and workforce. They own and control the commercial media. They also have the money to finance the nonprofit organizations that influence educational policy and shape public opinion. They can use their wealth and power to influence the outcomes of elections. Thus, the government is basically their servant, instead of being the instrument by which the people as a whole can keep the wealthy in line. Thus, the Establishment would love for the general public to think that capitalism is the servant of the people and that the government is a threat to the people and must be kept small enough to be drowned in a bathtub.

Real conspiracies do occur. Thus, some theories about conspiracies do turn out to be correct. However, a theory about a conspiracy should have to meet the same standards of proof as any other theory. Is the theory logical? Is it supported by evidence? Does that theory provide the simplest explanation that accounts for all of the available evidence? Many theories of conspiracy fail in that regard. Then why do people persist in believing them? I think that it's often because people don't understand how to tell a good theory from a bad theory or because they don't know much about how the world really works. In other words, they haven't had a proper education in the liberal arts, the humanities, or the arts and sciences.

People who have such a profound misunderstanding of how the world works are unable to solve real political problems. They may attack irrelevant targets, like Don Quixote when he attacked a windmill, thinking it to be a giant. When Timothy McVeigh bombed the Oklahoma City Federal Building, he presumably intended it as a strike against what the members of the militia movement called the Zionist Occupation Government. In reality, he killed a bunch of human beings with little or no real power—children in day-care, lower-echelon bureaucrats, and clerical workers. Fortunately, however, most conspiracy theorists engage in no real political activity at all, out of the belief that the supersecret society that is running the world is so all-powerful that resistance is futile.

The Skeptics complain about the gullibility of people who believe fringe theories. However, history tells me that the gullibility of people who accept conventional wisdom at face value is far more dangerous. I don't know of anyone who has died because of the belief that the remains of space aliens are being stored at Area 51,

but I know that war is a racket that has killed many millions of people and impoverished millions more. If we hope to have peace and
justice in the future—if we even want Earth to remain livable for
future generations—we need for the majority of the population of
the most powerful nation on Earth to learn to think rationally about
how and why things happen.

PART IV: *The Politics of Education*

As I explained in Chapter 1, one way to suppress education is by preventing people from going to school. But if you do that, the people quickly realize that you are their enemy. Thus, they may get organized politically to change educational policy to serve their own interests. If, on the other hand, you work behind the scenes to make the public schools ineffective, then people will blame the students and maybe the teachers. If a wealthy philanthropist has a good public relations agency, he could gain public acclaim for supporting the schools, even as his philanthropy is being used in ways that undermine public education.

In the next few chapters, I explain how wealthy and powerful people have used their wealth and power to erode the quality of public education, especially in poor neighborhoods. I explain that the poor performance of our public schools should be viewed as the end result of a series of institutional failures. I explain that those institutions are created by the public and can be disciplined through democratic political means. To explain the problems that we face in US public education, I'll start by discussing the troubling legacy of our most highly acclaimed philosopher of education: John Dewey.

CHAPTER XVII

The Legacy of John Dewey

I first became aware of John Dewey's role in reshaping American education from reading Harper Lee's largely autobiographical novel *To Kill a Mockingbird* in high school. The novel is a narrative from the point of view of a six-year-old girl named Scout. On Scout's first day of school, her first-grade teacher, Miss Caroline Fisher, is horrified to discover that Scout can already read. Miss Fisher says,

> Now you tell your father not to teach you any more. It's best to begin reading with a fresh mind. You tell him I'll take over from here and try to undo the damage... Your father does not know how to teach. You can have a seat now.

Later that day, Scout's brother explained to her,

> "I'm just trying to tell you the new way they're teachin' the first grade, stubborn. It's the Dewey Decimal System." Having never questioned Jem's pronouncements, I saw no reason to begin now. The Dewey Decimal System consisted, in part, of Miss Caroline waving cards at us on which were printed: "the," "cat," "rat," "man," and "you." No comment seemed to be expected of us, and the class received these impressionistic revelations in silence. I was bored, so I began a letter to Dill. Miss Caroline caught me writing and

told me to tell my father to stop teaching me. "Besides,"
she said. "We don't write in the first grade, we print.
You won't learn to write until you're in the third grade."

I knew that the Dewey Decimal System isn't a method of teaching
reading. It is a system for shelving library books. There must have
been some other "Dewey." When I looked up "Dewey" in the ency-
clopedia (there was no Internet back then), I found that there was a
John Dewey who was a philosopher of education.

At first, I found it hard to believe that anyone who promoted the
teaching methods that Harper Lee described could have been
respected as a philosopher of education. What kind of philosopher
would think that it's bad if a child can already read and write on the
first day of first grade? Unfortunately, it was obviously someone with
long-lasting nationwide influence. Harper Lee was writing about
things that happened in Southern Alabama in the 1930s, but I had
similar experiences when I started school in Ohio in the mid 1960s.

Like Scout, I'd learned to read before I started school. Although
my parents read to me, they hadn't tried to teach me to read. I just
figured out somehow that letters stand for sounds. I may have gotten
the idea from the older children in the neighborhood. When I was
four years old, I stunned my parents by pointing to the milk carton
at breakfast one morning and sounding out the name of the dairy.
When my mother was later criticized by a school administrator for
having taught me to read "too early," she could only say, "I didn't
teach her. She just learned."

What kind of "expert" on education would expect children to
learn to read by memorizing the overall shape of whole words,
instead of by sounding out each word letter by letter? I knew at age
four that children need to sound out the words in order to learn to
read. That's how I taught myself to read. How could an educated
grownup think otherwise?

The idea that an "expert" on education could have such stupid
ideas about reading is a paradox—a set of facts that don't seem to
mesh together to make sense. Yet as I learned more about Dewey, I
found paradox after paradox. To resolve these paradoxes, I had to

read what Dewey wrote. I couldn't go by what other people wrote about him. That's because people either swear by Dewey or swear at him, but hardly anyone reads his work. Perhaps it's because he was such a bad writer.

John Dewey was the most famous American philosopher of the early 20ᵗʰ century. He was a public intellectual who was involved in many social and political causes. For example, he was a founding member of the National Association for the Advancement of Colored People and the American Civil Liberties Union. He was also active in the founding of the New York Teachers' Union. Dewey was an early member of the Socialist Party, but he later joined the Progressive Party and supported Robert "Fighting Bob" LaFollette when LaFolette ran for President.

Given these liberal credentials, it's not surprising that liberals tend to admire Dewey. Unfortunately, few liberals realize that some of the educational policies that Dewey advocated have been a disaster, especially for poor, black children. Conservatives, on the other hand, tend to misunderstand Dewey's politics. I've seen conservatives complain that Dewey was promoting radical, anti-American views or even that he was secretly an agent of the Worldwide Communist Conspiracy. But as far as I can tell, Dewey was voicing the mainstream views of the educated Americans of his day, which is why so many educated Americans took him seriously.

Dewey expressed standard Enlightenment ideas about science and democracy and human rights. These ideas had inspired people like Benjamin Franklin and Thomas Jefferson and Thomas Paine and were still commonplace among educated Yankees like Dewey in the early 20ᵗʰ century. If Dewey's views seem radical today, it's only because a peculiar coalition of atheists and Evangelical Christians on the political right have had worked so hard reshape public opinion. If you don't like Dewey's politics, you wouldn't have liked Benjamin Franklin's and you would have despised Thomas Paine's.

Why would a first-grade teacher use flashcards with whole words, instead of cards with individual letters and then single syllables, to teach children to read? John Dewey had persuaded American schoolteachers to resurrect the whole-word teaching method that had been such a disaster in Massachusetts in the 1840s. If Harper Lee's school had been using "the Dewey system" for teaching reading, it's no wonder that so many of her classmates were repeating first grade because they hadn't learned anything the previous year.

Lee makes it clear that these children weren't stupid. When Miss Caroline Fisher told the class that she was from Winston County, the children became worried. These first graders all knew the legend of the "Republic of Winston"—that when Alabama seceded from the Union in the Civil War, Winston County seceded from Alabama. Clearly, these children already knew a lot about history, geography, and politics. They just weren't learning to read. As a result, their education was being derailed.

How could someone who advocated the whole-word method for teaching reading be taken seriously as a philosopher of education? The whole-word method is based on a ridiculous theory, and its results had been shown nearly a century earlier to be disastrous. Intensive phonics, which was the method that had been used since the invention of the alphabet, is clearly the superior way to teach reading. There has never been any justification for replacing it or even just watering it down a little with "sight words." So why would Dewey, who was supposedly an expert on logic as well as education, have made such a seemingly irrational choice of teaching methods? It's a paradox.

Another paradox concerns Dewey's role as teacher and his role as a parent. Dewey was a high school teacher for two years before he went to graduate school to study philosophy. Dewey had six children with his first wife. After her death, he adopted two more children with his second wife. Dewey also founded the University of Chicago's laboratory school and went on to teach at Columbia Teachers College, which also had its own laboratory school. And yet, when I read Dewey's writings about education, I don't find any stories about actual children.

In what I've seen of Dewey's writing, I see lots of discussion of "the child" and "pupils" and "the young" as abstractions, but no stories about any actual child or any real classroom. I never see any discussion about what any actual child did or learned. I never see any discussion about any educational approaches that unexpectedly turned out badly or any practical problems that were solved. Nor does Dewey ever report what any real children had to say about anything. It is as if he had never met any actual children or observed an actual classroom. In other words, he doesn't sound like any teacher or parent or researcher I've ever met.

Yet another paradox concerns Dewey's philosophy. People tell me that Dewey is the most important figure in a particularly American school of philosophy called pragmatism. According to my dictionary, pragmatist philosophers believe that the function of thought is to guide action and that the truth of a belief is to be tested by its practical consequences. Yet when I read Dewey's writings on education, I find them filled with abstract theorizing that is so vague that it's often meaningless. I don't see reports of actual consequences, not even in his later works. In particular, I don't see any discussion of how a method that sounded good in theory failed in practice. A genuine pragmatist would be particularly interested in that kind of thing.

The sheer vagueness of much of Dewey's writing helps to explain another important paradox: why people such as Noam Chomsky credit a Deweyite progressive school for the excellent education they received in their youth while other people complain that Deweyite schools fail to teach children much of anything. Dewey's writings were so extensive and so unclear that people could cite Dewey to justify nearly anything they want to do in a school setting.

If you want to keep poor whites in southern Alabama from learning to read well, you could cite Dewey to justify using the whole-word method for teaching reading. If you want to allow the children of college professors to develop independence of mind by pursuing their own academic interests, you could cite Dewey to justify that, too. Perhaps the vagueness of Dewey's writing style was deliberate. Maybe he wanted his writings to be like Rorschach inkblots, so that people could read into them whatever they wished.

A genuinely pragmatic philosopher of education would be particularly concerned about the practical consequences of illiteracy and ignorance. Dewey had grown up in Burlington, Vermont, which at the time was an industrial city with a significant immigrant population. He spent most of his working life in New York City, at a time when waves of immigrants from Europe and the American South were flooding into the city. Thus, Dewey would have had plenty of opportunity to see the personal and social problems that result when people grow up uneducated.

Because of Dewey's involvement at Columbia Teachers College and the Lincoln School, Dewey also would have had plenty of opportunity to notice how poorly the whole-word method of reading instruction worked. Of John D. Rockefeller Jr.'s six children, the four sons who went to the Lincoln School all had serious difficulty in learning to read. The son and daughter who were educated elsewhere had no such trouble.

I suspect that Dewey didn't care about the poor reading skills of the children at the Lincoln School. Dewey had written that the emphasis on reading instruction in primary school seemed to him to be a "fetich" and the emphasis on literature to be a perversion. I know of no other writer who thinks that it's perverse to focus on literature.

When I read Dewey's writings on education, I find many passages in which he expresses contempt for literacy and academic learning. Consider this passage from *Democracy and Education*:

> Children doubtless go to school to learn, but it has yet to be proved that learning occurs most adequately when it is made a separate conscious business. When treating it as a business of this sort tends to preclude the social sense which comes from sharing in an activity of common concern and value, the effort at isolated intellectual learning contradicts its own aim.

What on earth did Dewey mean by that? Did he mean that children can learn only from group activities? Reading is a solitary activity. Did that mean that people can't learn from reading books? If Dewey really believed that, why did he bother to continue writing books?

Children probably do learn better if they are actively engaged in their schoolwork, and if their peers are, too. Yet isn't all academic learning ultimately something that goes on in the learner's own brain and is therefore not a social activity, even if the person is learning something from other people or for an explicitly social purpose? As the French philosopher and mathematician Blaise Pascal wrote, "*On mourra seul*"—each of us dies alone. Perhaps each of us must inevitably learn alone, as well.

Dewey's writings on education are peppered with passages that express hostility to literacy and literature and academic learning in general. Instead, he has warm praise for nonacademic activities in school, whether it's a social activity or some activity related to the mechanical or servile arts, such as cooking or sewing. Dewey seemed to expect that children would naturally learn skills like arithmetic while doing handicrafts that require them to do calculations, instead of by memorizing their multiplication tables and doing practice problems. Didn't Dewey realize that human beings had been cooking and sewing for thousands of years before the invention of mathematics?

If children aren't taught how to do arithmetic, how will they be able to do it when they need to do it? It's far more likely that the children will use their social skills to get a friend to do their arithmetic for them, instead of learning to do arithmetic themselves. Today, many "progressive" educators want children to be allowed to use calculators, instead of memorizing the multiplication tables.

Dewey thought that testing was bad and that children should be allowed to help each other in school. Yet if there are no tests and if children are allowed to help each other, how can anyone figure out whether a particular child is learning anything of value? The cooperation and lack of testing can provide a smokescreen that hides the fact that the children are not learning.

If Dewey were genuinely a pragmatist, he would have given clear, useful, evidence-based answers to practical questions about education. Perhaps the most important of these questions is this: What do children need to learn that they would not learn on their own? Another crucial question is this: How should those things be taught to the children? Dewey largely ignored the question of what should be taught. He gave a lousy answer to the question of how those things should be taught.

Dewey pointed out that education can be viewed in broad terms as the ways in which a society transmits knowledge and customs and so on from one generation to the next. Formal schooling is only one of the means of transmission. Yet Dewey seemed to be horrified by the idea of adults teaching things to children. Instead, he wanted children to construct their own knowledge through activities that they do voluntarily. This idea is called constructivism.

No one doubts that children learn better if they are interested in their schoolwork. However, children won't learn much about science if they have to discover everything for themselves. That would be like growing up in prehistoric times or the Dark Ages. Instead, educators need to understand an important lesson from Isaac Newton, who created the field of classical mechanics by working out the mathematics behind the Law of Gravity and the Laws of Motion. Newton explained, "If I have seen further it is by standing on the shoulders of giants." High school students shouldn't be expected to "construct" Newton's laws for themselves. Instead, the school should help the children climb up onto Newton's shoulders, and then Einstein's.

Dewey didn't seem to care about literacy and the arts and sciences. Instead, he was more concerned about children's social "success." While reading Dewey's writings, I get the distinct impression that he would admire today's popular football players and cheerleaders, even if they are ignorant or even functionally illiterate, but he would look down his nose at the nerdy kids in the Advanced Placement classes.

Dewey's emphasis on the student's social "success" at the expense of academic learning could help to explain why school, and especially high school, is such a miserable experience for so many smart kids in the United States. Paul Graham, who had been an unpopular "nerd" in high school and eventually got a doctorate in computer science from Harvard and made millions in the computer industry, sheds light on this problem. In his essay, Why Nerds Are Unpopular, he explained,

Being smart doesn't make you an outcast in elementary school. Nor does it harm you in the real world. Nor, as far as I can tell, is the problem so bad in most other countries. But in a typical American secondary school, being smart is likely to make your life difficult. Why?

Graham said that nerds are unpopular because they think about something other than the vicious struggle for position within the social hierarchy of their school:

> The main reason nerds are unpopular is that they have other things to think about. Their attention is drawn to books or the natural world, not fashions and parties. They're like someone trying to play soccer while balancing a glass of water on his head. Other players who can focus their whole attention on the game beat them effortlessly, and wonder why they seem so incapable.

Temple Grandin has an interesting perspective on the same problem. Grandin is an autistic woman with a doctoral degree in animal science. She has revolutionized the meat industry by designing humane systems for animal handling. She is also a prominent authority on autism. Grandin notes that all of society's material progress has depended on the work of people who are, as she puts it, "interested in *things*." These people are the scientists and engineers who invent new technologies and in general keep things running. Unlike Dewey, Grandin feels that the people who are interested in something other than "social chit-chat" are the people who ultimately have the most to offer to society.

Like many "nerds," Grandin was subjected to horrible "teasing" when she was in high school. Her only escape from it was in interest-oriented activities such as horse-back riding, electronics club, and model rocket club. Grandin argues that autistic children, in particular, should be encouraged to cultivate these interests, which often lead to a rewarding and satisfying career and often to friendships in adult life.

Most parents want their children to have friends at school. No decent person would want a child to be unpopular and to be shunned, teased, and bullied. Yet I think that most adults would be horrified by the suggestion that school is primarily a social club, instead of the institution where children are supposed to learn reading, writing, mathematics, science, history, and so on. Most taxpayers would be furious to think that their tax money had been spent on schools that neglect academic learning because they are run by people who agreed with this passage from Dewey's *The School and Society*:

> The mere absorbing of facts and truths is so exclusively
> individual an affair that it tends very naturally to pass into
> selfishness. There is no obvious social motive for the
> acquirement of mere learning, there is no clear social gain
> in success thereat.

Why did Dewey think that academic learning should take a back seat to social success in school? I think that it was because he was expressing the worldview of the ruling class of his day. Back in Dewey's time, *whom* you knew mattered far more than *what* you knew. The country was being run by wealthy individuals who were linked through family ties and long-term friendships. These individuals served on the boards of directors of the railroads and the banks and the trusts, the largest of which was the Standard Oil trust. The people who owned those corporations ran the business world. They also had enormous influence on other aspects of society, through their philanthropy.

Dewey himself owed his success not to any outstanding personal accomplishments or any special genius, but to the fact that he'd managed to gain a prominent position in academic institutions being funded by the world's richest man: John D. Rockefeller Sr., the founder of the Standard Oil trust. Dewey's ideas about education were then spread through the Rockefellers' General Education Board, which set about remaking the entire American educational system, from kindergarten through graduate and professional school.

Dewey saw to it that the people he liked got teaching jobs at teachers' colleges and normal schools all over the country. That's how Dewey's stupid method of teaching reading made it all the way from New York City to southern Alabama. Thus, it must have seemed obvious to Dewey that the ability to cultivate relationships with the right people was the real secret to success.

Dewey's approach to teaching reading is still widely used in the United States, and it is the primary reason why we have such a problem with functional illiteracy and dyslexia in the United States. Some people hope to solve our educational problems by punishing the teachers when students score poorly on standardized tests. Yet anyone with even the slightest understanding of quality control methods would realize how stupid that approach is.

In manufacturing, you cannot improve the quality of a sample by testing it. Tests merely provide data. It still takes human intelligence to figure out what, if anything, those data reveal about the manufacturing process. If the workers in a factory are required to use bad methods for manufacturing the product, then management, not the workers, should be held accountable for the poor quality of the product. Similarly, it is silly to blame a schoolteacher for problems that resulted because the people who run the school system have chosen an ineffective curriculum or have failed to solve problems that occur before the student reaches that teacher's classroom.

Middle and high school teachers tell me that the biggest problem that they face is that their students can't read well. History teachers tell me that many of their students can't read their textbooks. Math teachers tell me that some of their students can do the mathematical calculations just fine but can't read the "word problems" on the tests. Dewey's whole-word approach to teaching reading is the main cause of this problem. This whole-word approach has had numerous incarnations. It has been called "look-and-say," or "sight-reading." It involves the use of "sight words" or "Dolch words." It's a cornerstone of "whole language." The latest incarnation of the whole-word approach is "balanced literacy."

The whole-word method persists because the people who train the teachers and the people who force the teachers to use a particular curriculum have decided that the whole-word method should be used. Unfortunately, the people who make this decision are never held accountable for the failure of the method. Instead, the teachers and the students and the students' families are blamed.

Some children do manage to learn to read even if a whole-word approach is used in their school. Like Scout, I learned to read before I started school. Harper Lee said that Scout didn't remember how the text turned into words, but I do remember. Somehow, I realized that letters stand for sounds. I may have gotten that idea from the older kids in the neighborhood. I then worked at figuring out the letter-sound relationships in the books that were being read to me. Before my parents realized what was happening, I could read. Other children probably figure out the letter-sound relationships in school, even if their teacher is using a whole-word method. Thus, many children learn despite the teaching method that is being used. Unfortunately, their success is hiding the failure of the teaching methods being used in their schools.

Standardized tests might be able to show how *well* a group of children can read. However, those tests don't reveal *how* any of those children learned to read. In a middle-class population, many of the children will end up learning to read outside of school. These children get tutoring, either directly from a family member or from a tutor whom the family hires. As a result, the schools in affluent neighborhoods will seem to be more effective than they really are. They take credit for the work done by the families and the private tutoring services. If you want to see how bad a teaching method is, see how it performs in a school where the children have no other educational resources to fall back on. A method that doesn't work in a school that serves low-income students is a method that doesn't work.

Since I started writing this book, I have heard from many people who had trouble learning to read in school or whose children were failing to learn to read in school. The cause of the problem was always the same: the children weren't being taught phonics. The solution was always the same as well: the parents got the child some tutoring in phonics outside of the school system. Unfortunately, that's not the approach that most school systems use.

School administrators generally assume that dyslexia is a genetic brain disorder, not a result of the ineffective teaching methods they require the teachers to use. Thus, the administrators assume that the problem is in the child, not in the teaching method. Once the child gets labeled as disabled, then federal money can be used to pay for special services for the disabled. Unfortunately, the remedial reading instruction that the supposedly disabled child receives is just an even larger dose of the teaching methods that didn't work to begin with. Money changes hands, and the children are marked for life as somehow defective, but the children still might not learn much.

John Dewey was supposedly an expert on education and an advocate for democracy. Yet he seems to have failed to grasp something important about the role of education in promoting democracy. Democracy means rule by the people. If the people are to rule, they must achieve consensus about what should be done. They can achieve this consensus only through a process of civilized public discussion.

The ancient Athenians realized that public discussions were much more productive if people knew how to tell a good argument from a bad argument, and if people knew how to avoid being swept away by an appeal to their emotions. To help their children develop these skills, the ancient Athenians taught them reading, grammar, logic, and rhetoric. They also taught them mathematics, geometry, music, and astronomy. The Romans called these studies the liberal arts because they were considered appropriate for free people, as opposed to slaves. Dewey suppressed the teaching of the liberal arts. Instead, he argued that children should be kept busy with social activities and the servile arts.

During the Renaissance, the wealthy families of northern Italy faced similar concerns about promoting productive discussions within their social set. For that reason, they created a larger curriculum, which they called the humanities. In addition to the classical liberal arts, the humanities included languages, literature, the arts, history, and philosophy. To engage in productive political discussions today, a person would also have to know a lot about science and economics.

To take a meaningful part in important political discussions today, a person must have learned a lot of skills and facts and ideas in
school. These are not the sort of skills and facts and ideas that one
learns through cooking and sewing and chatting with friends. Otherwise, the United States would have had Founding Mothers instead
of Founding Fathers. In reality, most of the Founding Fathers of the
United States had precisely the kind of education that John Dewey
disparaged.

As one of Dewey's critics explains, "Since at least the time of
Aristotle, the greater societies have always been grounded in tradition as well as having an active/educated citizenry. Dewey knew this
from his own education but promoted what he called progressive
education completely devoid of the base and basics from which to
progress."[1]

Reference

1. O'Mara K. John Dewey and the decline of American education: how the patron
saint of schools has corrupted teaching and learning [book review]. Eclectic
Homeschool Online.

http://eclectichomeschool.org/reviews/individual _review2.asp?revid=2465

CHAPTER XVIII

Traditional or Progressive?

For decades, Americans have been debating about whether to take a "traditional" or "progressive" approach to education in the public schools. I can't take either side in this debate. I know that many "traditional" strategies and tactics were invented fairly recently, and for a bad purpose. I also know that some of the supposedly "progressive" strategies and tactics make it difficult for children to progress. If we want to figure out how to improve education in the United States, we need to have a completely different discussion.

The usual debate is between people who want to emphasize basic skills and people who want children to develop higher-order skills. I was stunned to see that people actually argue about how much classroom time to take away from teaching basic skills in order to teach higher-order skills, as if it were a matter of robbing Peter to pay Paul. These arguments make no sense to me. It would be like a music teacher taking time away from teaching basic music theory in order to teach advanced jazz improvisation.

Great jazz musicians become great through careful study of music theory and countless hours spent practicing scales and other musical elements. The great jazz clarinetist Benny Goodman practiced his scales every day until the time of his death at age 77. Many people who think of themselves as progressive educators disapprove of this sort of emphasis on memorization and drills. I suspect that John Dewey would have been particularly horrified by the idea of music

students spending so much time "in the woodshed," in solitary practice. He thought that worthwhile learning could take place only in a
social setting. Yet no serious musician wants to play in an ensemble
with a person who hasn't been "woodshedding." You need to spend
a lot of time practicing by yourself if you want to get the chance to
play with good musicians. Dewey didn't understand that principle.
Perhaps it was because he had no musical training and had a reputation for being tone-deaf.

There's no tradeoff between basic skills and higher-order skills.
You can't develop higher-order skills without first developing basic
skills. What we need to do is figure out which of the basic skills
children need to master if they are to go on to develop higher-order
skills. If we can teach those basics with a minimum of fuss and
bother and at the right time and in the right order, the children can
progress more quickly and easily.

When most people talk about the problems in our educational
system, they tend to focus on children. For example, they look at
how poorly children do on standardized tests or count the number
of young people who drop out of high school. My perspective is
different. I focus on the results of education in educated adults. I
don't know whether their schools were "traditional" or "progressive,"
but I can't help noticing how much they learned and what they failed
to learn. That's because I end up "grading their papers." I'm an
editor, and I have to edit their manuscripts before the articles and
books they wrote get published.

I've worked as an editor in various aspects of medical publishing
for more than 20 years. I've also edited some college textbooks. This
means that I've ended up teaching remedial English to people who
have succeeded at the highest levels in the US educational system.
I've seen a lot of bad writing from educated Americans. I've also
edited many manuscripts from authors from Europe or Asia. The
writing from the Europeans and Asians is generally surprisingly
good, even if English is their second, third, or fourth language.
They may have trouble with figures of speech, and their writing may
be a bit stilted, but it's generally understandable. In contrast, many
educated Americans have trouble writing coherently in their first

language. Hardly any of them can function at all in any other language. These observations made me wonder what's going wrong in our English and foreign language classes.

When I was trained as an editor, I was taught that I shouldn't suggest any editorial change unless I could explain exactly why that change is needed. When I talked with the authors about these changes, I often ended up explaining basic grammatical concepts, such as dangling participles or parallel structure. Many of the authors told me that they were never taught these things in school. I was inclined to believe them. These authors were the sort of people who remember what they were taught in school. That's how they made it into and through medical school and how they managed to pass their board exams. They also tended to remember and apply the lessons I taught them. As a result, their writing improved dramatically.

When it was my turn to supervise entry-level editors, I developed a system for training them as efficiently as possible. I had them study a Web site that reviews the parts of speech and shows how to diagram sentences. Then I gave them a handout with some simple rules of thumb for turning bad sentences into good sentences and how to punctuate correctly. If someone from my staff came to me for help with a troublesome sentence, I'd usually just point to one of the words in the sentence and ask, "What part of speech is this?" Sometimes, I'd ask the person to diagram the sentence. That was usually enough to enable the person to figure out the problem and the solution by him- or herself. I got such a good reputation for turning bad writers into good writers that I was asked to write a column on grammar and writing for the *American Medical Writers Association Journal*.

As I was doing research for my column, I searched for the answer to a simple question: Why did American grammar schools stop teaching grammar? The short answer is that some people who were influential in the National Council of Teachers of English decided in 1963 that grammar lessons were not only boring and pointless but probably harmful.[1] On the basis of their advice, public schools all over the country stopped teaching grammar.

What happened after the schools stopped teaching grammar? Did the scores on the verbal portion of Scholastic Aptitude Test (SAT) go up, or at least stay steady? Nope. In 1963, the scores on the verbal portion of the Scholastic Aptitude Tests (SATs) began a sharp and unexpected 16-year decline. This decline was *not* the result of a larger percentage of students taking the test. Test scores had remained remarkably stable between 1952 and 1963, when the percentage of high school students taking the SATs increased dramatically. One study linked the decline to an earlier "dumbing-down" of textbooks.[2] I suspect that the abandonment of grammar instruction made things worse.

After watching verbal SAT scores decline steadily for 16 years, the NCTE started back-pedaling a bit, by publishing Constance Weaver's *Grammar for Teachers* in 1979. Weaver argued that teachers need to know key aspects of grammar in order to teach writing more effectively. In 1996, Weaver extended those ideas in her book *Teaching Grammar in Context*. This book seemed to give English teachers permission to resume teaching some grammar lessons, as long as the grammar was taught "in context." What did she mean by "in context"? (I had always thought that grammar should be taught "in English class"!) What she meant was that grammar should be taught in the context of writing and editing, which is the only context in which I could imagine teaching it.

Maybe some English teachers did need to be told to teach grammar in the context of writing. Some of the authors I've worked with over the years have told me that they did learn some grammatical concepts in school. For example, they knew what a preposition was. They even knew that some people will try to "correct" you if you put a preposition at the end of a sentence. (Winston Churchill is rumored to have called that kind of hypercorrection an "offensive impertinence, up with which I shall not put!") However, nobody ever told them that they should avoid putting a potentially adjectival prepositional phrase after a noun unless they want it to modify that noun. Nor did anyone tell them to avoid putting an adjectival phrase at the beginning of a sentence unless they wanted that phrase to modify the subject. It's as if someone gave them a box of tools and told them the names of some of the tools but then didn't show them how to use the darn tools.

I have always taught grammar specifically to help people improve their writing. Thus, I have always taught grammar "in context." Grammar should be taught in the context of writing. It should also be taught in the context of thinking. People need to understand some basic grammatical concepts before they can even begin to study logic, which is the study of arguments. People need to study logic before they can begin to study rhetoric.

As I explained in Chapter 11, there are three modes of persuasion: *ethos, pathos,* and *logos. Ethos* refers to the character of the speaker, *pathos* is an appeal to the emotions, and *logos* means logic and reason. Of those three modes of persuasion, *logos* is the only one that should matter in a scientific discussion. *Logos* should be important in other kinds of discussions as well. If you can't respond appropriately to logic and reason, the only means of persuasion left are ethos and pathos. In other words, if you can't respond to logic, you'll be easily manipulated by propaganda.

I think that the lack of instruction in grammar, logic, and rhetoric in American public schools goes far toward explaining why political discussions in the United States tend to be so ugly and pointless. If logical arguments don't work, then the only modes of persuasion that are left are name-calling, flag-waving, fear-mongering, and hair-pulling.

Within the past few years, the NCTE has published some material on what they call rhetorical grammar. This material argues that careful attention to word choice and sentence structure can help people become more persuasive. Of course it would. What bothers me is that they've turned the trivium into a bivium. Why talk about grammar and rhetoric but leave out logic? That omission seems creepy to me.

When I talk with people about some of the irrational aspects of education policy, they often tell me that the problem is politics. I've heard more than one person say, "We have to get the politics out of education!" But education has always been a central concern for the entire population. Thus, it's precisely the sort of thing that *should* be a subject of political discussions. Education has always been politicized. Back in 399 BC, the philosopher Socrates was given the death penalty because of a political offense related to education.

Socrates had long been known to have contempt for the liberal democratic government of Athens. His aristocratic students were known for their pro-Spartan sympathies. His student Alcibiades eventually betrayed Athens to Sparta and later participated in the coup that overthrew Athenian democracy for a few months in 411 BC. Socrates' student Critias was the worst of the Thirty Tyrants who overthrew Athenian democracy again in 404 BC, launching a reign of terror in which thousands of Athenians were killed or banished. Historians do not know to what degree Socrates was personally involved in those events. They do know that he was neither killed nor banished during the reign of the Thirty Tyrants.

Because of a general amnesty that was passed in 403 BC, after the restoration of democracy, Socrates couldn't be tried for treason in connection with the events of the previous few years. In 399 BC, however, a jury of 500 Athenians decided that he continued to "corrupt the youth" and they sentenced him to death. On one hand, I agree with Socrates that his death penalty brought shame on Athens. On the other hand, I'm amazed that the Athenians let him live as long as he did.

Unlike Socrates, I think that democracy is a good thing. I feel that people should participate in making the decisions that affect them. I think that it's best if people know what's going on. I don't think that people should be manipulated by Noble Lies from an oligarchy. I agree with the ancient Athenians that the best way to preserve democracy is for its citizens to be literate and to have a well-rounded education, with a solid grounding in the study of grammar, logic, and rhetoric.

Democracy literally means rule by the people. It means a lot more than casting a ballot once every few years. If a society is truly democratic, ordinary people become informed about the issues and become active politically in pursuing their interests and those of the general public. The people elect representatives who genuinely represent their views and hold those representatives accountable for their actions. Policy decisions are made in a fair and open way after public discussions where any point of view can be represented. Even if a society has a republican form of government instead of a direct democracy, that society can be democratic if government policy reflects the will of the people.

Democracy can survive only where there are open and well-informed political discussions. Unfortunately, many Americans were brought up to believe that it's impolite to talk about politics. That advice must have been dreamed up by people who think that the important decisions should be made in secret by a small number of powerful people. The Thirty Tyrants would have had no need to destroy the Athenian constitution if they could have persuaded the Athenian citizenry that it's impolite to talk about politics.

The discussions about traditional versus progressive educational policy provide a good starting point for having productive political discussions. When I listen to the people on either side of the debate, I find that most of them are sincere in their concern for children and society. Thus, we have the potential to build a consensus that would serve the common good. The problem is that I find bits of truth and lots of nonsense on both sides of the divide. The biggest challenge will be in persuading people to set aside their egos and preconceptions so that they can deepen their understanding of the problems affecting education. Only then will we be able to make real progress in reforming education in the United States.

Progressive educators need to realize that many of the policies that have been implemented in the name of progressive education have been a disaster. Chief among these is the insistence on teaching children to read by memorizing whole words, instead of by learning to sound words out letter by letter. The Boston Schoolmasters warned us in the 1840s that the whole-word method was based on a ludicrous theory and had disastrous results. Dr. Samuel Orton warned us in the late 1920s that the whole-word method had unleashed an epidemic of dyslexia and behavior problems, which could be reversed through direct instruction in intensive phonics.

The progressives claim that their policies are based on scientific research. Yet they don't want to accept blame for the problems that have predictably resulted from some of the policies they championed. The decline in verbal SAT scores during the 1960s and 1970s was only one example. Another was the whole-language catastrophe in California. After the whole-language curriculum was imposed on public schools throughout California in 1989, California's children's reading scores dropped to the third worst in the nation, ahead of only Louisiana and Guam.

The disaster in California was completely foreseeable and avoidable and is therefore inexcusable. Yet instead of admitting the error of their ways and embracing direct instruction in intensive phonics, many advocates of whole language backed off only a little. Their fallback position was called balanced literacy. It's just another variation on the theme of whole-word instruction, and it too is far less effective than direct instruction in intensive phonics. Unfortunately, the same sort of thing has happened repeatedly before, and no one seems to learn from this history.

In 1955, Rudolf Flesch's book *Why Johnny Can't Read* became a bestseller. In that book, Flesch explained that in his native Austria, all children who could see and hear and who weren't otherwise noticeably mentally disabled learned to read. Dyslexia and other problems with learning to read were unknown. The epidemic of reading difficulties in the United States was due to the use of the whole-word approach to teaching reading. *Why Johnny Can't Read* unleashed a storm of controversy. Yet nothing really changed as a result. In 1983, Flesh published *Why Johnny Still Can't Read*, which explained how the educational establishment had preserved the whole-word approach, despite public outrage. Unless some major changes take place, this problem will remain unsolved.

To me, it seems that the problems with the progressive approach to education boil down to a simple misunderstanding of how children learn. Progressives know that toddlers acquire their first language naturally and effortlessly just by having normal social interactions. Progressives want children to learn other kinds of things in the same natural and effortless way. The problem is that while spoken language (oral or sign language) is a natural product of an inborn human drive, reading and writing and arithmetic are not. They are technologies that must be taught and practiced. Otherwise, they cannot be learned.

The traditional idea of schooling is based on three basic assumptions. The first is that adults know some things that children need to learn. The second is that adults should use their authority to teach those things to children. The third is that children must be asked to do some things that they wouldn't necessarily choose to do of their own free will. John Dewey took issue with all of those assumptions, but I think those assumptions are reasonable.

Children do not have the knowledge or the judgment to make certain kinds of decisions for themselves. Adults have not only the right but the responsibility to use their authority to protect children and to promote and guide their development. I also think that it is good for children to be asked to do something besides following each momentary whim. Children do need to learn how to do what they *need* to do, as opposed to merely what they *wish* to do. The ability to delay gratification is a skill that can be taught and learned. Children who learn to put off receiving a reward in order to receive a greater reward later are more likely to succeed in many aspects of life as they grow up.

I realize that I've just trashed the progressives pretty badly. I'm afraid I have some strong criticism for the traditionalists as well. The traditionalists are right that using the methods that have been used for several thousand years to teach reading and writing and arithmetic and so on are far better than what the progressives have been advocating for the past 100 years. However, the traditionalists need to recognize that much of what we think of as traditional schooling was imported from Prussia in the 1840s.

The Prussian system was designed to turn the population into effective, obedient soldiers and efficient, docile workers with no mind of their own. Much of what some progressive educators want to do is get away from that model. Progressives have some valid concerns about the kinds of assignments and the amount of homework that children are given in school. When I was in school, my classmates used to complain about "busywork"—pointless assignments given just to keep us "busy."

Some of the ideas that motivate progressives really are important. For example, educational strategies should be based on an understanding of how children really learn. For example, we need to recognize that cramming a set of unrelated facts into a child's short-term memory, just so the child can pass a test, is almost certainly a waste of time. We need to think about the value and relevance of what is taught in school. For example, calculus seems to me to be of less value for the average person than statistics. Yet calculus is much more commonly taught in high school. We also need to think about how to lay the groundwork in the earlier grades for the more challenging work that will be done later on.

The support for direct instruction in intensive phonics and a general improvement in educational standards, at least with regard to basic skills, tends to come from conservatives. Unfortunately, this completely reasonable plank is built into an education platform that contains some elements that would not improve education.

For many conservatives, a dislike of the public schools comes from a general ideological opposition to government and contempt for government employees. Many elements within the Republican Party are currently trying to dismantle the public employees' unions, including the teachers' unions, and trying to find ways to use charter schools and a voucher system to dismantle public education. However, there is no reason to believe that dismantling the public school system or destroying the teachers' unions would improve education. In Finland, which has the world's best educational system, the schools are public and nearly all of the teachers are union members.

Another problem is the conservatives' support for extensive standardized testing. In the 10 years following the passage of the No Child Left Behind Act, the number of standardized tests that American children have to take exploded. Yet their achievements in math and science, as measured by the Programme for International Student Assessment, actually declined while their reading scores stayed low. Part of the problem is that teachers had to take valuable class time to prep students for the tests. To help the children pass the tests, teachers often end up stuffing random facts into children's short-term memory, which is a complete waste of time. The tests themselves teach nothing and their results have questionable validity. Finnish schools, in contrast, have virtually no standardized testing.

If traditionalists want progressives to embrace phonics and basic skills, traditionalists must also think about how to make our schools more humane. Progressives raise some important points about the social environment in schools. A school doesn't have to be like a prison or a factory. A school should be an inspiring and nurturing learning environment where every child is valued and every child can feel safe from bullying—from teachers and principals as well as from other students. There's no excuse for the use of corporal punishment in the schools, even though it remains legal in much of the United States.

There are certainly other ideological and cultural differences between progressives and traditionalists, but I think that people can begin to work to find workable solutions to those problems if they can put aside their differences long enough to solve a simple problem like teaching children to read. In this chapter, I've emphasized that political discussions are desirable and should be civilized and productive. In Chapter 19 and Chapter 20, I'll give some insight into how so much of educational policy has been made in secret, by institutions that are not accountable to the public.

References

1. Braddock R, Lloyd-Jones R, Schoer L. Research in written composition. Champaign, IL: National Council of Teachers of English, 1963.

2. Hayes DP, Wolfer LT, Wolfe MF. Schoolbook simplification and its relation to the decline in SAT-Verbal scores. *Am Educ Res J.* 1996;33(2):489-508.

CHAPTER XIX

How Foundations and Corporations Suppressed Phonics

I ntensive phonics is far more effective than whole-word methods for teaching children to read English. So why did the whole-word method become the main method for teaching reading in the United States? I can sum up the main reason in two words: oil money. Why does whole-word persist, even after it has been repeatedly discredited? I can sum that up in three words: the publishing business. I've heard some people insist that the whole-word method was promoted by a communist conspiracy to destroy the United States by ruining our public schools. Yet when I look at actual history, I find that the opposition to phonics came from people who owned or were funded by major corporations. It was perpetuated by an unhealthy relationship between the publishing companies and the faculties of the schools of education.

To a casual observer, the educational system in the United States may seem to be extremely decentralized. Education has largely been the responsibility of state and local governments, and teachers theoretically control what goes on in their classrooms. Yet it has long been possible for a relatively small number of people to wield enormous influence on what goes on in classrooms throughout the country, by controlling the training of aspiring teachers and influencing the content of textbooks. In the early 20th century, the most powerful of these influences was the General Education Board that was created by John D. Rockefeller Sr. and his advisor Frederick T. Gates in 1902.

Rockefeller eventually gave the General Education Board $180 million, nearly all of which was spent by 1950. Not only was $180 million a breathtaking sum in the early 20th century, but Rockefeller's advisors thought carefully about how to use leverage to make sure that Rockefeller got the biggest possible bang for all those bucks. That huge sum of money from the world's foremost practitioner of monopoly capitalism was the wind beneath John Dewey's wings. If Dewey had not been so prominently positioned in institutions funded by the Rockefellers, no one would ever have heard of him.

By the end of the 19th century, John D. Rockefeller Sr. had become the world's wealthiest man. If you take inflation into account, he might still be considered the wealthiest person in US history. Rockefeller's wealth came primarily from being the founder and major shareholder of the Standard Oil Company, which gained control over much of the transportation, refining, and marketing of oil in the United States. Of course, Rockefeller used some of his gains from the oil business to invest in other areas of the economy. For example, the Rockefellers' control of Colorado Fuel and Iron in the early 20th century meant that about 10% of the population of Colorado was directly or indirectly on their payroll.

When Rockefeller's philanthropy came to public attention in his later years, many people assumed that he was trying to curry favor with the public or to ease a guilty conscience. They were mistaken. Rockefeller had always shown an odd mixture of greed and generosity, and most of his early philanthropy was done discreetly.

Rockefeller saw nothing wrong with his ruthless business practices. He had a high opinion of his own moral code, and he had always given money to what he considered the deserving poor and worthy causes. Before the Civil War, Rockefeller was a supporter of the abolitionist wing of Abraham Lincoln's Republican Party. Before Emancipation, Rockefeller gave money to a Black man in Cincinnati to enable the man to ransom his wife from slavery. After Emancipation, Rockefeller provided major funding for a college for Black women in Atlanta, Georgia. It was named Spelman College, after his abolitionist in-laws.

Much of Rockefeller's early philanthropy was given to individuals, often to the poorer members of his church. Yet after Rockefeller became the world's richest man, he was so overwhelmed with "begging letters" that he had to "Standardize" his philanthropy, as his Standard Oil Company had "Standardized" the oil industry. He had to go from "retail" philanthropy to "wholesale" philanthropy. Much of this "wholesale" philanthropy was dedicated to furthering the goals of the Efficiency Movement.

The Efficiency Movement was a major movement among the political elites of the industrialized nations, including Britain and the United States, in the early 20th century. The captains of industry knew that skilled engineers and administrators enabled them to wring more profits out of their businesses. Thus, wealthy people wanted to make not just their private businesses but their entire societies efficient from their perspective. In other words, they wanted to set up not only their businesses but their entire society and even the wider world to serve their needs as efficiently as possible. The Efficiency Movement gave rise to the Progressive Era in the United States but lost favor in the 1930s, when some stupid things that were done in the name of efficiency deepened the Great Depression.

To understand the Efficiency Movement, you must realize that efficiency is a mental construct. How you construct your idea of efficiency depends on your point of view. It depends on what you include and exclude in your calculation of costs and benefits. For example, if you are a manufacturer, you would make more profit if you cut your workers' wages. Thus, low wages may seem more efficient than higher wages. Yet you'd still be using the same number of person-hours to get the work done. From a societal perspective, a cut in wages isn't a more efficient use of labor, it's just a redistribution of wealth.

To understand the Efficiency Movement and the Progressive Era, you have to understand two things: what wealthy people consider to be a problem, and how wealthy people solve their problems. Like anybody else, wealthy people are concerned about problems that affect their personal and economic interests. For example, a factory owner's income comes from revenue minus costs, and those costs include wages. Thus, the factory owner has higher profits if the workers' wages are low. The low wages might be a serious problem for the workers, but they are not a problem for the factory owner. Instead, low wages are a solution to the factory owner's own problem of how to maximize profits. To a factory owner, low wages are never a problem, but labor unrest can be a serious problem.

To keep wages low, the factory owner needs to promote an educational system that prevents workers from questioning the status quo or working together to create a system in which they get to enjoy more of the fruits of their own labor. Thus, factory owners have an economic incentive to promote the mechanical arts and suppress the liberal arts in public education. That's why the wealthy people of Massachusetts became interested in the Prussian model for public education when they were confronted with labor unrest in the textile factories in the 1830s and 1840s.

To solve problems, wealthy people can use either their money or their personal influence. With their money, they either buy things or pay people to do things. They can hire ordinary workers to do ordinary work. They can also hire highly educated people to do more specialized kinds of work. For example, they can hire lawyers to solve their legal problems. Because science and engineering developed so rapidly starting in the late 19th century, they could hire scientists and engineers to solve technical problems. With the rise of the social sciences in the late 19th century, they could also hire other kinds of experts to find solutions for social problems.

The other important thing to understand about wealthy people is how often they do things together. Rugged individualism is a myth that was created to keep poor people divided and conquered. A wealthy individual may brag about being self-made, but wealthy Americans have always made heavy use of their social and business connections. Wealthy people invest in each other's businesses. They serve on each other's boards of directors. They belong to the same churches and clubs and serve on the same committees in charitable, social, and political organizations. They consult with each other to preselect the candidates who will appear on the ballot in political elections. They do many things behind the scenes, so that the results seem as if they just happened, like the weather, instead of being the result of planning and purposeful action.

The Efficiency Movement and the Progressive Movement both represented attempts to apply the lessons learned from scientists and engineers to solve various problems in business, government, and society at large. At the time, this was a new and, for many people, disturbing development. Up until the 19th century, most of the scientific community in Europe and the United States looked to the Bible as a source of scientific truth. They believed that religious devotion was the best way to solve personal problems. They believed that religious revival movements were the way to solve social problems. By the early 20th century, however, powerful people were turning to secular experts in the natural and social sciences instead of to clergymen for solutions to practical problems.

Many devout Christians were troubled by how badly the influence of the Bible, the clergy, and religious institutions were eroding. Some people explained this erosion as the work of a personified evil: Satan. Others explained it in terms of a reified, foreign evil: communism. Since the Rockefellers made such heavy use of scientific experts, many people concluded that John D. Rockefeller Sr., who was in reality the world's foremost practitioner of monopoly capitalism, was secretly part of the Worldwide Communist Conspiracy. Likewise, nearly any advocate of science, social reform, or secularism was likely to be labeled a communist—which to many people simply meant an atheist, if it meant anything at all. Yet John D. Rockefeller Sr. was a devout Baptist.

The Rockefellers and their advisors tried to use the Rockefellers' millions to solve what they considered to be problems. One problem that John D. Rockefeller Jr. and steel magnate Andrew Carnegie addressed was the poor quality of medical education in the United States. The Carnegie Foundation funded a major study, *Medical Education in the United States and Canada*, which was published in 1910. It is often called the Flexner Report, after its author, Abraham Flexner.

The Flexner report revealed that many medical schools in the United States were for-profit institutions with extremely low standards for admission and graduation. Flexner recommended that such schools be closed. He recommended that the Johns Hopkins

University School of Medicine should serve as the model for medical schools in the United States. Within a few years after the Flexner Report was issued, half of the medical schools in the United States closed and most of the rest were substantially improved. Many of the improvements that were recommended in the Flexner report were funded by the Rockefellers.

Another of the problems that the Rockefellers addressed was the low productivity of Southern agriculture. The Rockefellers provided funding for demonstration farms established by the US Department of Agriculture. In 1909, John D. Rockefeller Sr. provided $1 million in funding for the Rockefeller Sanitary Commission for the Eradication of Hookworm Disease. Hookworm is an intestinal parasite that was called "the germ of laziness" because it often caused severe, debilitating anemia and could stunt the physical and mental development of children. The Sanitary Commission helped state medical associations organize campaigns to find and cure cases of hookworm infection. It also supported local educational campaigns to teach people how using properly designed privies and wearing shoes could stop the transmission of the parasite. By 1914, hookworm was nearly eradicated, thus leading to gains in agricultural output in areas where the parasite had been common.

Rockefeller's General Education Board also provided funding for state universities and for state boards of education in the South to send out representatives to persuade local communities to establish high schools. It also provided funding for schools for blacks, especially for training black teachers.

Many people are aware that wealthy philanthropists have given a lot of money to support educational institutions. However, few people stop to think about what a captain of industry might want to achieve through such donations. The General Education Board candidly expressed its goals in 1913, in the first of its "Occasional Papers":

> The present education conventions fade from their minds, and unhampered by tradition, we work our own good will upon a grateful and responsive rural folk. We shall not try to make these people or any of their children into

philosophers or men of learning, or men of science. We
have not to raise up from among them authors, editors,
poets or men of letters. We shall not search for embryo great
artists, painters, musicians nor lawyers, doctors, preachers,
politicians, statesmen, of whom we have an ample supply...
The task we set before ourselves is very simple as well as a
very beautiful one, to train these people as we find them
to a perfectly ideal life just where they are. So we will
organize our children and teach them to do in a perfect
way the things their fathers and mothers are doing in an
imperfect way, in the homes, in the shops and on the farm.

Rockefeller already had an ample supply of adequately trained doctors, lawyers, engineers, geologists, and other useful experts because of the money he'd given to colleges and universities. His goal
in promoting education for the general public was not to provide
opportunities for the "grateful and responsive rural folk" to learn
how to use their political power to improve their lives and the lives
of others like themselves. It was merely to make them fulfill their
existing roles in society more efficiently. Thus, the General Education Board's vision of the purpose of education is the exact opposite
of the American dream.

Rockefeller and his advisors did not want education to give individual members of the working class the opportunity for upward
social mobility. Nor did they want education to promote freedom,
equality, and democracy. Instead, the General Education Board's
stated goals were the same as those of the Prussian educational system: to promote efficiency but to suppress thought and free will
among the lower classes.

As one might expect, the high school education that the General
Education Board promoted tended to be heavily vocational. It
emphasized the mechanical arts, not the liberal arts. In fact, the
Rockefeller philanthropies tended to suppress the liberal arts for the
general public by helping John Dewey promote educational methods
that suppressed literacy and academic learning. Through these
methods, the kind of education that was traditionally considered

appropriate for free people was ultimately reserved for a privileged elite, while the vast majority of people got the kind of education that was traditionally considered appropriate for slaves.

The Rockefellers' advisors should have known by 1930 that whole-word reading instruction would be a disaster. They had funded Dr. Samuel Orton's research, which incriminated the whole-word method of reading instruction as the cause of dyslexia. Orton found that the more "sight words" that children were asked to memorize before they learned any phonics, the higher their risk of dyslexia was. The Rockefellers should also have learned from their family experiences. Four of John D. Rockefeller Jr.'s six children went to the Lincoln School, which was run by Columbia Teachers College. The four boys who went to the Lincoln School had serious lifelong problems with reading, mainly because nobody bothered to teach them how to read; the other two children, who were educated elsewhere, had no difficulty with reading.

Rockefeller's General Education Board was not the only way in which wealthy and powerful people have undermined public education. Another example was the campaign to suppress Harold Rugg's social studies textbooks.

Harold Rugg had originally been trained as a civil engineer. He then went on to study psychology and sociology and got a doctor of philosophy degree in education. He developed a particular interest in curriculum design and was one of the founders of social studies, which the National Council for the Social Studies defines as "the integrated study of the social sciences and humanities to promote civic competence."

Starting in 1929, Rugg introduced a set of social studies textbooks for junior and senior high schools. The textbooks were popular with teachers, students, and parents. Unfortunately, they pointed out that American society had weaknesses as well as strengths. One of the books even mentioned that the cost of advertising was passed on to the consumer. Thus, Rugg's textbooks provoked a furious backlash from the National Association of Manufacturers, the Advertising Federation of America, and the American Legion, among others. The American Legion distributed a pamphlet that claimed that Rugg planned to indoctrinate students to turn away from Americanism to Socialism or Communism. Yet when a school board committee in Washington DC reviewed Rugg's text, it could find no mention of communism, or even a suggestion of it. Nevertheless, Rugg's textbooks were banned in many school districts.

Wealthy industrialists used their wealth and influence to re-shape what children learned in school. They also invested heavily in efforts to reshape what people learned in church. John D. Rockefeller Jr. was a heavy promoter of what came to be called Modernist Christianity. Meanwhile, his opponents in the Fundamentalist camp weren't exactly free from the influence of oil money. Lyman and Milton Stewart of Union Oil anonymously funded the publication of *The Fundamentals*, a 12-volume publication that became the foundation of the Fundamentalist Christian movement. Thus, the Fundamentalist-Modernist debate, which was the major theological debate in the early 20th century in the United States, turned out to be a proxy war between rival oil magnates.

During the 20th century, wealthy people spent a lot of money to make religious organizations more efficient, at least from their perspective. They did not want the churches to preach that the love of money is the root of all evil or that it is easier for a camel to pass through the eye of a needle than for a rich man to enter the Kingdom of God. Thus, the wealthy people used their money and influence to turn the churches away from the Gospels toward a theology that was more in line with their needs. That was a truly mind-bending accomplishment.

To make religion efficient in serving the needs of the wealthy, one must make Christians ignore what the Bible in general and the Gospels in particular say about the rich and the poor. One must also keep people from understanding something that the French philosopher Rousseau explained in his Discourse on Inequality about why some people are rich and others are poor: the very notion of property rights is a social construct.

Rousseau explained that there are two kinds of inequality, natural and political. Natural or physical inequality is a product of nature. For example, one man may be physically stronger than another.

Political inequality, however, results from differences in wealth and influence. That type of inequality is established by social convention. As Rousseau explained,

> The first man who, having fenced in a piece of land, said "This is mine," and found people naïve enough to believe him, that man was the true founder of civil society. From how many crimes, wars, and murders, from how many horrors and misfortunes might not any one have saved mankind, by pulling up the stakes, or filling up the ditch, and crying to his fellows: Beware of listening to this impostor; you are undone if you once forget that the fruits of the earth belong to us all, and the earth itself to nobody.

According to Rousseau, the decision that land and the fruits of labor belong to some people and not to others is the result of a political process. Inequalities of wealth and power can exist only as long as the consensus of public opinion allows them to exist.

Capitalism is an economic system in which the productive assets of a society are owned privately—by individuals or corporations, but mainly by people other than the ones who are doing the actual productive work. Yet that kind of economic system cannot exist independently of a political system that allows a tiny minority to gain control over the fruits of other people's labor and that allows that tiny minority to impose its decisions on other people. In other words, capitalism is a peculiar form of "golden rule": he who has the gold makes the rules. In contrast, democracy allows people who don't have any gold to participate in making the decisions that affect them, including the decisions of how the fruits of their labor are to be distributed.

If you read the Gospels—and especially the passages in red type, which represent the words of Jesus—you'll find that they describe Jesus as someone who would take a dim view of capitalism. If you realize that capitalist accumulation means that a few powerful individuals get to impose their decisions on the rest of the population, you realize that there is something fundamentally undemocratic about capitalism. Thus, the big accomplishment of the propaganda system in the 20th century was to get the population of the United States to imagine that Christianity, democracy, and capitalism were all on the same side — and that all three meant more or less the same thing.

We still have problems with good textbooks being suppressed for political reasons. For example, conservatives on the Texas State Board of Education have tried to prevent children from learning in school that many of the Founding Fathers were Deists rather than Christians and that the Founding Fathers deliberately set up a secular government based on Enlightenment principles, rather than a religious government based on Biblical principles. In 2010, an activist group called the Texas Freedom Network reported that the Texas Board of Education tried to remove the Enlightenment from the high school history curriculum:

> Board member Cynthia Dunbar wants to change a standard having students study the impact of Enlightenment ideas on political revolutions from 1750 to the present. She wants to drop the reference to Enlightenment ideas (replacing with "the writings of") and to Thomas Jefferson. She adds Thomas Aquinas and others. Jefferson's ideas, she argues, were based on other political philosophers listed in the standards. We don't buy her argument at all. Board member Bob Craig of Lubbock points out that the curriculum writers clearly wanted students to study Enlightenment ideas and Jefferson. Could Dunbar's problem be that Jefferson was a Deist? The board approves the amendment, taking Thomas Jefferson OUT of the world history standards.

It would be bad enough if a cabal of zealots in a state with a small population, such as North Dakota or Vermont, were trying to distort the curriculum in their public schools. Unfortunately, Texas is the second most populous state in the United States. The Texas Board of

Education buys so many textbooks that it has enormous influence over the content of the textbooks that are used all over the country. The textbook publishers, being for-profit businesses, are likely to degrade their textbooks, so as not to offend the sensibilities of a handful of far-right extremists in a big state. As a result, students in American public schools end up learning practically nothing about science or history or political economy.

The textbook publishers' need to pander to the right-wing extremists in Texas degrades textbooks in a way that stupefies the entire nation. Just as one example, Americans are encouraged to "remember the Alamo." Yet hardly any white Americans have any idea what the defenders of the Alamo were really trying to achieve: they wanted to reestablish slavery in what was then part of Mexico.

Slavery had been declared illegal in Mexico in 1810 and was gradually wiped out in practice by around 1821. That historical fact makes Texas and the United States look bad by comparison. It's contradictory to the idea that the United States is a "City on a Hill" that is supposed to inspire the rest of the world with its goodness. The idea that the United States lagged so far behind Mexico in an important advance in human rights is literally unthinkable for many people. Thus, this obvious historical fact is downplayed or never even allowed to enter consciousness. So is the fact that the British and French empires abolished slavery long before the United States did.

The campaigns to keep the public schools from teaching important facts about history, economics, biology, and so on have also undermined public support for higher education. What young people learn in college is often radically different from what is taught in high school. As a result, many people suspect that there's something fishy about college and college professors.

Political conservatives often complain that college professors are socialist or that colleges promote a socialist agenda. Yet as far as I can tell, not one of the colleges in the United States has ever been run by socialists or communists. Public and private colleges and universities are generally run by a board of trustees, most of whose members are wealthy businessmen and -women. Even the trustees who are scholars or scientists understand how heavily their institution depends on the generosity of wealthy people for funding, and they quickly learn that he who pays the piper generally calls the tune.

Colleges and universities have to train the people who will become the doctors and lawyers and scientists—the experts whom the wealthy people will need as advisors. Thus, colleges and universities must teach at least some of their students the liberal arts and the humanities, as well as the arts and sciences. These are the studies that are generally reserved for the privileged, not taught to the general public. Thus, these subjects contain ideas that are unfamiliar and often disturbing to the general public.

The fact that the textbook publishers are for-profit businesses goes far toward explaining why whole-word methods of reading instruction have been promoted and intensive phonics has been suppressed. The whole-word method of reading instruction may be inefficient from the perspective of someone who is trying to teach first-graders to read. However, it is highly efficient way to get schools to buy more textbooks and workbooks.

You need very little in the way of curriculum materials to use intensive phonics to teach reading. Colonial Massachusetts achieved high rates of literacy while using little more than *The New England Primer* and the Bible. After the Revolutionary War, Webster's blue-backed speller took the place of *The New England Primer*. In contrast, the whole-word curricula involve a lot of expensive, extensively illustrated textbooks, plus workbooks that have to be replaced every year.

The whole-word method was introduced in the 1830s, but it wasn't widely used throughout the United States until in the 1930s, when Scott Foresman introduced the Dick and Jane books. The Dick and Jane books were co-authored by William S. Gray, who served for many years as the Director of Research in Reading at the Graduate School of Education at the University of Chicago ("Mr. Rockefeller's University"). As such, Gray had presumably read the existing scientific literature on reading instruction. Thus, he should have known that intensive phonics was clearly superior to the whole-word method. Scientific research had already established that fact by the 1890s.

Nevertheless, as the co-author of the Dick and Jane books, Gray made a lot of money from promoting whole-word reading instruction.

The widespread use of the whole-word method led to major outbreaks of "learning disabilities." In 1955, Rudolf Flesch published the bestseller *Why Johnny Can't Read*. In it, Flesch explained that the whole-word method was causing seemingly normal children to fail to learn to read. Flesch's book created a public outcry. In response, William S. Gray used his money and influence to launch an antiphonics lobbying group called the International Reading Association. As a result, little changed between 1955 and 1983, when Flesch published *Why Johnny Still Can't Read: A New Look at the Scandal of Our Schools*.

Because of the use of whole-word methods for reading instruction, a staggering number of American schoolchildren fail to learn to read well. Yet whether you consider this widespread failure to be a problem or an opportunity depends on your point of view. The failure of our schools to teach reading, writing, and arithmetic has led to the development of specialized "remedial" instruction programs. The status of the people who develop these programs and the funding for the people who work in them would erode sharply if schools started using effective teaching methods from the beginning.

Many Americans have been indoctrinated with the idea that "market-based" solutions are the best. Unfortunately, they have no idea how many of their problems result from corporations maximizing profits. Americans have been encouraged to believe that private charity is better than government programs. They seldom stop to think that private charity is inadequate and is often structured to serve the interests of the philanthropist, rather than the interests of the people whom the charity is supposed to help. In contrast, a government program can be held accountable to standards of fairness. Americans have been told that government should be shrunk until it is small enough to drown in a bathtub. They have no idea that a democratic government is their only defense against the people who control the commanding heights of the economy.

CHAPTER XX

Why Bad Teaching Methods Persist

Teaching English-speaking children to read English is easy. From the 17th to the 19th century, schoolteachers with little more than a primary school education themselves managed to do it in North America. All they had to do was teach children the letters of the alphabet and the sounds that those letters represented. Then, the students were taught how to combine those letters to make syllables. The syllables were then combined to make words. Once children know how to "sound out" words, they can read tens of thousands of words, even words they'd never before seen in print. The children can even make a reasonable guess about how to spell thousands of words they've never seen in print. In other words, intensive phonics is the time-tested, quick, and effective method for teaching English speakers to read and write.

Up until the 20th century, if an English-speaking person couldn't read, it was usually because he or she had never been to school at all. Nowadays, however, millions of people who have spent many years in US public schools that were staffed by college-trained, state-licensed teachers still can't read. What went wrong?

The problem was that the professors of education at some prestigious universities and state teachers' colleges started telling teachers not to use intensive phonics to teach reading. Instead of teaching children to sound out the words letter by letter, teachers were told to have children learn to recognize whole words by sight. With that method, however, even a good student might memorize only a few hundred words per year. After several years of that kind of teaching, even a good student would still be unable to read an ordinary book or newspaper. Of course, some children learn to read even if the whole-word teaching method is used. Either they figure out the letter-sound relationships on their own or they learn it from their parents or a private tutor. The other children remain "learning disabled."

In the 1920s, an epidemic of "congenital word blindness"—what we now call dyslexia—broke out in many communities in the United States. By the late 1920s, it was clear to anyone who read the medical literature that the epidemic was due to the use of the whole-word method, as opposed to intensive phonics, for teaching children to read. Yet instead of abandoning the whole-word method as a tragic mistake, the educational establishment in the United States went on to promote it even more enthusiastically.

How can such a stupid idea be promoted by presumably educated people? How can a problem like this persist, even after it has been exposed in bestselling books, such as Rudolf Flesch's *Why Johnny Can't Read* (published in 1955) and his *Why Johnny Still Can't Read* (published in 1983)? Why do the people who are running our educational institutions insist on promoting teaching methods that have been so clearly shown to be ineffective? To understand why problems like this persist, you have to understand how decisions get made. Once you understand that, you'll have a clear understanding of the nature of oppression.

Before you can start to solve a problem, you have to figure out what kind of a problem it is, and for whom it is a problem. Is illiteracy a problem in the United States? If so, what kind of problem is it? For whom, exactly, is it a problem? Who benefits from the fact that lots of people can't read?

Merriam-Webster's Web site defines the word *problem* to mean, among other things, "an intricate, unsettled question; or a source of perplexity, distress, or vexation." For people who are illiterate in the United States today, illiteracy is definitely a source of perplexity, distress, or vexation. Most illiterate Americans are so ashamed of their illiteracy that they try to hide it. However, our epidemic of illiteracy in the United States is not an "intricate, unsettled question." The causes of illiteracy are obvious. Some people, mainly immigrants, cannot read because they never had a chance to go to school. However, most of the illiterate people in the United States today have spent many years in school. Unfortunately, their schools used bad methods for teaching reading.

What should we call something that causes "perplexity, distress, or vexation" but is not an "intricate, unsettled question"? What label should we apply to a problem that can be solved but hasn't been solved? It would depend on who has the ability to solve it. If you have a problem that you caused for yourself and that is within your power to solve, it's a personal problem. But if the problem is someone else's fault or if you have to depend on someone else to solve it, then it's a political problem.

If a problem is a political problem, then it requires a political solution. When you want to figure out how to solve a political problem, you have to figure out not only who is causing the problem but who benefits from its existence. If powerful people benefit from the cause or the consequences of a problem, then solving the problem will be politically difficult, even if the solution is technically easy. It's easy to teach English-speaking children to read English. It will be hard to get the schools to stop using an ineffective teaching method that has been promoted for political reasons.

Illiteracy is distressing to the people who cannot read. It's also distressing to other people in their lives, especially their children. However, one person's illiteracy can be an advantage for somebody else. Slumlords are at an advantage if their tenants cannot read their leases. Sweatshop owners benefit if their employees cannot read their employment contracts. A tyrannical government can get away with murder if the populace cannot read books or newspapers and therefore has no idea what is going on. If knowledge is power, then functional illiteracy is disempowerment. If disempowerment is being imposed on some people by other people, then it is oppression.

People often resist oppression, at least if they understand what is happening to them. The harsher and more obvious the repression is, the more likely its victims are to resist. The fact that obvious, heavy-handed oppression tends to provoke a particularly lively resistance is called the paradox of repression. It's far easier to keep people oppressed if they blame themselves or their bad luck for their situation. Once they realize that many of their personal problems are really the result of political problems—i.e., that "the personal is political"—then they can undertake political action to solve those problems. As long as people think that their children's failure to learn is the child's fault, and not the fault of the educational establishment, there will be no political pressure to reform the educational establishment.

To understand why bad teaching methods have been used so widely in the United States, it's important to understand where the bad methods come from and how they manage to outcompete the more effective alternatives. Let's start with the schools of education.

The schools of education in the United States are not just supposed to train teachers. They are also supposed to do research into how to help teachers teach better, so that students end up learning more of what they need to know. Yet what happened when the public schools started replacing traditional methods, such as intensive phonics, with the unproven methods that were heavily promoted by the teachers' colleges, such as whole-word reading instruction? The children ended up learning less than children did when a schoolmarm with little more than a primary school education herself used the *New England Primer* or Webster's blue-back speller to teach the ABCs. What happened after language arts teachers in the United States followed expert advice to stop teaching grammar? Verbal aptitude scores dropped and have never recovered.

When the dyslexia epidemic broke out in the 1920s, after schools started using whole-word methods, it should have been a wake-up call.[1] So should the sharp and prolonged decline in verbal SAT scores starting in 1963.[2] These problems were so serious and so widespread that they should have prompted an attempt to find out what was going wrong in the educational system. It's important to understand why they did not. The problems in public education in the United States resulted from a combined failure of academia, philanthropy, government, industry, and journalism.

The whole-word methods of reading instruction were developed and promoted by professors at teachers' colleges. Many of these professors doubtless thought that their methods would work. Unfortunately, their methods were imposed on teachers and students without having been tested or even after they had been found to be ineffective. Often, the methods were supported by nothing but their creators' massive egos. Tragically, the whole-word methods were promoted even though their rationale makes no sense and there was already plenty of historical and scientific evidence to show that they wouldn't work. Unfortunately, this meant that schoolteachers have been taught and often forced to use ineffective teaching methods.

It's important to understand that many of the educational approaches used in public schools in the United States are created at the top of the educational establishment and imposed on the people underneath, rather than being created on a grassroots level and spreading laterally and percolating upward if they are successful. Methods survive or die out on the basis of how well they serve the people at the top of the educational establishment, not on how well they serve the students.

Unfortunately, the methods of successful teachers are unlikely to be widely shared. Tragically, the successful teachers are often punished for their success. Bullying of teachers by administrators and even by other teachers is a major problem. As in any workplace, competent and ethical workers are the most likely targets of bullies. The competent and ethical teachers should be getting the full support of their administration, instead of being fired or driven out of the profession.

You might imagine that it would be hard for an ineffective curriculum to survive in this era of extensive standardized testing. Yet the tests are generally not being designed or used for evaluating curricula or textbooks or even educational approaches. Besides, there is no need to use standardized testing to see whether intensive phonics or whole-word is a better way to teach reading. The answer to that question was clear enough by the 1840s. Instead, the standardized tests are used for sorting, ranking, and punishing children and schools. They also serve to line the pockets of the people who supply and process the tests themselves.

A teaching method becomes popular if it gains support from other education professors, from bureaucrats at major foundations, and from textbook publishing companies. The methods that are endorsed by education professors and educational foundations might then be adopted by bureaucrats in the state departments of education and local school boards, who then impose those methods on the teachers. Only rarely do outside experts intervene, such as when 40 of the world's top experts in linguistics and psycholinguistics wrote to the Massachusetts Commissioner of Education in 1995, warning him that the whole-language approach to language arts education is based on a misunderstanding of linguistics and psychology and has led to serious declines in reading achievement.[3] Often, curricula and instructional methods are chosen by people with no experience as classroom teachers.

Although I place a lot of blame on many of the professors at the teachers' colleges, I don't want to absolve the bureaucrats at the foundations and the departments of education. Many of these people were educated people who should have known better. Certainly, the outbreaks of dyslexia starting in the 1920s and the decline of verbal SAT scores starting in 1963 should have prompted some of them to step back, do some background reading, and figure out what was going wrong.

Teachers in many public schools in the United States today have little control over what and how they are to teach. To ensure that the teachers follow orders to use the methods that the administrators have chosen, many school districts buy curriculum materials that have the methods built into them. Some of these materials are even designed to be "teacher-proof"–providing scripts for the teachers to follow on a day-to-day basis. Of course, these materials are far more expensive than a copy of Webster's blue-backed speller and a set of graded reading books like the old McGuffey Readers. The sad thing is that the expensive materials are far less effective because the teaching methods that are built into them are defective.

I once asked a high school English teacher whether he teaches his students to diagram sentences. His eyes went wide in a classic involuntary fear response. He told me that if an administrator happened to see even a fragment of a diagram on the blackboard, he'd be fired. Schoolteachers are at the bottom of a chain of command. It would make no sense for the educational establishment to blame its failings on the teachers, any more than it would make sense for a general to blame his private soldiers for being badly trained and badly led.

Since the publishing companies are for-profit businesses, publishing executives want to publish the materials that will yield the most profit. Whether children actually learn from using those materials makes no difference to the publishing company's bottom line. The publishing companies can afford to hire the professors at the teachers' colleges to help develop and promote materials for the companies to sell. The professors then gain prestige as well as fees and royalties from their relationship with the publishers, and the professors and publishers can be expected to link arms to suppress any criticism. Thus, this system represents a self-reinforcing closed loop. In other words, the development and propagation of ineffective teaching methods can be viewed as an example of institutional failure.

By institutional failure, I don't mean that an institution itself goes bankrupt or stops producing goods and services. I mean that the institution fails to achieve the purposes that an ordinary member of society would want and expect that institution to fulfill. This kind of institutional failure is a matter for political concern. Institutional failure means a failure to serve the public. The institutions themselves were created or chartered by the government, and thus by the people. Theoretically, the people thus have the power to discipline or dissolve institutions that are not serving the public.

Although a corporation is owned by private stockholders, the corporation owes its very existence as a corporation to the government. Corporations are created by government to serve public purposes. The corporate charter gives the corporation's owners certain benefits, especially a reduction in the amount of personal liability that the shareholders would have for the corporation's liabilities. In exchange, the corporation is expected to do things that directly or indirectly benefit the public, such as producing goods and services and providing employment. If the corporation ends up producing more harm than benefit to the public, the government can revoke the corporation's charter, thus dissolving the corporation.

A teachers' college has failed as an institution if it trains aspiring teachers to use teaching methods that do not work. If a teachers' college fails to train teachers adequately, the government might be able to fire the college's administration, cut the college's funding, remove its accreditation, or even revoke its charter. Yet a teachers' college is never judged on how well its alumni's students learn. Instead, a teachers' college is likely to be judged on how many articles its faculty members publish in the education literature and on how successful its graduates are at getting jobs as schoolteachers in public schools and as professors at other teachers' colleges.

A publisher of schoolbooks has failed as an institution if children don't learn much or are misled by those schoolbooks. Yet as a for-profit business, the company is judged only on how much money it makes from selling those books. The company can be richly rewarded for producing materials that satisfy the faculty at the teachers' colleges and the bureaucrats in the foundations and in the state and local boards of education, regardless of whether the textbooks help children learn.

A charitable organization has failed as an institution if it just performs favors for its wealthy backers and enriches its employees, instead of solving problems that affect the general public and especially the poor. A charitable organization is particularly easy to discipline if it has to depend on the general public for funds. A simple exposé in the press or an effective social media campaign can cause contributions to dry up. Even if an organization exists to do the bidding of a single wealthy donor, it could be disciplined by loss of its tax-exempt status. In the United States, a charitable organization can apply for tax-exempt status under section 501(c)(3) of the Internal Revenue Code. However, the organization can lose that tax-exempt status if the organization is found to be organized or operated for the benefit of private interests, or if the organization gets too involved in political or legislative activities or violates the public trust. During World War II, the IRS shut down the Ku Klux Klan, which was interfering with the war effort, by hitting it with a $685,000 tax lien.

A state board of education or a local school board fails as an institution if it forces teachers to use lousy textbooks and ineffective teaching methods and if it fires good teachers for political reasons. Schools may suffer because of policies at the state or local level. Local control of the schools could enable a community to protect its schools from bad decisions made at the state level. However, it leaves the school vulnerable to the problems resulting from the personal and political relationships that principals and school board members may have with mayors and local political bosses. Nor does it eliminate the possibility that publishers and their agents could buy influence over local school board members.

Governmental institutions such as school boards are created by the people to serve the people. The individuals who are involved in making government policy related to education are either elected by the people or appointed by elected officials. This means that a well-informed public could use its power as voters to bring about major changes in educational policy.

The people can use their political power to police the institutions in their society, but only if they know what is going on within those institutions. Theoretically, journalists have the responsibility to expose institutional failure, so that the public can use its political power to correct the problem. Yet journalists rarely provide an accurate account of the underlying problems in public education in the United States. The problems are usually portrayed as the failures of the children and their families or a failure of the teachers. When questions such as the use of phonics versus whole language arise, journalists tend to take a false-balance approach, pretending that the question cannot be resolved because the arguments supporting both sides are equally compelling.

In other words, the public's failure to understand the problems in the public school system are the result of yet another institutional failure — the failure of fourth estate, the press. If the problems in the educational system were creating inconvenience for the rich and powerful, then the press would rapidly bring those problems to light. The press would also work to build consensus for solutions that meet the needs of the wealthy and powerful people who own the press and its advertisers. In other words, the press is likely to promote the solutions that serve the rich and powerful, not the solutions that are needed by the poor and oppressed.

Who suffers as the result of an institutional failure? The institutional failure of the teachers' colleges, educational philanthropies, state and local boards of education, and textbook publishers would do no harm to wealthy and connected people's children. In fact, privileged people's children would actually benefit from the failure of the public education system. The failure of the schools that serve the general public means that the children of the well-to-do face less competition. The children whose education was enriched, in comparison to what the average child gets in public school, will find it easier to get into a good college and then into law school or medical school. As long as the children of the lower classes are getting enough of an education to prepare them for the lower rungs of the workforce, the wealthy people will have no incentive to improve the schools in the poor neighborhoods.

The professors at the teachers' colleges are not held accountable for training teachers to use teaching methods that predictably don't work. Neither are the bureaucrats at the foundations and the state departments of education held accountable for promoting ineffective teaching methods. The publishing companies are never sued for producing defective instructional materials. The administrators who force teachers to use ineffective teaching methods are never sued for malpractice. In fact, the only people who regularly get punished for the poor performance of our public schools are the students. Lately, many people have expressed the desire to punish the teachers as well.

Some teachers do resist the pressure to use ineffective teaching methods. Unfortunately, those who resist may face the wrath of the school administrators. Nor are high-performing teachers always encouraged or even allowed to share their teaching methods with their colleagues. Instead, they are likely to be attacked by jealous peers and administrators. Even if the teacher's job is protected by tenure, the teacher's working life can be made miserable by bullying from the administration and from other teachers. These facts may help to explain why schoolteachers make up such a high percentage of the people who seek advice about how to deal with bullying by coworkers and supervisors. The bullied teachers' most common complaint is that their union does nothing to protect them.[4] That's yet another example of institutional failure.

If you don't understand the nature of a problem, you can easily be tempted to try the wrong solution. Lately, many conservatives have been trying to persuade the American public that the problems in our public schools result from the fact that they are public, or the fact that many teachers are union members, or the fact that public schools are no longer permitted to promote Protestant Christianity. Yet the best schools in the world are the public schools in Finland, where nearly all of the teachers are union members. Nor is it likely that religious instruction or observance in school makes a positive difference. Some extremely secular nations such as Japan and Sweden have high educational standards and are in general much safer, cleaner, and healthier than the United States and have lower rates of teen pregnancy.

Currently, the people of the United States are being bombarded with propaganda intended to persuade them to abandon their public schools in favor of charter schools and private religious schools or even schools run by for-profit companies. In fact, much of the rhetoric that blames the teachers' unions comes from the advocates of for-profit schools—people who would reap higher profits if teachers got paid less. Yet none of the problems in the schools result from the fact that they are nonprofit or public or secular or staffed by union members. Some of the problems that the schools in poor neighborhoods face are due to unequal funding, which in turn results from the fact that schools are being funded by local property taxes instead of getting most of their funding from the federal government.

It is ironic that so many poor children are asked to pledge allegiance to the flag of the United States of America in school, and to the republic for which it stands, while that republic does so little to ensure that those children get a decent education or even that they have health care or a roof over their heads. In 2011, the National Center on Family Homelessness reported that 1.6 million children in the United States were homeless. Children in other democratic societies never have to swear a loyalty oath of any kind in school, and they certainly do not have to repeat the oath on a daily basis. Yet they typically get a better education, better nutrition, and free healthcare.

Given the struggle for school desegregation during the Civil Rights era, it seems foolish to me to give up the idea of common schools—schools open to every child in the community, regardless of race, color, creed, or social class. I think that our public schools are worth saving and worth improving, and the improvements should start with a curriculum that works. That means improving the curriculum in the schools that train our aspiring teachers as well as the schools for our children. It means creating a dignified professional atmosphere for teachers as well as a safe and supportive learning environment for children. To achieve these goals, education activists will have to investigate every aspect of the educational establishment and mobilize the populace to demand real, productive change.

References

1. Orton ST. The "sight reading" method of teaching reading, as a source of reading disability. *J Educ Psychol.* 1929;20(2):135-143.

2. Hayes DP, Wolfer LT, Wolfe MF: Schoolbook simplification and its relation to the decline in SAT-verbal scores. *Am Educ Res J.* 1996;33(2):489-508. http://educationconsumers.org/research/briefs_0801.htm.

3. Bach E, Calabrese A, Caplan D, et al. Standards for reading instruction in Massachusetts [letter to Robert V. Antonucci, Commissioner of Education, Commonwealth of Massachusetts. http://listserv.aera.net/scripts/wa.exe?A2=ind9608e&L=aera-c&P=684.

4. Information for teachers and lecturers experiencing workplace bullying. BullyOnline. http://www.bullyonline.org/workbully/teachers.htm.

CHAPTER XXI

Equality, Meritocracy, and Elitism

At the beginning of Chapter 1, I mentioned that education can serve more than one purpose. Education can prepare the student for a particular occupation. It can also help an individual become a good person and a good citizen. Both of these purposes of education have important political implications.

If you control access to education, you can control who gets to enter which occupation. Thus, you can control who gets to enter the middle class. For example, the purpose of segregation in the public schools was to make sure that black people stayed at the bottom of the labor market and on the lowest rungs of society. Educational segregation was also used against women. Until 1972, female students were routinely excluded from many kinds of schools and training programs. Many Americans are aware that Title IX of the Education Amendments that were made in 1972 to the federal Higher Education Act provided a major boost to women's sports programs. However, Title IX also made it possible for large numbers of women to go to law school or medical school.

Control over education also means control over the distribution of power within society. That's because education has a profound effect on a person's ability to understand current events and to make a meaningful contribution to politics. Inequality and injustice can persist only if enough people believe that the status quo is normal and acceptable, or at least inevitable. The easiest way to get people to accept an unjust status quo is to indoctrinate them with social mythology instead of teaching them the liberal arts, the humanities, and the social sciences.

As I explained in Chapter 2, advisors to the King of Prussia designed a new approach to public education in the wake of Prussia's humiliating defeat by Napoleon's army in 1806. The King of Prussia needed loyal and capable military officers and civil servants. He also wanted the vast majority of the population to be efficient workers and effective soldiers who were mindlessly loyal to him personally, rather than to the local aristocracy. Thus, the Prussian educational system was designed to serve the needs of a militaristic totalitarian industrial state. A Prussian-style educational system tends to breed fascism. It's partly because the regimentation within the schools encourages conformity. It's also because the curriculum was designed to promote mindless obedience, not to cultivate wisdom and freedom of thought.

Many education reformers have expressed concern about the regimentation within public schools. They point out that this regimentation serves the needs of the institution, not the needs of the student. Yet many of the educational reformers who have advocated an end to this kind of regimentation have also worked to suppress the liberal arts and the humanities—even though those are the disciplines that were developed to prepare people to participate in a democratic or republican society. Some educators, such as John Dewey, have opposed any kind of drills in skills, regardless of the value or political significance of those skills.

Education reformers have also expressed concern that the public schools could have an unfair influence on what kinds of jobs children will have in the future. They're worried that the public school system could create social inequality by teaching more to some children than to others. The system could do this by providing good schools in some neighborhoods and bad schools in others. It can also do it within a school by sorting the children into "tracks." Although the theory behind "tracking" was to allow children to learn at their own speed, the tracking system often assigns children inescapably to a particular curriculum. Although the criteria used for assigning children to one track or another are often arbitrary or irrelevant, the consequences of this assignment can be serious. Being assigned to the lower track can demoralize a child and derail his or her education. It destines the child for the lower classes.

The theory behind tracking is that some children learn faster than others. You wouldn't want the fast learners to be held back by the other children. Nor would you want children to give up completely if they can't keep up with the rest of the class. I feel that the solution, in either case, is to find ways in which children can learn at a reasonable speed, rather than remaining in lock-step with the rest of their class, or even just with the rest of their track, for their entire educational career.

Of course, some teachers do want the faster children to be held back by the other children. I learned that first-hand as one of the faster children in my classes in school. I didn't understand why I couldn't just be left alone with a textbook, to learn at my own pace. Instead, I had to sit there, bored and miserable, while I waited for the rest of the class to learn things that I already knew. I suspect that some teachers thought it was unfair for me to learn more than the other children did. I think that's why some people are opposed in principle to meritocracy.

Concerns about equality of educational opportunity are important because of the role that schooling plays in preparing people for work in modern society. Also, this concern raises questions about elitism and meritocracy. Elitism and meritocracy are two different kinds of aristocracy. Elitism involves aristocracy based on birth, and meritocracy is an aristocracy based on achievements.

If you were born in the Middle Ages, your role in society would be determined far more by who your parents were than by your personal talents and achievements. During the Middle Ages, most people didn't need schooling to prepare them for their life's work. Instead, children learned by working alongside their parents. If your parents were farm laborers, you'd probably become a farm laborer, too. If a boy's father was a baker, the boy would probably become a baker, too. That's why so many surnames are words for occupations: Baker, Butcher, Brewer, Smith, and so on.

If a tradesman didn't have enough children to follow in his footsteps, he would take in other people's children (usually sons) as apprentices and teach them the business from the ground up. The apprentice provided labor in exchange for room and board and training. Sometimes, families would have to pay the tradesman a fee to take one of their children as an apprentice. At one time, even the professions, such as law and medicine, were generally learned through apprenticeship rather than in a school.

Industrialization brought about a major shift in how people in the United States were trained for work. Production shifted from small workshops to major factories, and training for many kinds of work shifted from home and small workshops to schools. Training for the professions shifted to universities and graduate schools. This caused a major shift in the perceived purpose of university education.

Harvard College was established to train young men for the ministry. Colleges also taught young gentlemen the liberal arts, including mathematics. Nowadays, the main purpose of a college or university education is to prepare young men and women for secular occupations. The most common major in colleges and universities in the United States today is business administration.

During the Colonial era, the classical education that a gentleman received was intended to make him a wiser, better person and a better Christian. However, a gentleman's training in mathematics could give him important power over other people. For example, knowledge of spherical geometry enabled the officers of a ship to do celestial navigation. Although the sailors on a ship knew how to operate the sails and steer the ship, they didn't know how to figure out where they were, or how to set a course to where they wanted to go. To be able to get back home, or at least to some safe refuge, mutineers would need the cooperation of at least one of the ship's officers. The same kinds of mathematical skills that are useful for navigation are also useful for land surveying, which was a crucial skill for a real estate speculator such as George Washington.

When I look at history and in particular at the history of education, I see three basic systems of social organization: aristocracy based on birthright, aristocracy based on personal achievement, and egalitarian democracy. Each system perpetuates itself through a different approach to education. Since all social systems are essentially the result of a social consensus, the powerful people within each system tend to promote a social mythology that encourages other people to accept the status quo as natural, normal, or at least inevitable.

The feudal system was based on an aristocracy by birthright. The high-ranking persons were the eldest surviving sons of the previous generation of rulers. In that kind of society, education consists mainly of religious indoctrination. The purpose of the indoctrination was to get people to accept the idea that God wanted the king and the nobles to be wealthy and powerful. If the common people accepted their humble station in this life, they'd get to enjoy a good afterlife. To support the institution of monarchy, the Catholic Church developed the idea of the divine right of kings. John Calvin's ideas about predestination and the elect could be used to justify social inequality in a Protestant republic.

Christianity is not the only religion that has been used to serve the wealthy at the expense of the poor. Many Eastern religions taught that wealthy and powerful people deserved their wealth and power in this life because they earned it by building up merit in past lives. It's not surprising that religions often teach poor people to revere the rich. In general, rich people use their wealth and power to support the theologians who are on their side. That's why religious institutions often serve the interests of the rich, even if they have to ignore their own scriptures to justify doing so.

An aristocracy based on birthright might work well enough in a small kingdom, where a wise king can select clever advisors whom he knows personally. However, it is simply impractical in a larger empire, which needs a huge staff of capable bureaucrats. An aristocracy by birthright becomes even more impractical in an industrial society, which needs capable scientists, engineers, and so on. In that situation, the people who will play important roles in society must be chosen by ability, not by pedigree. To solve that problem, the ancient Chinese came up with a system that we call meritocracy.

To enter the civil service in Imperial China, a man had to pass a series of examinations that were open to practically anyone—that is, to anyone except the sons of prostitutes and entertainers or low-level government employees. In practice, of course, only someone whose parents could afford to provide a good education could actually pass the exams.

The idea of meritocracy and a professional civil service reached Europe in the 17th century, when the writings of Confucius were translated into Latin. These ideas were particularly well-received in France and Britain, which needed a corps of well-trained civil servants to administer their far-flung empires.

The Industrial Revolution meant that the emerging industries were also going to need a large and growing corps of engineers and accountants and so on. These people needed special occupational training and certification. Yet at the same time, the gentlemen who were to supervise all of these various technical professionals were still expected to have a classical education, to give them training in strategic thinking and the social graces. The result was a three-tiered educational system: a liberal arts education for the children of the wealthy and powerful, a technical education for those with aspirations of joining the middle class, and a system of indoctrination and training in the mechanical and servile arts for the ordinary workers.

As the privileges of royalty and the nobility were eroded by industrialization, the emerging capitalist class needed to promote a new kind of ideology that would persuade people to accept the new social order. Religion no longer filled the bill, partly because more and more people from the lower classes could read the Bible for themselves. Thus, they knew what Jesus had said about rich people. So instead of distorting Scripture to serve their political purposes, the new ruling class distorted science. They used a misinterpretation of Darwin's theory of natural selection to justify the wealth and power of the captains of industry.

The apologists for the new social order of industrial society used Social Darwinism (a political ideology that wasn't actually based on Darwin's theory) to say that rich white people were superior to poor whites, who in turn were supposedly superior to people of color.

Social Darwinists argued that the wealthy and powerful people had "evolved" out of the rest of humanity, as humanity had evolved from monkeys. Social Darwinists even managed to believe that men were more "evolved" than women.

Of course, to embrace Social Darwinism, you had to ignore history. For thousands of years, the Northern European homeland of the white "race" was a primitive backwater while the major achievements in science and technology and the arts were being made in Africa and Asia and Southern Europe. In other words, anyone with a classical education should have been able to see that Social Darwinism is nonsense. Of course, anyone who had actually understood Darwin's work would have rejected Social Darwinism because it is based largely on a Larmackian theory of inheritance.

Steel magnate Andrew Carnegie was a particularly devoted adherent of Social Darwinism. It eased his conscience about rising to the top of a dog-eat-dog social order. Carnegie was also a major philanthropist who had an enormous impact on education in the United States. Thus, it is hardly surprising that Social Darwinist principles are used even today to justify the inequalities in the public education system in the United States. When poor black and Latino children do poorly in school, their poor performance is blamed on their genes instead of on their schools. These inequalities are bad for the poor, but they are beneficial to the upper middle class because of the way the upper middle class is created.

Meritocracy is based on the idea of social mobility. Unfortunately for the children of the upper middle class, social mobility runs in both directions. Meritocracy provides opportunities for ambitious poor people. However, it poses a threat to the status of the children who were born to the members of the upper middle class.

The son of a Chinese peasant could theoretically rise to a position of wealth and power and prestige within Imperial China. Yet he could not pass his government post to one of his own sons. His sons would have to earn their own place in the system by performing well in the Imperial examinations. The children of today's upper middle class face the same problem. The children of doctors, lawyers, and business executives don't automatically become doctors, lawyers, and business executives. Meritocracy makes it hard for the upper middle class to reproduce itself as a class. To keep their children from sliding back into the working class, the members of the upper middle class must use their economic and social advantages to tilt the playing field in their children's favor.

Many upper middle class people firmly believe that they and their own children are genetically and morally superior to poor people. But in fact, they're generally not. Privileged people tend to underestimate the importance of the advantages they've had. They also overestimate the degree to which intelligence and other psychological traits can be inherited.

The insecure social position of the children of the upper middle class explains why the upper middle class does not use its political power to improve the schools in poor neighborhoods. Privileged children benefit from the fact that poor children get poor schooling. Thus, the poor schools in the inner city serve the wealthy people in the suburbs quite well. That's the main reason why the problems in our inner city schools go unsolved. These problems will remain unsolved until the people who suffer as a result of them get informed and get organized into a national movement that demands real reform.

The biggest obstacle that this movement will have to overcome is the notion that the liberal arts are "elitist" and should therefore be abandoned. Although it's true that the liberal arts have traditionally been reserved for gentlemen, it's because the liberal arts are politically empowering. If we want to have democracy, we must incorporate the liberal arts into the education for the general public.

Even if we manage to create a public education system that provides equal opportunities for everyone, some children will still end up learning more than others do. Likewise, even if we give everyone a library card, some people will end up reading more library books than others do. It's inevitable. The question is whether it is a problem. I think that it isn't. If you try to suppress high achievers within the public school system, you'll merely open up more slots at

Harvard for the kids who went to elite prep schools. You won't solve the problem of social stratification that way. You'll merely restrict social mobility for some public school kids.

Some people feel that meritocracy poses a threat to democracy because it means that people with more impressive achievements end up with the better jobs. Yet I think that society is best served if the jobs that require the most training and skill go to highly qualified candidates. What really matters is if this system of job assignments ends up causing other kinds of problems. It doesn't bother me if only the people who have passed the bar exam get to serve as lawyers or judges. What would really bother me is if only rich white men got to go to law school or if only rich white men got to vote or serve on juries. History teaches us what is wrong with a system like that.

Education shouldn't just prepare you for work. It should also prepare you for citizenship. It should prepare you to participate in the democratic process of public decision-making. The public school system cannot prepare everyone to be a rocket scientist or a brain surgeon. Nor should it even try. There simply isn't that much need for rocket scientists or brain surgeons. However, the public school system can give the general public a good enough education that they can use their political power to ensure that everyone can make a decent living and that those who can't work can live in dignity.

CHAPTER XXII

Willful Ignorance as a Strategy for Success

Several comedians such as Howard Stern and Jay Leno have done "man-in-the-street" style interviews where they ask ordinary Americans simple questions about history and geography and other things that they should have learned in grade school. These interviews often reveal shocking ignorance and stupidity.

One man was baffled when Jay Leno asked, "In what country would you find the Panama Canal?" Leno then asked, "In what country would you find the Great Wall of China?" The man answered, "Most likely China." Leno then repeated the question, "In what country would you find the Panama Canal?" The man then ventured a guess, "China?" The man did not know that the Panama Canal is in Panama, and he could only guess that the Great Wall of China must be in China. He probably didn't know that Panama is a country.

Educated people watch clips like this with a mixture of amusement and horror. Of course, many Americans probably answer these questions correctly, and their footage ends up on the cutting room floor because it has no value as comedy. Nevertheless, surveys have shown that many high school and college graduates in the United States really are that ignorant.

What I find most disturbing is that the interviewees usually come across as sincere and completely unashamed of their ignorance. They're like Adam and Eve before they tasted the fruit from the Tree of the Knowledge of Good and Evil. They're completely unaware that they should be embarrassed about their nakedness.

It's okay to laugh at them. They're laughing, too. So we're "laughing with" them, not "laughing at" them.

In one of his "Jaywalking" segments, Jay Leno asked a woman who was wearing a cap and gown at a graduation ceremony, "What was the Gettysburg Address?" Leno properly put the stress on the second syllable of Address: ad*dress*. The woman whispered "Gettysburg address" to herself, as if trying to jog her memory. Then Leno added, "Have you heard of it?" The young woman responded scornfully, "Yes I've heard of it! I don't know the exact *ad*dress." In other words, the woman thought that Leno was talking about the street address of a building. She had no idea that he was asking about one of the most famous speeches in US history.

The Gettysburg Address was the speech given by President Abraham Lincoln at the dedication of a cemetery in Gettysburg, Pennsylvania. The cemetery contained the bodies of soldiers who had died four and a half months earlier at the Battle of Gettysburg. That battle, where Union Armies defeated Confederate armies, marked the major turning point in the Civil War (or as Southerners call it, the War Between the States).

In the days before "progressive" education, schoolchildren (at least in the North) were often asked to commit the entire speech to memory. At the very least, they were expected to understand the meaning of the first and last lines. The opening line of the Gettysburg Address alludes to the Declaration of Independence, which was adopted by the Continental Congress on July 4, 1776: "Four score and seven years ago our fathers brought forth on this continent, a new nation, conceived in Liberty, and dedicated to the proposition that all men are created equal." The speech concludes, "we here highly resolve that these dead shall not have died in vain; that the nation, shall have a new birth of freedom, and that government of the people by the people for the people, shall not perish from the earth."

Other Jaywalking segments showed Americans who didn't know what happened on July 4, 1776. In other words, even if they had the text of the Gettysburg Address in front of them, along with the date on which it was given, they wouldn't have been able to associate it with the Declaration of Independence. As I explained in Chapter 4,

David Mulroy asked college students to rewrite the first sentence of the Declaration of Independence, the one that begins "When in the course of human events…" None of the students seemed to recognize the sentence. Only a few understood its meaning, which is that when people decide to break free from an existing political union, they should explain why they are doing so. Many of the students thought that the sentence was about the breakup of a romantic relationship, or about theology or the environment.[1]

The Gettysburg Address used to be included in the curriculum to teach children that their forefathers didn't fight for a flag (an idea that smacks of idolatry). Nor did their forefathers fight to serve their "commander-in-chief" (a disturbingly fascist idea). In the Gettysburg Address, Lincoln argued that the Revolutionary War was fought to create and preserve a government that was of, by, and for the people—a government based on the idea that all men are created equal. In other words, Lincoln was saying that Union soldiers who died at Gettysburg had given their lives in the defense of freedom, equality, and democracy.

Of course, the real cause of any war is far more complicated than that, and no one should take any justification for a war at face value. Nevertheless, a high school graduate in the United States should know, at the very least, that the Gettysburg Address was a speech given by Abraham Lincoln about the Battle of Gettysburg. A college graduate should know a great deal more.

At least the woman who was asked about the Gettysburg Address had the decency to pretend that she does know something. As I watch other Jaywalking segments and similar "pop-quiz" style interviews of ordinary people in the United States, I can't get over the fact that so many of the people who are interviewed are not only unashamed of their ignorance, they seem proud of it.

Some of the people who are being interviewed in the Jaywalking segments look to their friends for moral support. They are pleased to see that their friends are equally ignorant, and pleased to see that their friends also think that the whole thing is funny.

Why are so many people in the United States ignorant of things that they should have learned in school? And why do they think it's funny and cool to display their ignorance on national television? Perhaps it's because they learned in school that the "cool" kids are ignorant and the kids who get the right answers aren't "cool." In fact, as Paul Graham has explained, being smart in high school in the United States *makes* you unpopular.[2] Being smart also makes you a target for bullies, most of whom are your fellow students, but a few of whom are your teachers.[3]

The people whom Leno interviews may actually feel an odd sense of relief when they can't answer his question. Their ignorance marks them as not a nerd, which means that they are cool, which means that they will have friends and the bullies will leave them alone.

Since the massacre at Columbine High School in 1999 and especially since the rise of social media, people in the United States have been paying increasing attention to the issue of bullying in schools. The social cost of bullying is often expressed in terms of the number of young people who lose their lives. Some children commit suicide when they can no longer stand the torment. A few die at the hands of their fellow students, who snap after years of abuse. However, I think that these tragic deaths are only the most visible aspect of the harm that bullying does.

Bullying directed at smart children and at good students derails the entire academic mission of the school. I've known many teachers who work hard to inspire a love of learning in their students. Yet their hard work can easily be undone by the misbehavior of a few emotionally disturbed children, especially if nothing is done to stop that misbehavior. All the time and money spent on enriching the curriculum will be wasted if students learn that engaging with their schoolwork will make them unpopular and even vulnerable to attack. Even befriending a smart child can make one unpopular, or even expose one to attack by bullies. Thus, children know that being smart in school will make them social outcasts.

Most children care far more about their popularity in the present than they care about their economic prospects in the future. Thus, they may decide to sacrifice learning on the altar of popularity. In other words, they use willful ignorance as a strategy for social success. This strategy may enable them to have fun in junior high and high school, but it could ultimately limit their career choices to burger-flipping. Worse yet, children who learn in school that cruelty is acceptable and that intellect is uncool will go on to create a cruel and stupid society as adults.

When people talk about the social problems at a junior or senior high school, they often talk about the effects of puberty and hormones and sex drive. Clearly, sexual drives are important, but I think that people underestimate the young people's need for social connection, for friendship and membership within a peer group. This drive for social connection can be stronger than sex drives. Why else would straight boys in junior and senior high spend so much of their energy in jockeying for social position among other boys, instead of spending as much time as possible chatting up the girls? It is irresponsible of adults to make young people choose between doing well academically or being popular.

Children who know that they would have to pay a heavy social price for being a good student may resist doing schoolwork. Parents and teachers may think that such a child is lazy or has a learning disability when the child is simply choosing the strategy that solves his or her most pressing problems. How many children are given a psychiatric diagnosis such as attention-deficit disorder or oppositional defiant disorder when the real problem is that the child knows that being a good student would make him or her unpopular?

Parents and teachers and school administrators need to understand that bullies play a powerful role within the school society. Bullies are disciplinarians. They make and enforce rules. They punish the weak and the nonconformists. I suspect that bullies may even view their role as enforcers in a positive light, especially when they attack the people who are vilified by their parents or their church, such as the black kids or the gay kids or the Jews or the girls who step out of line in some way.

We really must think carefully about how our culture is being transmitted from one generation to the next. If you listen to how children of immigrants speak, you quickly realize that children adapt to match their peer group, rather than retaining their parents' accent. Children adopt the culture of their peers because their peers represent the future, while their parents and other adults represent the past. Thus, we really ought to find ways to enable children to influence each other in desirable ways, rather than allowing some children to destroy others.

Often, the adults turn a blind eye to bullying, even when it escalates to the point that the bullies are committing felonies (robbery, aggravated assault, kidnapping, rape). By doing nothing to stop the bullying, adults teach bullies that bullying behavior is acceptable or even desirable. I feel some pity for the kids who turn 18 and suddenly face serious lifelong consequences for doing the same sort of thing that they've been doing openly for years. Their behavior should have been corrected much earlier.

Sometimes, I suspect that the bullies might even be right. Maybe some adults do nothing because they like what the bullies are doing, just as some police departments seemed mysteriously unable to solve the murders of civil rights activists. Rather than putting a stop to the bullying, some adults even egg the bullies on.

When I was in school, most of the bullying that I observed took place out of the earshot of any adults. Yet a lot of it took place on the school bus, which was driven by an adult, who never did anything to intervene and probably never reported anything. On those occasions when I knew that the teachers did see or hear something, they didn't seem to know what to do. It made me wonder, just what had they been taught in teacher school? Surely an age-old problem like this would have been covered in at least one of their classes. Why didn't they know what to do?

Part of the problem is that many adults blame the target rather than the bully. For example, articles in newspapers and magazines often say that children with autism-spectrum disorders are often bullied because of their poor social skills. What? Isn't it the bullying that is the shockingly inappropriate social behavior? Why criticize the autistic child for "poor social skills" when it's the bullies whose social behavior is appalling? Often, the autistic child merely got caught in cross-hairs of a serial offender.

I'm glad that people are finally paying attention to the torment that young people are suffering in school at the hands of their peers and even some of their teachers. However, I think that many influential people remain apathetic about the problem because they don't realize what's at stake. It isn't just the happiness or even the lives of a few unpopular children. It's the educational mission of the entire school.

No matter how much money is spent on the schools, most children won't try to learn if they think that learning will make them unpopular. As long as adults allow emotionally disturbed children to set the rules, most students will continue to choose willful ignorance as a strategy for success.

References

1. Mulroy D. *The War Against Grammar*. Portsmouth, NH: Boynton/Cook Publishers, 2003.

2. Graham P. Why nerds are unpopular. Paul Graham. http://www.paulgraham.com/nerds.html

3. Twemlow SW, Fonagy P, Sacco FC, Brethour JR Jr. Teachers who bully students: a hidden trauma. *Int J Soc Psychiatry*. 2006 May;52(3):187-98. http://isp.sagepub.com/content/52/3/187.long.

CHAPTER XXIII

A Man's a Man for A' That

One of my favorite songs was written in 1795 by Robert Burns, a Scottish poet and lyricist who is known in Scotland simply as The Bard. It's sometimes called *Is There for Honest Poverty*, which is the first line of the first verse. The song is more commonly known as *A Man's a Man for a' That*. Here's the third verse:

> Ye see yon birkie, ca'd a lord,
> Wha struts, an' stares, an' a' that;
> Tho' hundreds worship at his word,
> He's but a coof for a' that:
> For a' that, an' a' that,
> His ribband, star, an' a' that:
> The man o' independent mind
> He looks an' laughs at a' that.

Here's a translation into standard English:

> You see that fellow called 'a lord,'
> Who struts, and stares, and all that?
> Though hundreds worship at his word,
> He is but a dolt for all that.
> For all that, and all that,
> His riband, star, and all that,
> The man of independent mind,
> He looks and laughs at all that.

In Burns' time, people were expected to regard the aristocracy as superior beings, and to be impressed by the badges of knighthood and so on (ribands and stars). Yet Burns argues that nobody of independent mind would be impressed by such nonsense. The song concludes with this verse:

> Then let us pray that come it may,
> (As come it will for a' that,)
> That Sense and Worth, o'er a' the earth,
> Shall bear the gree, an' a' that.
> For a' that, an' a' that,
> It's coming yet for a' that,
> That Man to Man, the world o'er,
> Shall brothers be for a' that.

This song declares that honesty and dignity are priceless virtues that have nothing to do with social rank, and that we can hope for equality and brotherhood in the future. Burns set it to a catchy tune, but I find the song impossible to sing. The words affect me so deeply that I have trouble breathing.

When I hear the debates about whether children should learn grammar in school, and whether children should learn Standard English, I don't think so much about Black English, which is mainly what people are arguing about. I think about Robert Burns. Would *A Man's a Man for a' That* be less compelling if written in Standard English? Burns obviously didn't think so. His letters reveal that he could write beautifully polished Standard English. He had also studied Latin and French in childhood. Yet he chose to use the language of his youth—the language of common people—when he wanted to sing about honesty and dignity and justice and the brotherhood of man.

It was a bit daring for Burns to write in Scottish, and thus to celebrate the Scottish language. Although Scotland and England had been ruled by the same monarch since King James IV, King of Scots, was crowned King of England in 1603, Scotland and England were considered separate kingdoms until the Acts of Union a century later. In Burns' time, many Scottish people still mourned the loss of their independence and the erosion of their language, which was partly due to the use of the English-language King James Bible.

The people of the Scottish Highlands traditionally spoke a Celtic language, like that of Ireland and Wales. In contrast, the people of the Scottish Lowlands, including Robert Burns, spoke a Germanic language. Like Old English, the medieval Scottish language was descended from the languages of the Germanic tribes that migrated to Great Britain starting in the fifth century. The language of the Scottish Lowlands evolved side by side with English. However, the guid Scots tongue was eventually overshadowed by English, especially after the King James Version of the Bible, which had been commissioned by King James I, was adopted by Protestants in Scotland.

It was even more daring for Burns to express contempt for aristocracy and respect for the dignity of common people in 1795. Those ideas were associated with the French Revolution. Not only had many French aristocrats just lost their heads to the guillotine in the Reign of Terror, but Great Britain was at war with France.

Much of what Burns wrote in his poems needs no translation for a modern American audience:

> O my Luve's like a red, red rose,
> That's newly sprung in June:
> O my Luve's like the melodie,
> That's sweetly play'd in tune.

Burns' poetry is mainly in a "light" Scottish dialect that is easily understood by an English or American audience. In contrast, "broad Scots" would be far harder to understand. This fact raises a question that is hard to answer: did Burns write his poems in English? Of course, a Scot would probably say that Burns wrote in Scottish. Yet that answer raises another question: Is Scottish a separate language from English, or are they two dialects of the same language? Is that question even meaningful? How do we decide what is and is not English? How do we decide whether someone is speaking a separate dialect of English, and who is simply speaking a variety of English? Who is to say which is "proper" English? Arguments over what kind of English is proper and correct have been bitter and have led many people to argue that schools should abandon the teaching of grammar altogether. Yet I think that would be the worst solution to the problem.

In my opinion, the English curriculum in public schools in the United States ought to have two major aims. One is to enable the student to read and write and speak Standard English, which has become the international language of many fields, including science, medicine, aviation, etc. If you are going to learn to function in only one language, it ought to be Standard English. The second major goal is to give the student an appreciation of how English has varied over time, and how it varies geographically.

The English that Shakespeare wrote is different from the English that is commonly used today. Yet nobody asks which variety is "right" and which is "wrong." Instead, students learn that the rules of grammar and usage are, to some degree, arbitrary and subject to the whims of fashion. To understand Shakespearean English, students need to become acquainted with words such as "thou." They need to understand that the meaning of some words, such as *nunnery*, have changed over time and mean different things to different people.

The lesson that students can learn from Robert Burns is that nonstandard dialects of English are perfectly legitimate means of expression, and the people who speak those nonstandard dialects are fully human and therefore fully deserving of respect. The same principle applies to the way that many African-American children speak. The dialect that linguists have called American Plantation Creole and that many people call Black English is just as legitimate a means of expression as the guid Scots tongue. If people feel differently about Black English than they do about the guid Scots tongue, it's because they feel differently about black people than they do about Scottish people. In other words, they are racist. I'm not sure what to do about that problem. Perhaps teachers who don't respect black children should simply be encouraged to find another way to make a living.

Some of the people who want schools to stop teaching grammar are concerned that differences in how children use English serve as markers of social class. They think that if we stop telling children that certain ways of using English are "right" and others are "wrong," then we will stop having problems with discrimination. Yet by stripping the grammar lessons out of the language arts curriculum, they are making it difficult for children who grow up speaking some other variety of English to learn to read, write, and speak Standard English. If poor children and children of color are deprived of the opportunity to develop strong skills in Standard English, they have even more difficulty in overcoming discrimination.

Children in the United States do need to develop skills in Standard English because it is a world language. It would also be nice for them to learn to speak a foreign language as well. They should develop the ability to speak in different tongues for different purposes, as Robert Burns did. For children who grow up speaking a nonstandard variety of English, this may mean specific instruction in how their form of English differs from Standard English. In other words, they may need instruction in Standard English as second dialect. The purpose is not to eradicate the children's version of English but to help the children become fluent in Standard English, regardless of how they choose to speak with their friends and relatives.

Language has long been an excuse for political repression in the United States. After the Indian Removal Act of 1830, indigenous people in the eastern United States were forced to abandon their farms and villages and were sent to reservations on the far side of the Mississippi. To avoid being dispossessed and sent far away, people of mixed heritage denied their ancestry and avoided speaking their indigenous language in public. Up until the 1980s, it was common for Native American children to be forcibly taken away from their families and sent to boarding schools, where they were often beaten for using their native language.

The use of other European languages has also been suppressed by state and government action in the United States. In the 1880s, Wisconsin and Illinois passed laws requiring English-only instruction in parochial as well as public schools. In 1896, under the Republic of Hawaii, English became the primary medium of schooling for children in Hawaii. After the Spanish-American war, English was declared the "official language of the school-room" in Puerto Rico. The United States made English the official language of the Philippines after the Philippine-American War. During World War I, a widespread campaign against the use of the German language stifled German cultural organizations.

Today, there is still a vocal movement for "English only." I think that this movement flies in the face of the First Amendment. Freedom of speech should include the right to speak in whatever language you wish. Furthermore, some of the organizations promoting "English only" have even been classified as hate groups by the Southern Poverty Law Center. At the very least, the proponents of "English only" are trying to solve an imaginary problem while failing to help solve real problems.

Believe it or not, English is alive and well and doesn't need any help from the "English only" movement. In reality, English tends to expand and replace other languages. Adults who move to the United States have always had difficulty in learning English, but their children usually learn English quite well. The grandchildren of immigrants are typically unable to speak more than a few words of their grandparents' language.

We don't really have a problem with children learning to speak English. What we have is an illiteracy problem that is particularly severe in immigrant populations because they have limited resources and thus are less able to compensate for inadequate schooling. The most intelligent solution to that problem is to teach immigrants to read in their native language. It takes only a few months to teach a Spanish-speaking person to read Spanish. Once Spanish-speaking people can read in Spanish, they can use their Spanish literacy to help them learn English.

Lately, I've also heard a lot of people complaining that the "language" that children are using when they text or tweet each other is corrupting the language. Such complaints make me LOL. Textspeak isn't really a language. It's just shorthand. For decades, the world's best secretaries used shorthand, and nobody thought it impaired their ability to edit and proofread the correspondence they typed.

Education has always been part of the American Dream. Education has enabled the children of poor immigrants to get the kinds of jobs that would allow them to enter the middle class. As a result, many people think of education as a way to prepare for work. Yet for thousands of years, education has been intended to serve higher purposes. People learned to work at home. They went to school to become wise and good. The education in ancient Athens was intended to help a boy grow up to become a good citizen. The public schools that were established in colonial Massachusetts were intended to teach every boy and girl to read the Bible, to help children become good Christians.

One of the purposes of the liberal arts is the cultivation of virtue. The word *virtue* came from the Latin word meaning man. It originally meant manliness, or how a good man was expected to behave. Of course, the behavior that was considered good depended on the person's station in life. A "good" slave did exactly as he or she was told. Free men, in contrast, were expected to think for themselves and to apply moral principles when making decisions. In the next few chapters, I'll explain how the study of grammar and logic provide a solid basis for the study of morality.

CHAPTER XXIV

I and You, We and Them

Many people imagine that grammar involves memorizing a bunch of pointless rules of "correctness" that have nothing to do with how people really speak. In childhood, many people were annoyed by adults who corrected them for saying "Me and Jim went to the park" instead of "Jim and I went to the park." Many people are so wary about saying "me" that they often use *I* inappropriately, such as saying "between you and I." (It should be "between you and me" because *me* is an object of the preposition *between*.)

Since the 1960s, many English teachers have become convinced that the study of grammar is pointless and probably harmful. Unfortunately, children who never learn the rules for when to say *I* and when to say *me* will have an even more difficult time when they try to learn a highly inflected foreign language, such as German. They will also be deprived of the opportunity to think carefully about pronouns such as *I* and *you* and *we* and *them*. As I explain in this chapter, those simple words are a good starting point for the study of morality, which is covered by a branch of philosophy called ethics.

The rules about when to say "I" and when to say "me" depend on grammatical case. Grammatical case refers to the role that a noun or pronoun plays in a sentence. Modern English has just two cases. The nominative case is used when the noun or pronoun is the subject of a verb. The objective case is used for everything else (direct or indirect objects or the objects of prepositions).

Like speakers of modern German, speakers of Old English altered the endings on their nouns and the associated adjectives to indicate how each noun was related to a verb. This alteration is called declension. Modern English has lost most of its declensions. The only declensions left are for pronouns. We use *I, you, he, she, it, we, they,* or *who* when the pronoun stands for the subject of a verb and *me, you, him, her, it, us, them,* or *whom* for everything else.

Modern English is perfectly understandable even though we don't decline nouns for case. Likewise, people can speak perfectly understandable English without following the standard rules for declining pronouns. The use of *whom,* in particular, seems to be on the way out. Nevertheless, it's probably a good idea to make sure that children who have English as their native language learn the *I/me* and *who/whom* distinction, even if they'll never say "whom" in ordinary conversation. Learning the concept of grammatical case in their native language will make it easier for them to learn highly inflected languages, such as German or Russian, which decline their nouns as well as their pronouns for case.

The question of whether to say "I" or "me" is a matter of grammar. However, the question of whether to say the other person's name before you say "I" or "me" isn't governed by a grammatical rule. It's a social convention intended to cultivate and convey modesty. It's a way of showing respect to others. Such displays of respect help to smooth out social relationships.

I started thinking about using grammatical analysis for clarifying social relationships and morality when I read Martin Buber's classic book *I and Thou.* In the original German, this was *Ich und Du.* It was translated to *I and Thou* as opposed to *I and You* because the ways that people say "you" in German are complex. First, let me explain a little bit about how people have said "you" in German and English. Then I'll explain the moral implication of these ideas.

Buber was writing about theology. Thus, it makes sense to translate *du* as *thou.* Many English-speaking people use the word "thou" for "you" when praying or when talking about religion. That's because they learned to use *thou* from reading the King James Version of the Bible. However, there are other reasons for the translators to use *thou* instead of *you.* Using *thou* implies intimacy.

In Standard English, we use the same second-person pronoun (you) for any number of individuals and any degree of formality. In German, however, the second-person pronouns are tricky because you have to decide whether to use an informal or formal pronoun. The informal pronouns (*du* for singular and *ihr* for plural) suggest a close relationship. Germans use the informal pronoun *du* to address God, a child, a pet, or a close friend or family member. The formal pronoun *Sie* (which is treated as a plural even if you are addressing just one person) is used for addressing anyone else.

The formal pronoun *Sie* is derived from *sie*, which means they. The only difference is the capitalization of the first letter. There's no difference in pronunciation or verb conjugation. Thus, when someone is talking, you have to figure out from context whether that person is talking to you or talking about someone else. Thus, to address someone as "*Sie*" implies a certain social distance. For German speakers, the question of whether to address someone as *du* or *Sie* is a tricky point of etiquette. "*Sollen wir uns duzen?*" means "should we call each other *du*?"

In Shakespeare's day, which was when the King James Version of the Bible was published, the English would use *thou* where Germans would use *du*. Thus, people would address God as "Thou," and God would also address an individual as "thou." In the King James Version, when someone is speaking to a close friend or to a servant or when God is giving commands that are binding on everyone individually, some variation of *thou* is typically used: "*Thou* shalt not make unto *thee* any graven image... *Thou* shalt not bow down *thyself* to them nor serve them: for I the LORD *thy* God am a jealous God."

In Shakespeare's day, the second-person plural pronoun was ye/ you: That's why you often see crowds of people being addressed as "ye" in the King James Version: "But seek *ye* first the kingdom of God, and his righteousness; and all these things shall be added unto *you*." Notice that *ye* is the subject of a verb (nominative case) and *you* is the object of a preposition (objective case). English speakers of Shakespeare's day often used a plural form of the second-person personal pronoun when they were speaking to an individual of high social standing. So you might see a single high-ranking person being addressed as "ye" or "you" instead of as "thou" or "thee."

Don't get confused with the "ye" that is sometimes used to mean *the*, as in "Ye Old Curiosity Shoppe." Older forms of English used a letter called a *thorn* (þ) to indicate the hard *th* sound at the beginning of words like *the* and *that*. Unfortunately, the fonts for the printing equipment that William Caxton and other early English printers imported from the continent of Europe didn't include a thorn character. Since the handwritten version of the thorn looks kind of like a *y*, the word *the* sometimes got printed as *ye*. But it was still pronounced "the." Nowadays, we use the letters *th* where people used to use a thorn. That's why words like *thou* and *that* begin with a hard "th" sound but words like *thorn* and *think* begin with a soft "th" sound. Those two different sounds were originally spelled differently.

I and *thou* are both singular pronouns. Each of them refers to only one person at a time. They are also both in the nominative case. They are in the same grammatical form (i.e., they are parallel) because both represent the subject of a verb. I think it's significant that Buber puts both of these words in the nominative case. It's "ich und du," not "ich und dich" (which would imply that I am the subject but you are the direct object) or "ich und dir" (which would imply I am the subject and you are the indirect object).

Martin Buber pointed out that simple words like *I, thou, he, she,* and *it* can express something profound about relationships:

> If I face a human being as my *Thou*, and say the primary word *I-Thou* to him, he is not a thing among things, and does not consist of things. This human being is not *He* or *She*, bounded from every other *He* and *She*, a specific point in space and time within the net of the world; nor is he a nature able to be experienced and described, a loose bundle of named qualities. But with no neighbour, and whole in himself, he is *Thou* and fills the heavens. This does not mean that nothing exists except himself. But all else lives in *his* light.[1]

In other words, the words *I* and *Thou* capture something that is unique and important about the relationship that one person is having with another particular human being in the present moment, as opposed to how he or she interacts with a thing at any point in time.

Philosophers from many different cultures have insisted that at the core of the I-Thou relationship is some sort of mutual responsibility. This reciprocity is often stated as the Golden Rule: Do unto others as you would have others do unto you. It is sometimes stated in a negative form: Never impose on others what you would not choose for yourself.

After the horrors of World War II, the newly created United Nations passed a Universal Declaration of Human Rights, which was the first global expression of the rights to which all human beings are inherently entitled. The declaration was written by a committee that was chaired by former First Lady Eleanor Roosevelt. The preamble starts with the following clause: "Whereas recognition of the inherent dignity and of the equal and inalienable rights of all members of the human family is the foundation of freedom, justice and peace in the world..." Thus, this important document implies that humanity must recognize the fundamental equality of the I-Thou relationship if there is to be freedom, justice, and peace. The Universal Declaration of Human Rights boils down to a simple principle: human beings should be treated as human beings, not as things or as livestock.

Thinking about the pronouns *I* and *Thou* is obviously an important way to approach moral questions. You can address some even more difficult questions by thinking about the pronouns *we* and *they*, and *us* and *them*. The pronoun *I* is a difficult enough concept. *I* is how the individual who is thinking or speaking refers to him- or herself. The problem is that you can't just make *I* plural, as if it were a matter of putting two apples instead of one apple in a basket. To construct the concept of *we*, you must include some persons in a group with yourself, while excluding other persons from that group. Likewise, you can't construct the concept of *they* without assembling some group of persons that excludes yourself and the people to whom you are speaking.

Sometimes, the word *they* isn't intended to mean a specific group of persons. Sometimes it's used in an indefinite sense, to mean people in general. "They say that you can't go home again." I try to avoid this kind of usage. I like to specify exactly whom I mean by *they*.

The word *you* is also often used in an indefinite sense. You could use the indefinite pronoun *one* instead, but it sounds a bit distant and formal.

How do you decide who is part of *we* and who is part of *they*? Can you make those decisions without betraying the *I-Thou* relationship that you would otherwise have with each of the persons involved? Let's look at this problem in the context of human rights.

According to a story from the Book of Judges, the inhabitants of Gilead once inflicted a military defeat on the tribe of Ephraim. To prevent the Ephraimites from escaping across the River Jordan to their home territories, the Gileadites stopped everyone who was trying to cross the river and asked them to say the word *Shibboleth*. The Ephraimite's language didn't contain a "sh" sound. Anyone who couldn't say the "sh" sound was presumed to be an Ephraimite and killed on the spot. Under ordinary circumstances, only a psychopath would kill a defenseless human being just because that person couldn't make a "sh" sound. Yet the concept of "we" and "them" that was generated by the war made it possible for the ordinary Gileadites to do precisely that.

Unfortunately, events like those didn't occur only in a distant or mythologized past. In October 1937 in the Dominican Republic, Dictator Rafael Trujillo ordered his soldiers to slaughter all of the Haitian civilians living in the parts of the Dominican Republic near the Haitian border. To determine whether a person was a Dominican or a Haitian, the Dominicans would ask the person to say the Spanish word for parsley. Individuals whose "r" sound in the word *perejil* sounded French instead of Spanish were killed on the spot. Thus, the decision of whether to have an I-Thou relationship or an I-it relationship with another human being hinged on the pronunciation of a single letter. Roughly 20,000 persons were killed in the course of five days, either shot to death, clubbed to death, or hacked to death with machetes and knives. The killings were carried out by soldiers, local government officials, and civilians.

The Haitians could be differentiated from the Dominicans by language. However, the killers and the victims in the Rwandan Genocide of 1994 had a common language and a common religion and often common ancestors. What marked someone for death was a set of three strikeout lines as follows in the "ethnicity" section of an identity card: ~~Hutu~~, Tutsi, ~~Twa~~, ~~Naturalisé~~.

Although the concept of Hutu or Tutsi identity had existed earlier, these concepts were more like social castes than like nationalities or ethnic groups. The political significance of Hutu or Tutsi identity was a product of Belgian colonialism. Not only did the Belgians assign an ethnic identity to individuals on their ID cards, the Belgians created a system of discrimination through employment and education quotas. The churches reinforced this system by favoring one group or another at various times. Thus, a piece of paper could destroy the basis of the I-Thou relationship, transforming a human being into an entity that was classified as unequal.

Nationalism and ethnic identity both derive from an attempt to make a plural out of *I*. Racism and genocide result when the I-Thou relationship is destroyed by making *I* plural (*we*) and not only making *Thou* plural but putting it into the third person (*they* or *them*). Note that the second person is used for people, but the third person doesn't differentiate people from things.

Never underestimate the power of simple words like pronouns to shape human thoughts and behavior. In Rwanda, the Hutus were urged to think of Tutsi not as fellow human beings but as cockroaches that must be exterminated. That kind of thinking led to the slaughter of 800,000 men, women, and children within the space of about 100 days. Without these ideas about "we" and "them," how could so many seemingly normal people hack their neighbors to death with machetes?

Reference

1. Buber M. *I and Thou*. Edinburgh, UK: T &T Clark, 1937:8.

CHAPTER XXV

He, She, and They

In Chapter 24, I explained that much of morality springs from the I-Thou relationship and that the careless use of the words *we* and *them* can lead to irrational thinking that can lead to distorted and unhealthy relationships between human beings, and even to crimes against humanity. In this chapter, I wish to point out that the words *I* and *Thou* (or *I* and *you*) are not marked for gender in English. Whether you are male or female or somewhere in between, you still refer to yourself as "I" and I would still address you as "you." I feel that the moral responsibilities inherent in the *I-Thou* relationship should transcend the biological sex of either person. Politically, we should relate to each other first and foremost as human beings.

Like the words *we* and *them*, the simple words *he* and *she* can also distort thought processes. Often, we can get around these problems by using the word *they* as a neuter pronoun of indefinite number, as great English writers have been doing for hundreds of years.

Political problems that arise from the use of gender in language have been obvious from the very beginning of US history. The Declaration of Independence, which the Continental Congress issued on July 4, 1776, states,

> We hold these truths to be self-evident, that all men are created equal, that they are endowed by their Creator with certain unalienable Rights, that among these are Life, Liberty and the pursuit of Happiness.

It is an inspiring statement, as it was intended to be. However, it raises two troubling questions. What did they mean by "all," and what about women?

Many of the men (yes, all of the members of the Continental Congress were male) who drafted and signed the Declaration of Independence owned slaves. The slave-owners did not intend to declare that their slaves were their equals. Nor did they intend the Declaration to grant their slaves liberty or the right to pursue happiness. So by *all*, they didn't necessarily mean *all*. But what about the word *men*? Are women female men? Does a statement about "all men" apply to women? Does a statement about mankind say anything about womankind?

On March 31, 1776, Abigail Adams wrote the following in a letter to her husband John, who was in Philadelphia serving in the Continental Congress:

> I long to hear that you have declared an independency. And, by the way, in the new code of laws which I suppose it will be necessary for you to make, I desire you would remember the ladies and be more generous and favorable to them than your ancestors. Do not put such unlimited power into the hands of the husbands. Remember, all men would be tyrants if they could. If particular care and attention is not paid to the ladies, we are determined to foment a rebellion, and will not hold ourselves bound by any laws in which we have no voice or representation.

In fact, it took a long and courageous struggle for women to get the right to vote. It took a much longer and even more courageous struggle for black women, along with black men, to get the right to vote. That struggle is still not over.

The 19th Amendment to the Constitution, which was ratified on August 18, 1920, said, "The right of citizens of the United States to vote shall not be denied or abridged by the United States or by any State on account of sex." In reality, however, many black women still couldn't vote.

The Fifteenth Amendment, which had been ratified on February 3, 1870, said that "The right of citizens of the United States to vote shall not be denied or abridged by the United States or by any State on account of race, color, or previous condition of servitude." But it wasn't until after the Voting Rights Act of 1965 was passed that black women and men in many parts of the South were able to vote. Unfortunately, after the passage of the Voting Rights Act, the War on Crime and the War on Drugs were used in a racially biased way to take away the voting rights of millions of people of color. Florida is a "swing state" only because so many black men have been deprived of their right to vote.

Careless use of the words *we* and *them* have led to biased thinking about identity. Problems with the words *he* or *man* or *mankind* can also cause distorted thinking that can lead to injustice. The question of whether women are included in mankind is just one of the many problems posed by the use of gender in language. The use of masculine pronouns such as *he* and such masculine suffixes as *–man* and *–boy* can hide the very existence of women and girls.

I've been a medical editor for many years. The American Medical Association's *Manual of Style* gives medical writers clear guidelines for avoiding the use of language that can distort thinking about sex and gender, as well as about age, ethnicity, and so on. The main concern in medical writing isn't "political correctness" but scientific accuracy.

One of the problems that English-speaking people have to face when they are dealing with issues related to gender and sex bias is the nature of the English language. In English, gender normally relates only to biological sex. Thus, when English-speakers use a gender-specific pronoun, they seem to be specifying male or female, even if they didn't intend to do so.

Many European languages, including Latin and German, have three genders: masculine, feminine, and neuter. Nouns and many third-person pronouns are marked for gender. The neuter nouns from Latin generally became masculine in the modern Romance languages, such as Spanish and French. The gender of a noun may have no connection with biological sex. Inanimate objects often get marked as masculine or feminine, and a noun's gender may have more to do with the history or structure of the word than with the biological sex of its referent. For example, the word *Mädchen* in German means maiden, or young woman. However, *Mädchen* is a neuter word because of the *–chen* diminutive ending. In contrast, *Männlichkeit*, or manliness, is feminine because of the *–keit* ending, which is equivalent to *–ness* or *–hood* in English.

In his essay *The Awful German Language*, Mark Twain shows how odd the gender-specific pronouns in German sound to an English-speaker. Twain notes that the word *wife* is neuter, *fish* is masculine, and *scale* is feminine, and so on. Then he gives this "translation" of a story that he made up. Notice that he capitalized all the nouns, as Germans do:

> It is a bleak Day. Hear the Rain, how he pours, and the Hail, how he rattles; and see the Snow, how he drifts along, and of the Mud, how deep he is! Ah the poor Fishwife, it is stuck fast in the Mire; it has dropped its Basket of Fishes; and its Hands have been cut by the Scales as it seized some of the falling Creatures; and one Scale has even got into its Eye, and it cannot get her out. It opens its Mouth to cry for Help; but if any Sound comes out of him, alas he is drowned by the raging of the Storm.

In English, we don't mark nouns for gender, although some words refer specifically to persons or animals of a particular biological sex, such as woman or girl, man or boy, cow or bull, mare or stallion, and so on. We do have separate pronouns (*he, she,* and *it*) for masculine, feminine, and neuter for the third-person singular. We use *he* and *she* to indicate the sex of a person or of some higher animals, espe-cially domestic animals. We use *it* for inanimate objects and other animals and sometimes for babies or small children.

The fact that grammatical gender in English is so tightly connect-ed to biological sex can raise some problems. What do you do when you are talking about a hypothetical or unknown person who could be male or female? The easiest solution is to rewrite the sentence so that it talks about more than one person. The third-person plural pronoun *they* doesn't specify gender. Regardless of whether you are talking about a group of men, a group of women, or a group that includes men and women, you can use the pronoun *they*.

But what if you really do mean just one hypothetical person, but you don't know, or don't care, whether the person turns out to be male or female? This kind of problem crops up when you are talking about unknown people or hypothetical situations. In medical writing, it's a common problem when you are writing about patients or research subjects. If you are writing about a condition that affects women only, you can refer to a hypothetical patient as "she." If you are writing about something that affects males only, you can refer to the hypothetical patient as "he." If the person could be male or female, you say "he or she."

A particular problem arises with the use of indefinite pronouns that are singular in construction. I mean words such as *everyone, anyone, nobody,* and *no one* that take the singular form of verb. What possessive adjective do you use to refer back to the indefinite pronoun? For example, should you say "Everyone should bring his driver's license" if some of the people included in "everyone" are women?

There are two obvious solutions to this problem. Since the 16th century, good writers have been using *they, them,* and *their* in this situation. Since the 18th century, however, some grammarians have insisted that we should say *he, him,* and *his.* They argued that people would get confused about number (even though they didn't worry about number with *you*) but would not get confused about gender. They were wrong.

The use of a masculine pronoun to mean a male or a female created confusion for legislators and lawyers. To clear up the confusion, they had to specify "he or she," "him or her," and "his or her." All of this "he or she" and "his or her" bogged down the language so much that the British Parliament specified in the Interpretation Act of 1850 that "he" means "he or she" unless otherwise specified. Of course, the legislation that is passed by the British Parliament has no effect in the United States. In 1879, a motion to admit women to the Massachusetts Medical Society was blocked by men who argued that the by-laws describing membership referred to a member as "he."

Even if people agree that *he* will be interpreted to mean *he or she* unless someone specifies that it means males only, the use of *he* to refer to a person who turns out to be female sounds odd. Using *he* instead of *he or she* or *they* can also distort thinking. It encourages people to think only of men and boys when they ought to be thinking of all of humanity.

When I train copyeditors and proofreaders, I explain that in an ideal world, we'd be allowed to use *they, them, their,* and *theirs* when we're talking about just one person of unknown gender or an indefinite number of persons. Unfortunately, we do not live in an ideal world. Instead, we live in a society where some of the few grammar rules that people do know are unreasonable. Thus, we need to say "he or she" or use a plural pronoun to avoid confusion over gender.

Although we rarely mark English nouns for gender, some English nouns imply a particular biological sex. Careless use of these words can also distort people's thinking about males and females. During the 1970s, the Women's Liberation movement in the United States started calling attention to the effect of gender-linked words for occupations. People in the women's movement realized that the masculine or feminine names for some occupations caused people to think of those jobs as "for" men or "for" women. This bias in thinking could then lead to bias in hiring.

To eliminate this bias in thinking, stewardesses are now called flight attendants. Mailmen are now called letter carriers. Actresses are now called actors—except when they get a Best Actress or Best Supporting Actress Oscar, because those gender-specific terms are part of the proper name of the award. Many words that once ended in "-man" now end in "-person." We are used to this kind of usage now, but it initially sounded strange.

The Women's Liberation movement also introduced the use of "Ms" as an honorific for a woman. They pointed out that the honorific "Mr." doesn't mark a man as married or unmarried. Women also need an honorific that doesn't mark them as married or unmarried.

Some feminists play with words to highlight how our language shapes our ideas about girls and boys and women and men. One example is the use of the word *herstory* to refer to history written from a feminist perspective. The word *herstory* is a play on the word

history and is intended to highlight the fact that history has traditionally been about the activities of men, that in a sense history has
been "his story" as opposed to "her story." The novelist Umberto Eco
has complained that the use of the term *herstory* is a wrong-headed
hypercorrection that reveals an ignorance of the Greek root of the
word *history*. He doesn't seem to realize that the intention is not to
"correct" or replace the word *history* but to broaden the minds of
historians so that they also think about women.

I once edited an article by a transsexual gynecologist. Her work
taught me a lot about the thoughtful use of *he* and *she*. The American
Medical Association's *Manual of Style* explains that sex and gender
are two different things. Sex is a biological concept that is related to
genes and anatomy. Gender, on the other hand, is a social construct
and has to do with how individuals view themselves and present
themselves to the world. Most children are assigned to one gender
or the other at birth, on the basis of their external anatomy. However,
the concept of biological sex and gender can be far more complicated
than that.

At birth, some children have sex organs that aren't typically
male or female. That condition is called an intersex state. However,
most of those individuals will eventually choose to identify as male
or female. The Intersex Society of North America says that children
should be assigned a gender at birth. The choice should be based on
the gender that a child with those biological and anatomic traits will
most likely choose. However, children should not undergo surgery
to change the appearance of their private parts. Such surgery cannot
be undone and the results cannot be easily corrected if the surgeon
made the wrong choice.

Biological sex is a matter of the primary and secondary sexual
characteristics, the things that make a person look male or female.
Yet gender involves the brain activities that make a person perceive
him- or herself to be male or female. Gender involves more than
biological sex. It's a social construct that includes how a person
perceives him- or herself. Thus, it makes perfect sense to me to refer
to a person with the gender of pronoun that he or she prefers. It's
the respectful and compassionate thing to do. It's the sort of thing
that an I-Thou relationship would require.

In this chapter and Chapter 24, I talked about how important it is for people to think carefully about the meaning of common words such as pronouns. I asked some basic questions that have profound implications for morality: Who are *we*? Who are *they*? Does mankind include women? These are just a few of the moral questions that you can approach through the study of grammar. In Chapter 26, I'll discuss commandments. What kind of sentences are they? What do they say? How can one decide whether to obey them?

CHAPTER XXVI

Thou Shalts, and Thou Shalt Nots

W hen people think about rules of morality, they typically think of lists of commandments, like the Ten Commandments. A command is an order to do something or not to do something. People generally use the word *commandment* for important commands that come from a high authority, such as God. The study of grammar provides important concepts that will help you analyze commands and other statements about morality and expectations. Thinking clearly about morality will help you avoid doing things that you will later regret. Thinking clearly about expectations can help you find inner peace, along with improving your relationships with other people.

Grammatically, commandments and commands are sentences of a particular kind. They are not statements of fact. They don't affirm or deny anything. Thus, they can't be true or false. A command might be wise or foolish. It might be obeyed or disobeyed. There may be rewards for obeying it or punishments for disobeying it. But since a command is not a statement of fact, it can't be true or false.

Since a command cannot be true or false, you cannot use it as a premise in an argument. It makes no sense to say, "since this command is true, then this statement of fact must be true." Nor does it make sense to say, "since these statements are all true, this command must be true." A command can never be true, and it can never be false. A statement of fact is an expression of what the speaker thinks is true or false. In contrast, a command is the speaker's attempt to influence someone else's behavior. You might give an argument to try to persuade someone to follow a command, but that's different from proving that the command is true.

In the operetta *The Mikado*, W. S. Gilbert made fun of this difference between a command and a statement of fact. The character named Koko had to explain why he had failed to follow an order from the emperor and then had lied to the emperor about it. Koko had told the Mikado that he had followed the Mikado's order to execute a man. Then he had to explain why the man was obviously still alive:

> When your Majesty says, "Let a thing be done," it's as good as done—practically, it *is* done—because your Majesty's will is law. Your Majesty says, "Kill a gentleman," and a gentleman is told off to be killed. Consequently, that gentleman is as good as dead—practically, he *is* dead—and if he *is* dead, why not say so?

In the topsy-turvy world of Gilbert and Sullivan, that line of reasoning satisfied everyone.

Like other kinds of sentences, a command consists of a subject and a predicate. However, the subject of a command is often left unstated. If I say to you, "Open the door," the implied subject is "you."

The difference between the command "(You) open the door" and the statement of fact "You open the door" is the mood of the verb. The verb in a command is in the imperative mood, which is used for giving orders and making requests. Some languages use special word endings to indicate when a verb is in the imperative mood. English doesn't. English speakers have to guess the mood of a verb from context.

Commands can be phrased in several different ways. They may have a verb in the imperative mood, or an auxiliary (helper) verb may be used to express the imperative mood. In English, the modal auxiliary verbs include *can, could, will, would, shall, should, may, might,* and *must*. These modal auxiliaries help to clarify whether the verb that they are helping is intended to be an order, a suggestion, or an expression of something that is possible or probable. However, the use of these auxiliaries doesn't necessarily make a verb imperative. *Shall* and *will* can also be used to express an action that will take place in the future.

British grammarians made up a complicated rule for using *shall* and *will*. They argue that when *I* or *we* is the subject, *shall* means the same as *will*. It's just a statement about the future. For any other subject, however, *shall* is used to imply what is going to happen, regardless of what the subjects want: "They shall not pass!" Thus, *shall* in the first person just means the future, whereas *shall* in the second and third person is used for making promises, commands, and threats. That's why *shalt* (which is the form of *shall* that goes with *thou*) was used in King James Version of the Ten Commandments. Americans rarely make this distinction between *will* and *shall*. Americans mainly use *shall* when they are trying to sound formal, stuffy, or British.

Even though modal auxiliary verbs are some of the most commonly used words in the English language, their meaning is sometimes unclear. Consider the word *can*. Sometimes it is used to mean ability, and sometimes it is used to mean permission. To clear up any possible confusion, some people insist on using *can* only for ability. To express permission, they prefer to use *may*. "Can I go to the park, Mom?" "Yes, you *can*. But no, you *may* not!"

The word *should* can also cause confusion because it can be used for several different purposes. British say *shall* more often than Americans do. Thus, they use *should*, which is the past tense form of *shall*, in ways that sound odd to Americans. For example, British people sometimes use *should* to express futurity from a point of view in the past. They often use *should* to express conditionality ("If I should die before I wake...") or to soften a statement or make a request sound more polite ("I should like..."). In the United States, however, *should* is mainly used either for expressing what is likely (probability) or what ought to be (obligation, propriety, expediency).

Modal auxiliaries are often used to phrase commands and requests indirectly, to make the requests sound more polite. At a restaurant, for example, you might say, "I would like..." or "Could I have...?" when you really mean "(You) bring me...!" The linguist

Deborah Tannen has written several books about the pitfalls of phrasing commands and requests directly or indirectly. Of course, you can't even begin to understand her work unless you know some of the basics of grammar and sentence structure.

When most Americans think of commands and moral rules, they think of the Ten Commandments. In particular, they think of the wording from the King James Version, with its *thou shalts* and *thou shalt nots*. The word *shalt* is the version of *shall* that goes with *thou*. In this context, *shalt* is clearly being used to give commands, and the adverb *not* turns the command into a prohibition. You never hear people say the word *thou* in ordinary conversation anymore, and *shall* is also becoming less common.

The King James Version of the Bible is a translation that was produced in Shakespeare's day. In contrast, recent translations use language that sounds more like the way people speak today. Instead of saying "thou shalt" or "thou shalt not," they may say "you must" or "you must not." You might think that "thou shalt" sounds better than "you must," but they both mean the same thing.

In a command, the subject (you) is often implied. Likewise, the identity of whoever gave the command is also often left unsaid. The author of the book of Exodus makes it clear that the Ten Commandments were made by God. "And God spake all these words, saying, I am the Lord thy God, which have brought thee out of the land of Egypt, out of the house of bondage." Yet the identity of the commander isn't part of the command itself: "Thou shalt not kill."

Grammatical analysis can help you clarify that a command is being made, and by whom. Sometimes, people make themselves miserable by making unreasonable commands, without even realizing that they're doing so. Cognitive behavior therapy teaches people to avoid "demand thinking," to avoid telling themselves that the world must and should and ought to be a certain way. These demands are commands that are phrased with a modal auxiliary verb.

Demand thinking tends to make people unhappy. People become frustrated and angry when their demands are not met. Cognitive behavior therapists teach their clients to replace these demands with statements about opinions and preferences: "It would be nice if" or "I would prefer if." I suspect that this method works by teaching people to correct an unhealthy sense of entitlement. You may certainly prefer things to be a certain way, but it's unreasonable to demand that the world be set up for your convenience. Coming to this realization can help you find inner peace.

Grammatical analysis can help you recognize when commands are being made. Grammatical analysis can also help you clarify whether the command is a suggestion, a request, or a demand. Once you realize that a demand is being made, you can try to figure out who is issuing the command and whether you wish to obey it.

A command is not a statement about what is. It's somebody's attempt to influence someone else's behavior. No argument can make a command true. By its very nature, a command can't be true. However, people often give arguments to persuade people to obey (or disobey) a particular command.

A command is often followed by some sort of "or else" clause. "Do this, or else…" An "or else" clause that contains some sort of threat is called an *ad baculum* argument. In Latin, *ad baculum* literally means "to the stick." In other words, do as I say or I will hit you with this stick. Although *ad baculum* arguments are not logically strong, and many people consider them to be morally repugnant, they can be persuasive.

In *Through the Looking-Glass, and What Alice Found There*, Lewis Carroll makes fun of the "or else" principle:

> "You are sad," the Knight said in an anxious tone: "let me sing you a song to comfort you."
>
> "Is it very long?" Alice asked, for she had heard a good deal of poetry that day.
>
> "It's long," said the Knight, "but it's very, *very* beautiful. Everybody that hears me sing it—either it brings the *tears* into their eyes, or else—"
>
> "Or else what?" said Alice, for the Knight had made a sudden pause.
>
> "Or else it doesn't, you know."

Once students learn enough about the imperative mood and modal auxiliaries to recognize commands, they are much better able to think critically about authority and power. Just who says that I should or must do something (or abstain from doing it)? Why are they giving me that command? What would happen if I disobey? Would something bad happen to me, or to somebody else? What kind of "or else" statement is involved? Is it an honest warning about a natural consequence? Or is it a threat? If it's merely a threat, do I wish to let myself be bullied? These are vital questions for anyone who cares about freedom and dignity.

Even people who have taken vows of obedience tend to pick and choose which commands to obey and which to ignore. A quick review of the Bible shows that even religiously devout people pick and choose which commandments to obey. Soldiers are supposedly even expected to disobey unlawful orders. The judges at the war crimes trials that were held after World War II insisted that "I was just following orders" is no defense. This raises the question of how or even whether people can decide whether a command is good or evil. The ancient Greek philosopher Plato dealt with this question in the Socratic dialogue Euthyphro.

In that dialog, Socrates is about to be taken in to court to face charges of impiety. Outside of the courthouse, Socrates meets a man (Euthyphro) who believes he has a clear understanding of piety, or dutifulness in religion. Socrates asks Euthyphro to tell him what makes pious things pious. Euthyphro says that piety is what is pleasing to the gods. After asking a series of other questions, Socrates poses the "Euthyphro dilemma." Monotheists state it as follows: Are moral acts good because they are willed by God, or are they willed by God because they are good?

Theologians have struggled with the Euthyphro dilemma for more than two thousand years. If things that are good are good only because God commands them, then morality means just following orders. There are no moral principles besides obedience. If that were true, then what does it mean to say that God is good? Yet if God commands good things because they are good, then human beings might be able to think through the moral principles for themselves. If that were true, would human beings even need divine commandments?

If there is any such thing as a moral principle, then it probably could be expressed in a sentence. In Chapter 27, I'll explore what grammatical analysis can tell us about how to think about moral principles.

CHAPTER XXVII

Grammar, Morals, and Principles

One skill that is essential for moral reasoning is the ability to parse, or to break a sentence down into its parts and see how those parts fit together. Chapter 26 explained the difference between a command and a statement of fact. A command is an attempt to get someone else to modify his or her behavior. Many statements that use modal auxiliary verbs, such as *should* and *must*, are really commands. Once you realize that a statement is a command, you can think about who is making the command, and for what purpose. Then you can decide whether you will obey. The decision of whether to obey any given command depends on a combination of practical concerns and moral principles.

Many commands are followed by an "or else" clause. Do this, or else… Sometimes, the "or else" clause describes a natural consequence. In that situation, the commands are made for the person's own good. For example, your parents and your dentist command you to brush your teeth. If you refuse to obey, your teeth will probably rot. In other words, some "or else" clauses are warnings of a natural consequence. On the other hand, some commands are backed up by a threat of an "unnatural" consequence: a punishment. Those are the kinds of commands that are important politically and morally.

Some kinds of commands provide warnings of natural consequences and are made to benefit the individual being commanded. For example, if you resist the advice to follow rules of ordinary politeness, you may end up friendless. Other kinds of commands are beneficial to society as well as to the individual. If you refuse to obey traffic signals, you could end up killing other people as well as yourself. Still other kinds of commands benefit other people or society in general but require some sort of sacrifice from the individual, such as when fire fighters are ordered to risk their lives to save other people's lives and property. Then, there are the commands that serve only a powerful person or a powerful group of people but are generally harmful for the ordinary person and for society at large. Such orders are tyrannical.

How will you decide whether to obey or disobey a particular command? Your decision will probably be influenced by your expectations. What do you expect will happen if you obey? What do you expect will happen if you disobey? In many situations, however, your decision will be based on a moral principle. Yet even when a moral principle is involved, the decision of when and how to make your stand can be a matter of strategy or tactics.

Where do our moral principles come from? Many people feel that moral principles come from divine commandment. Yet that raises the Euthyphro dilemma, which I mentioned in Chapter 26: Are moral acts good because they are willed by God, or are moral acts willed by God because they are good? If an act is moral only because God wills it, then obedience is the only moral principle. But if that is true, what does it mean to say that God is good? On the other hand, if God wills moral acts because they are good, then there should be some independent way of deciding whether an act is moral or not, which means that it is possible to develop a code of morality without reference to divine commandment.

An entire branch of philosophy has been dedicated to finding ways of judging which acts are moral under what circumstances. It's called ethics. Ethics is of practical importance because it deals with how actions in the present are likely to affect events in the future. It is of political importance because it deals with how one person's actions affect other people. Ethics often deals with some difficult problems, partly because the world is complicated and partly because no one can predict the future. Yet even when complicated math or science problems are involved, an ethical judgment is still influenced by the person's feelings, whether the person realizes it or not.

In his *Enquiry Concerning the Principles of Morals*, which was published in 1751, the Scottish philosopher David Hume explained that morality is guided by reason but determined by sentiment or feelings. Twentieth-century philosophers incorporated that idea into a view called emotivism: that ethical statements are not statements of fact but are expressions of emotional attitudes. This idea does make a lot of sense when you look at the structure of the sentences that express moral principles. These sentences tend to be statements about whether something is good or bad or attempts to influence other people's behavior. The statement "this is good" really means "I like this." The statement "that is bad" really means "I don't like that." The sentence, "You should (or must) do this" really means "I want you to do this." If there is an "or else" clause attached, the sentence could mean "I will punish you if you don't do as I say." If that threat of punishment isn't taken seriously, the person may make a bigger threat: "God will punish you if you don't do as I say."

When people say that something is good, they mean that they like it, or that most people seem to like it, or perhaps that they think that God likes it. Likewise, when they say that something is bad, they mean that they dislike it, or that most people dislike it, or perhaps that God dislikes it. It never ceases to amaze me how quick so many people are to speak on behalf of the Almighty, insisting that He shares their point of view and is taking their side in a conflict. It's as if they never read the Third Commandment: "Thou shalt not take the name of the LORD thy God in vain; for the LORD will not hold him guiltless that taketh his name in vain." When people insist that God is on their side, or threaten that God will smite the people they don't like, aren't they taking the Lord's name in vain? Aren't they breaking one of the Ten Commandments? Of course, once they've put one foot on that slippery slope, there's no telling where it will end. They might even end up cutting firewood on the Sabbath and making graven images!

The idea that our ethical judgments are expressions of feelings raises the important question of what shapes our feelings. A lot has been written about "primitive drives" such as hunger and greed and lust. The British philosopher Thomas Hobbes was convinced that human beings are so driven by such passions that they must submit to a strong ruler if they wish to live in peace. However, I think that besides having those selfish drives, normal human beings also have drives that are related to getting along with each other. Normal human beings desire companionship, friendship, and love. If individual human beings lacked such social drives, *Homo sapiens* would never have been able to survive as a social species. In fact, pro-social behavior can be important for the survival of an individual.

In 1976, Jane Murphy reported that people from distinctly different cultures tend to label similar kinds of actions as misbehavior that calls for social correction or even punishment.

> [The] Eskimos have a word, *kunlangeta*, which means "his mind knows what to do but he does not do it." This is an abstract term for the breaking of many rules when awareness of the rules is not in question. It might be applied to a man who, for example, repeatedly lies and cheats and steals things and does not go hunting and, when the other men are out of the village, takes sexual advantage of many women—someone who does not pay attention to reprimands and who is always being brought to the elders for punishment. One Eskimo among the 499 was called *kunlangeta*. When asked what would have happened to such a person traditionally, an Eskimo said that probably "somebody would have pushed him off the ice when nobody was looking."[1]

Scientific studies have shown that people all over the world have the same kinds of emotional responses to the same kinds of social contexts. When psychologist Paul Ekman was trying to see whether people in different cultures made the same facial expressions in response to the same emotional state, he asked them questions about social situations. The people from Papua New Guinea associated happy facial expressions with the statement "friends have come."

They associated a fearful expression with a story about a person being threatened by a wild pig when "there is no one else in the vil-
lage." They associated an angry glare with the statement that the
person is "about to fight." Sadness was associated with the death of
a mother, or of a mother's child.

Two of the basic emotions that Ekman identified have a particularly important role in moral reasoning: disgust and contempt. Disgust is the emotion that people feel when they encounter a bad smell
or contaminated food. When people feel disgust, they tend to wrin-
kle up their nose in a characteristic way. When something disgusts
them, they want to reject it and distance themselves from it. Contempt, on the other hand, has something to do with social hierarchy. People feel contempt when they see that someone has failed to
measure up in some way. (The emotion that people feel when they
accept other people's contempt is called shame. That explains why
people who have been mistreated often feel shame, even though
they themselves did nothing wrong.) When people feel contempt,
they tend to have a lopsided smirk on their face. Some people feel
that they are so superior to everyone else that their smirk becomes
more or less permanent.

Since contempt is specifically associated with social hierarchy, it
comes as no surprise that feelings of contempt and shame play an
important role in regulating social behavior. But so does disgust.
Although disgust may have originally been about rotten food, it is
now also about rotten treatment. Human beings show the facial expression characteristic of disgust when they are reacting to situations that seem to them to be unfair. The greater the injustice, the
more intense their expressions of disgust. Thus, it's no surprise that
people complain that unfair treatment leaves a bad taste in their
mouth.

A person's moral reasoning can also be influenced by empathy,
which is the ability to understand and share the feelings of another
person, or even of an animal. When a normal human being observes
someone in pain or sees people reacting to a bad smell, parts of that
observer's brain react as if the observer were experiencing the same
thing that the other people were experiencing. You wouldn't see the

same pattern of activation in the brain of a callous, uncaring person —which could explain why that person is so callous and uncaring.

What has long puzzled me is that people who are not necessarily callous or uncaring in general can end up doing uncaring things or supporting uncaring government policies. How could they feel good about doing things that seemed to me to be so obviously cruel and pointless? At first, I thought that it was merely that they were unaware of the effects that those policies were having on other people. Eventually, I realized that there was something different about the way that they formulated their rules of morality. Upon analysis, the differences turned out to be grammatical. Some people respond emotionally to the nouns and pronouns and adjectives of a sentence, rather than to the verbs and adverbs.

To me, questions of the ethics of interpersonal relations hinge on verbs and adverbs. For example, consider the sentence "A killed B." To me, the important part is the verb "killed." I always find it upsetting when one person kills another person, regardless of the circumstances. As the poet John Donne wrote, "any man's death diminishes me, because I am involved in mankind." The same thing goes for the death of women and children. The killing itself is a bad thing. To me, the identity of A and B don't matter, but the circumstances might. Those circumstances can be expressed with an adverb (such as "accidentally") or an adverbial phrase (such as "in self-defense" or "in cold blood"). The adverbs or adverbial phrases that modify the verb "killed" can tell you what kind of a bad thing it was—a tragedy or an outrage—but it remains bad.

To many people, however, the verbs in the sentence matter far less than nouns or pronouns, especially pronouns like *us* and *them*. As I explained in Chapter 24, the careless use of the pronouns "we" and "them" can distort a person's thought processes so badly that a seemingly ordinary person can end up hacking his neighbors to death with a machete, just because of the "ethnicity" recorded on their passports. That's an extreme situation, but the same kind of distorted thought processes lead to support for war and other injustices.

The feelings of identification with a "we" and the feelings that result from regarding "them" as if they were animals or inanimate objects also lie behind something that George Orwell called "the defense of the indefensible."[2] Things that "they" do to "us" provoke moral outrage. Yet when "we" do the very same things to someone else, the response is far different. "Our" actions were praiseworthy or at least understandable, or they are shoved so far down the "memory hole" that people deny that the events even happened. The famous linguist Noam Chomsky has developed a useful method for studying this kind of problem:

> One obvious way is to try to find more or less paired examples. History doesn't offer true, controlled experiments but it often comes pretty close. So one can find atrocities or abuses of one sort that on the one hand are committed by "official enemies" and on the other hand are committed by friends and allies or by the favored state itself.[3]

However, the "paired example" approach is persuasive only to people who are concerned about the verbs and adverbs, not to people who really care only about the "us" and "them." To people who care only about the "us" and "them," nothing that "we" do can be considered bad. Any criticism of "us" is intolerable, no matter what "we" have done. A person who thinks this way may be quite capable of pointing out the mote in his brother's eye, while ignoring the beam in his own. Some of these people may call themselves Christians, but Jesus Christ would call them hypocrites (Matthew 5:7). Yet they themselves do not think that they are hypocritical.

A hypocrite may genuinely believe that "we" are good people and that whatever "we" do is therefore good. The hypocrite may genuinely believe that "they" are bad people and that whatever "they" do is therefore bad. Hypocrites may think that goodness or badness is a characteristic of a person or a group, not a judgment of behavior. This kind of thinking may enable the hypocrite to do horrible things with a completely clear conscience.

The struggle for world peace is largely a struggle against the hypocrisy of the powerful. This is a particularly important lesson for the citizens of the world's greatest military power, the United States. As Noam Chomsky has explained, "Everyone's worried about stopping terrorism. Well, there's really an easy way: Stop participating in it." He and other American antiwar activists pose a challenging question: Are we in the United States really doing unto others as we would want others to do unto us?

To approach these questions of morality and hypocrisy, one needs to be able to parse—to analyze the structure of sentences. To be able to parse, one needs to know something about grammar. I find it disturbing that the National Council of Teachers of English in the United States decided at the height of the Cold War to stop teaching grammar in public schools. Without the ability to think clearly about simple words such as "us" and "them," how will students be able to see through hypocrisy and develop moral integrity?

Many people argue that we need to teach religion in school (always their own religion, for some reason) in order to teach people ethics. I see no need for religious indoctrination in public schools, and the Founding Fathers saw good reasons for opposing it.

Many Christians believe that without the code of rules put forth in the Ten Commandments, humanity would have no guide for morality. Without God telling people, "Thou shalt not kill," how would people know that killing is wrong? The problem is that God allegedly gave people lots of exceptions to this rule.

According to the Bible, God says that it is okay to kill temple prostitutes, an engaged woman who is seduced by a man other than her future husband, women who practice black magic, some women who are raped in urban areas, children who cursed their parents, some non-virgin brides, Jews who collect firewood on Saturday to keep their families from freezing, persons preaching another religion, persons worshiping some god other than Himself, strangers who entered the temple, and of course the soldiers of foreign armies and the civilian populations of any land whose real estate His people coveted. In other words, the Bible permits many kinds of killing that violate the criminal laws of secular states and some that violate international law. Thus, I think that implementing Biblical law would be a setback for humanity, not an advance.

Many Christians argue that the United States is a Christian country that was founded on Christian teachings and that therefore the public schools should preach the gospel and try to save the students' souls. Yet the men who actually wrote the Constitution felt otherwise.

Both Thomas Jefferson, who was the primary author of the Declaration of Independence, and James Madison, who is known as the Father of the Constitution, argued passionately that government should not be involved in religious matters. In 1785, Patrick Henry (the slave-owner who became famous for saying "Give me liberty or give me death") was trying to get the Virginia House of Delegates to pass a bill that would have taxed Virginians in order to support "Teachers of the Christian Religion." In response, Madison wrote a pamphlet titled *Memorial and Remonstrance against Religious Assessments.* Not only did Madison argue that every man has an "unalienable right" to exercise religion as "conviction and conscience may dictate," Madison insisted that state support for religion "is a contradiction to the Christian Religion itself, for every page of it disavows a dependence on the powers of this world."

In 1787, Thomas Jefferson explained in his *Notes on the State of Virginia* that it is better for the state governments to stay free of entanglements with religion:

> Our sister states of Pennsylvania and New York, however, have long subsisted without any establishment at all. The experiment was new and doubtful when they made it. It has answered beyond conception. They flourish infinitely. Religion is well supported; of various kinds, indeed, but all good enough; all sufficient to preserve peace and order: or if a sect arises, whose tenets would subvert morals, good sense has fair play, and reasons and laughs it out of doors, without suffering the state to be troubled with it. They do not hang more malefactors than we do. They are not more disturbed with religious dissensions. On the contrary, their harmony is unparalleled, and can be ascribed to nothing but their unbounded tolerance, because there is no other

circumstance in which they differ from every nation on earth. They have made the happy discovery, that the way to silence religious disputes, is to take no notice of them. Let us too give this experiment fair play, and get rid, while we may, of those tyrannical laws.

The first public schools in the English-speaking parts of North America were founded mainly for religious reasons, and most public schools continued to promote a nondenominational Protestantism until the mid 20ᵗʰ century. Many Protestant Christians are angry that the Supreme Court has decided that the public schools should not be involved in promoting religion. What these Protestant Christians may not realize is that many of the Supreme Court cases that ultimately led to these decisions were brought by Protestant Christians—Jehovah's Witnesses.

Jehovah's Witnesses were targeted for repression in Fascist Italy and Nazi Germany because they refuse to bear arms or swear loyalty to a state. In the concentration camps, the Jehovah's Witnesses' prison uniforms were marked with a purple triangle. Witnesses have also been resistant to injustice in the United States. Between 1938 and 1946, 23 separate First Amendment cases filed by Jehovah's Witnesses made it to the US Supreme Court. Justice Harlan Fiske Stone once joked, "I think the Jehovah's Witnesses ought to have an endowment in view of the aid which they give in solving the legal problems of civil liberties."

References

1. Murphy JM: Psychiatric labeling in cross-cultural perspective. *Science.* 1976;191(4231):1019-1026.

2. Orwell. Politics and the English language. *Horizon*, April 1946.

3. Achbar M, Wintonick P: Manufacturing Consent: Noam Chomsky and the Media [film]. New York: Zeitgeist Films, 1993.

I have never been a schoolteacher. Thus, I can't begin to tell anyone how to run a classroom full of children or adolescents. However, I have been an editor for many years, which means that I've done a lot of the kind of work that English teachers do—correcting mistakes in other people's writing.

Over the years, I've come to the realization that bad writers are bad writers because they don't understand things that I learned in seventh grade—things such as misplaced or dangling modifiers. I've learned through experience that bad writers become better writers after I teach them these concepts. I started teaching grammatical concepts through memos and handouts at work. Later on, I started writing a column about grammar for the *American Medical Writers Association Journal*. As I was doing research for that column, I started to ask why the educators in the United States decided that children should not be taught grammar in grammar school. That research ultimately led to this book.

In the next few chapters, I talk about how I help adults become better writers. I explain why grammar lessons are so helpful to writers. I introduce many basic principles of grammar and composition and explain why they are important and useful. You may pick up some useful pointers from these chapters, but I mainly want to inspire people to study the subject in more depth on their own. All I can do here is give an overview of what is important and why it's important.

CHAPTER XXVIII

Teaching Grammar, Teaching Writing

I n 1963, a report published by the National Council of Teachers of English (NCTE) suggested that formal lessons in grammar did not improve children's ability to write and might actually be harmful.[1] That report, among others, led to major changes in what children in public schools in the United States were taught about the English language, which for many of those children is the only language they will ever speak. As these changes were being made, students' performance on the verbal portion of the Scholastic Aptitude Test (SAT) began a sharp and completely unexpected 16-year decline that could not be explained by changes in the number of students taking the test.[2] The verbal SAT scores have not recovered in the more than 30 years since then. One possible cause of the decline was the general "dumbing down" of the textbooks before 1963, but the refusal to teach grammar in grammar school almost certainly made things worse. It certainly didn't improve matters.

The decision to stop teaching grammar was based on research that supposedly showed that teaching grammar to students doesn't help students become better writers. If you look at that research carefully, however, you might come to different conclusions. One is that teaching grammar *badly* doesn't help children become better writers. Another is that even teaching grammar *well* might not help them become better writers *right away*. Children need to understand a lot of grammatical concepts before they can begin learning to apply them. Yet another conclusion is that badly designed studies can produce misleading results.

If you want to measure the effect of teaching grammar, you have to design your experiments so that they reflect what happens in the real world. Nor can you depend on the results of just one kind of study. A short-term study might fail to pick up evidence of longer-term effects. You need to look at the evidence as a whole. If the small, short-term studies say one thing but the big, long-term studies say something completely different, there's probably something wrong with the design of the small, short-term studies. That's one of the lessons I learned from studying research design in school and from editing articles on epidemiology. Unfortunately, few of the people who are making educational policy know much about research design or epidemiology.

Many people insist that the scientific evidence shows that teaching grammar doesn't help students become better writers. Yet in my experience, the fastest way to help bad writers become competent writers is to teach them how to use a dictionary and how to diagram a sentence and then to give them some pointers on word order and parallel structure and so on. I'll explain these concepts in the next few chapters. If the opponents of grammar instruction were right, then the scores on the verbal SAT would have gone up after teachers all over the country started following their advice. Instead, the scores began a sharp 16-year decline and then stayed low.

Although some language arts teachers in the United States ignored the advice to stop teaching grammar, others embraced it, only partly out of respect for the NCTE. The decision to stop teaching grammar appealed to many teachers, students, and parents for bad reasons. Those reasons relate to what has been called the motivational triad.

All animals seek to experience pleasure, avoid pain, and conserve energy. Human beings are no exception. Opponents of grammar instruction seem to be promising that children would experience the pleasure of learning to write well without having to suffer the pain of being extensively corrected and without having to waste their energy on grammar drills. Likewise, the teachers would have the pleasure of seeing the children advance more quickly, but without having to expend so much energy in correcting children's mistakes. The teachers would also experience less conflict with students and their parents over grades.

Unfortunately, anything that sounds too good to be true is probably false. Teaching English well is extraordinarily hard work. Much of that work is the thankless toil of marking the mistakes in students' compositions. The "progressive" idea of ignoring students' mistakes must have been welcomed by those English teachers who didn't want to work terribly hard. Only a teacher with an independent mind and extraordinary professionalism would be able to resist the temptation to do less work. Unfortunately, the war against grammar has gone on so long that the younger generation of English teachers in the United States wouldn't be able to teach grammar even if they wanted to — many have never studied it themselves.

The war on grammar has been intensified by the advocates of "whole language" educational approaches. Whole language proponents believe that children will be able to realize, without being told, that they don't write well. This realization will supposedly inspire the children to seek out ways to improve their writing. The role of a teacher in a whole language classroom is to serve as a resource to children who are engaged in that self-directed quest. Unfortunately, this theory flies in the face of what psychologists know about how people assess their own grammar skills.

People who have poor skills in grammar and logic tend to be unaware of how bad their skills are. That's because their skills are so poor that they don't notice their own mistakes.[3] Since they don't realize that they make lots of mistakes, they have no motivation to work at improving their skills. Only after their skills improve (usually as a result of direct instruction) do they gain the ability to judge their own level of skill. By that time, however, the problem of poor skills has been solved.

Children can get better at grammar and logic and rhetoric only if they are directly taught the skills that they need to learn and only if they get honest feedback about their level of skill. This means having their mistakes pointed out to them. Unfortunately, many educators and parents resist pointing out a child's mistakes because they fear that honest feedback would dampen the child's self-esteem.

As a result, they are afraid to give children the kind of honest feedback that children need in order to develop intellectually, socially, and morally. The result, I fear, is that children will end up not only ignorant but arrogant—the sort of person nobody likes.

We need to rethink the popular assumptions about self-esteem. Why do people think that it is better for children to be arrogant than for children to be humble? Humble people aren't necessarily unhappy, and they may be more receptive to learning. I think that children would be much better served if they were loved and valued simply for being human, and if they were given honest feedback, along with encouragement and guidance for strengthening their skills.

If we want children to learn to write well, we need to do several things in the proper order. Step one is teaching children to read well. That means using intensive phonics to teach children to read by sounding out the words, not by having children memorize Dolch words or sight words. The use of sight words promotes dyslexia because it encourages children to use counterproductive strategies for decoding words. Instead of teaching children sight words, we can simply teach them the exceptions to the phonetic spelling rules. Step two is encouraging children to read a lot of good literature from many different writers. This experience will expose them to many different literary models. Step three is giving children a well-rounded general education, along with the opportunity to pursue their own special interests. Then they will have something to write about, and something interesting to say.

To become good writers, children also need to develop some practical skills on many different levels, from word choice, to sentence structure, to paragraph structure, to the structure of the overall work. That's a lot of material to learn, but children in a K-12 public school have 13 years to learn it.

I know something about how to teach writing because I've worked as a medical editor for more than 20 years. It has been my responsibility to turn bad writing about a matter of life or death into writing that's good enough for publication in a scientific journal or textbook. Over the years, I've seen a lot of bad writing, most of it from college graduates—some of it from people who tell me that they were English majors. From what I've seen, bad writers write badly because they don't think carefully about the meanings of the words they use and because they don't know how to use the rules of English grammar to put those words in an order that makes sense. As a result, their writing is gibberish.

Some critics of grammar instruction seem to think that grammar involves nothing more than a bunch of arbitrary rules. I agree that some grammarians have put forth some rules that are arbitrary and stupid, such as the rule against splitting infinitives. I see nothing wrong with saying, "to boldly go where no one has gone before." However, most of the problems that I see in bad writing from educated people result from grammatical errors that no one who has been graduated from eighth or ninth grade should make.

In the next few chapters, I'll explain the basic concepts and skills that people need to learn to become good writers, as well as how I go about teaching those concepts and skills to grownups. These fundamentals are simple, but they help people develop highly sophisticated skills. The first thing I teach is how to use a dictionary and a thesaurus, to help people choose their words more carefully. The second is how to diagram a sentence. Sentence diagramming helps people analyze how the various parts of the sentence relate to each other. Once people understand the mechanics of sentence structure, I teach them some simple rules of thumb for using word order and punctuation to clarify meaning. Then, I teach some principles for writing coherent paragraphs. Finally, I teach some basic "mind-mapping" skills for planning the overall composition.

By teaching these basic skills, I have helped many adults improve their writing. Fortunately, most of those adults had learned many grammatical concepts in childhood. For example, they already knew what nouns, verbs, adjectives, and adverbs are. It's much easier to build on existing skills than to start from scratch.

Although I've had success in helping adults learn to write better, it's far easier to learn language-related skills in childhood than in adulthood. For example, it's far easier for children than for adults to learn to speak a new language fluently and without an accent. Children should be taught language-related skills when such learning is easiest for them. Learning grammar and writing skills in grammar school will also enable children to get the best possible education in high school. At the very least, children need to develop good reading comprehension and good skills in grammar and writing before they take their SATs or write the essays for their college applications.

I'm alarmed that schools in the United States are failing to teach English grammar and foreign languages when the children are most able to learn them and when children need them the most. If people do not learn those things in childhood, they may never learn them. Justice delayed is often justice denied.

References

1. Braddock R, Lloyd-Jones R, Schoerr L. Research in written composition. Urbana, IL: National Council of Teachers of English, 1963.

2. Hayes DP, Wolfer LT, Wolfe MF: Schoolbook simplification and its relation to the decline in SAT-verbal scores. *Am Educ Res J.* 1996;33(2):489-508. http://educationconsumers.org/research/briefs_0801.htm.

3. Kruger J, Dunning D. Unskilled and unaware of it: how difficulties in recognizing one's own incompetence lead to inflated self-assessments. *J Personality Soc Psychol.* 1999;77(6): 1121–1134.

CHAPTER XXIX

Finding the Right Word

Mark Twain once explained that the difference between the right word and the *almost* right word is the difference between lightning and a lightning bug. The choice of words—especially with regard to correctness, clarity, or effectiveness—is called diction. The way to develop good diction is to make heavy use of a good dictionary and a good thesaurus.

When I work with people to improve their writing style, the first thing I do is teach them how to make full use of their dictionary and thesaurus. Since most people use a computer for writing nowadays, I strongly urge them to load an electronic copy of a good dictionary into their computer. At the very least, they should bookmark the Web site of a good dictionary, such as *Merriam-Webster's Collegiate Dictionary* or *The American Heritage Dictionary*. These electronic dictionaries also have a built-in thesaurus.

From my perspective, the main difference between those two popular dictionaries is that *Merriam-Webster's* lists the oldest definitions of a word first, even if that particular definition is obsolete. In contrast, *The American Heritage Dictionary* lists the most commonly used definition first. Note that the term *Webster's* isn't copyrighted. You can publish anything you wish to call a dictionary and name it "Webster's." Merriam-Webster is the company that is considered the intellectual heir of Noah Webster, the lexicographer who published America's first dictionary. A lexicographer is someone who compiles or edits dictionaries.

The medical publishing companies I have worked for have all used *Merriam-Webster's Collegiate Dictionary* as their standard dictionary for nontechnical words. The companies have also specified a preferred medical dictionary for medical terminology. However, I often ended up looking up medical terms in *Merriam-Webster's Collegiate Dictionary* as well as the medical dictionary. *Merriam-Webster's* sometimes gives me additional information. It may explain what part of speech a word is, and it may give the past tense of an irregular verb or the plural form of an irregular noun.

The best way to develop good diction is to get in the habit of looking up words that you think you know. Good editors are continually looking words up in the dictionary. In fact, my husband says that the definition of *editor* in the dictionary should be changed to this:

> **ed·i·tor** noun \'e-də-tər\ 1: the sort of person who would look this word up in the dictionary.

Having an electronic version of the dictionary loaded into your computer makes it particularly easy to look words up when you are using a word processor. You can also load an electronic dictionary into your e-book reader, to make it easy to look up words as you read.

The dictionary gives you several vital pieces of information. One is information about how the word is spelled. Sometimes, several alternative spellings will be listed. Editors need to make sure that all of the words in a published piece are spelled correctly. Editors also like to make sure that a word is spelled the same way every single time it appears in a publication. The easiest way to do that is to use the preferred spelling of a word, which is the spelling that's listed first.

Whole language teachers think that correct spelling is unimportant. In fact, they often teach children to use "invented spelling" or "inventive spelling" for words. Invented spelling doesn't mean that the child makes his or her best guess at spelling the word phonetically and then looks the word up in a dictionary later on (an approach that boosts reading skills as well as spelling skills). Invented spelling means a completely made-up way of spelling the word, with no particular relationship between letters and sounds. As a result, the words that the child writes are unreadable to anyone but the child. Even the child may be unable to read them.

When whole-language teachers talk about "invented spelling," they do not mean that the student makes an educated guess at spelling the word phonetically. They want the child to start off by using random letters in any order. They expect children to "progress naturally" through phases in which the child's spelling gradually starts to resemble readable English, as if the child is inventing written language from scratch. Eventually, the child is supposed to reach a point where his or her spelling is "usually correct." Whole-language teachers waste an enormous amount of time waiting for children to progress "naturally," instead of just teaching things to the children and telling children whether they are doing something correctly.

Why do whole-language teachers advocate invented spelling? It's because their students, having been taught to read by the whole-word method, do not know enough about phonics to spell words phonetically or to look them up in a dictionary. The problems that children in a whole-language classroom have with spelling are the flip side of the problem they have with reading. The fact that they have such trouble with spelling is a warning sign that they cannot really read and are unable to use a dictionary.

Besides showing how a word can be spelled, dictionaries generally break a word down into syllables. That's useful if you need to figure out where to put a hyphen to break a word at the end of a line. Notice that some words that are spelled the same can be hyphenated differently. For example, the noun *present*, as in birthday present, is hyphenated after the *s*. In contrast, the verb *present*, as in *Alfred Hitchcock Presents*, is hyphenated before the *s*.

Besides telling you how to spell and hyphenate a word, dictionaries tell you how to pronounce the word. Electronic dictionaries are particularly useful in this regard because they let you click on an icon and hear the word being pronounced by a human being.

The dictionary also tells you what part of speech a word can be, such as whether it can be used as a noun or a verb. If the dictionary doesn't list the word as noun, you should think twice about using it as a noun in formal writing. If it isn't listed as a verb, think twice about using it as a verb.

The dictionary also tells you how a verb can relate to the nouns in the sentence. Transitive verbs have a direct object; intransitive verbs do not. Some verbs can be used as a transitive or intransitive verb. For example, I can say "I eat" (intransitive). I can also say "I eat pie" (transitive). If the dictionary doesn't say that a verb can be used in a transitive sense, then you should think twice about giving it a direct object in formal writing. You should also avoid using it in the passive voice. Only transitive verbs can be used in the passive voice because the passive voice means that the direct object of a verb has become the subject of the sentence. (The pie was eaten by me.)

A dictionary can help you figure out whether a particular word is serving as a preposition or a conjunction in a particular sentence. That kind of information can help you solve lots of problems with grammar and sentence structure. When the editors and proofreaders I was supervising at work would ask me for help with a particularly tricky sentence, I'd often simply point at one of the words in the sentence and ask, "What part of speech is that?" Often, that was enough to enable the person to solve the problem.

Most dictionaries also tell you about the origin and history of each word. This information can help you extend your vocabulary by learning about the meanings of the prefixes, stems, and suffixes that occur in many English words. Many of those prefixes, stems, and suffixes come from Latin or Greek.

The information about word origins reveals one of the secrets of great orators like Winston Churchill. Consider this stirring speech, which Churchill gave on June 4, 1940—during the darkest days of World War II for the British:

> "We shall go on to the end. We shall fight in France, we shall fight on the seas and oceans, we shall fight with growing confidence and growing strength in the air, we shall defend our island, whatever the cost may be. We shall fight on the beaches, we shall fight on the landing grounds, we shall fight in the fields and in the streets, we shall fight in the hills; we shall never surrender."

Much of the power of this speech comes from the fact that he uses short, simple words. If you look these words up in the dictionary, you'll find that most of them came originally from Old English, as opposed to French or Latin. The exceptions are *France, ocean, confidence, defend,* and *surrender.*

Old English, which is sometimes called Anglo-Saxon, was a Germanic language. It was derived from the Germanic dialects that had been brought to Great Britain in the fifth century by tribes called the Angles, Saxons, and Jutes. In fact, the name *England* came from *Englaland,* which meant land of the Angles. On September 26 of 1066, however, England was invaded by William II, Duke of Normandy, which is on the northwestern coast of France. William and his knights quickly conquered England. William had himself crowned King William I of England on Christmas Day, 1066. William the Conqueror (who was also known as William the Bastard) took lands from the English nobility and gave them to his knights, who spoke the Norman dialect of French. As a result, the ruling class of England was replaced by a group of foreigners who spoke Norman French, not Old English.

The Norman Conquest of England had a profound effect on the English language. The common people still spoke a form of German, while the rich people spoke a form of French. That's why we use words derived from German to refer to refer to farm animals (cow, sheep, swine) but words derived from Norman French for the meat (beef, mutton, pork). Most of our obscene words also come from Old English.

Although a large percentage of the words in modern English come from French or Latin, the words that came to us from Old English are particularly powerful. They tend to be short, simple, common, lively words about things that matter to farmers and workers and other plain folk. For this reason, many style guides urge writers to use "Anglo-Saxon words" whenever possible. Why say "construct" when you could say "build"? Why say "principal" when you could say "first" or "main"? Why say "discontinuity" when you could say "gap"?

I've already gone on for several pages about how to use a dictionary, and I'm just now getting to the definitions. I find it useful to look at all of the definitions of the word. Sometimes, you'll find that a word has meanings and connotations that you didn't know about.

The literal meaning of a word is sometimes called its denotation. Words can also have other meanings associated with them. Those other meanings are called the connotation. For example, the president of one of the companies where I used to work hated the word *cubicle* because it reminded him of the comic strip *Dilbert*. For him, the word *cubicle* connoted a soul-destroying environment where intelligent workers had to follow stupid orders from idiotic managers. So he ordered us never to refer to our workstations as cubicles. Perhaps he thought that if we never uttered the word *cubicle*, we would never notice the similarities between our working lives and Dilbert's. I followed his order to the letter. I never once called our workstations cubicles. I didn't call them workstations, either. I referred to them as cells, stalls, pens, crates, lairs…

When you look up a word in a dictionary and find that it doesn't mean what you thought it meant, or if you simply want to find another word with a more appropriate connotation, use a thesaurus. You probably have a simple thesaurus built into your word processing program. You can also use the thesaurus built into an electronic dictionary.

Roget's Thesaurus, which was first published in 1852, was a book of synonyms and antonyms that were organized by concept rather than alphabetically. However, the name *Roget's* is not copyrighted. You can publish anything you would like to call a thesaurus and call it Roget's, if you wish. Note that the controlled vocabulary that is used for indexing certain kinds of information in a computer database can also be called a thesaurus.

A synonym is a word that has more or less the same meaning as another word. For example, the word *costly* is a synonym for *expensive*. An antonym is a word that has more or less the opposite meaning. *Cheap* is an antonym for *expensive*. If you want to find words with a similar meaning to a particular word, look up that word's synonyms. To find words that mean the opposite of that word, look up the word's antonyms.

There are two basic approaches to writing dictionary definitions. Some lexicographers think that the definition should show what a word ought to mean and how it ought to be used. Since these lexicographers are prescribing how a word should be used, their approach is called prescriptivism. Other lexicographers feel that the dictionary definitions should reflect how the word actually is used, not how people think it should be used. Since those lexicographers are merely describing current usage, their approach is called descriptivism.

Most large English dictionaries are descriptivist. However, they may provide some additional notes, such as a warning that a particular word is often considered offensive or substandard. Many dictionary definitions include specific examples, often from famous writers, of how that particular word is used in a phrase or sentence. I pay careful attention to those examples.

Many dictionaries provide extensive usage notes that describe the history of a particular word or the controversies surrounding its use. For example, the usage notes under the entry *they* in Merriam-Webster's Web site discuss whether you can use the third person pronoun *they* as a neuter pronoun of indefinite number. In other words, can you use *they* to mean just one hypothetical or unknown person, who might be male or female? Merriam-Webster's usage notes explain that good writers have been doing that in English for hundreds of years. The other alternatives are either awkward or potentially misleading.

I urge people to look words up in the dictionary if they have any doubt about how to spell a word, about what the word means, or about how the word should be used. I also strongly urge people to look up words in the dictionary if they are going to be defining that word in something they are writing. Your definition of a word should match the dictionary definition unless you have a really good reason for giving some other definition. If so, then you probably ought to explain how your definition differs, and why.

Be wary of using words in ways that aren't covered by one of the definitions in your dictionary, especially if you are writing for an international audience. I was one of only two native English speakers in one of the statistics courses I took in college. One day, the professor mentioned that the geneticist Gregor Mendel had probably fudged his data from his experiments with the peas. The professor was writing on the blackboard when he said this, so he didn't see that several students grabbed their dictionaries to figure out what "fudge" meant. I wrote "Fudge, noun: A type of chocolate candy. Fudge, verb: to lie about numbers" and handed it to the student sitting next to me. The note got passed all throughout the class and was greatly appreciated.

There are three basic kinds of definition that often differ from the dictionary definition. One is legal definitions. For example, if your town has a law that says that you cannot keep livestock in your neighborhood, does that mean you can't keep a miniature potbellied pig as a pet? To answer that question, a judge will probably look at how the word *livestock* has been defined in that law and how other judges have interpreted that word in that context.

Scientists also have special definitions for certain kinds of words. Consider, for example, the question of whether a tomato is a fruit or a vegetable. To a botanist, a tomato is a fruit because it is the ripened ovary of a seed plant. However, to nutritionists and to the Supreme Court, a tomato is a vegetable:

> Botanically speaking, tomatoes are the fruit of a vine, just as are cucumbers, squashes, beans, and peas. But in the common language of the people, whether sellers or consumers of provisions, all these are vegetables which are grown in kitchen gardens, and which, whether eaten cooked or raw, are, like potatoes, carrots, parsnips, turnips, beets, cauliflower, cabbage, celery, and lettuce, usually served at dinner in, with, or after the soup, fish, or meats which constitute the principal part of the repast, and not, like fruits generally, as dessert.[1]

Researchers in various fields must often use operational definitions in their research. An operational definition is based on some set of characteristics that you can observe, measure, or calculate. For example, if you are trying to figure out whether obesity is becoming more common in a population, you might define obesity as a body mass index of at least 30 kg/m². That is a useful definition for defining obesity in the general population, even though it would have falsely classified Arnold Schwarzenegger in his Mr. Universe days as obese.

Another kind of definition that may be different from a dictionary definition is the Socratic definition. Socrates liked to ask questions of the form "What is F-ness?" What is piety, what is courage, what is virtue, and so on. The point of asking a Socratic question is not to figure out the dictionary definition of a word, although that's a general starting point in that kind of discussion. The point of asking a Socratic question is to explore the concept that the word represents, especially with regard to other concepts. For example, how does courage relate to wisdom? If someone refuses to retreat from a battle, is it evidence of courage or stupidity? These are questions for which there are no easy answers.

In short, I urge you to use your dictionary and thesaurus heavily. Look up words that you think you know. Pay attention to what part of speech a word can be, and to the examples of how the word has been used. Refer to the usage notes for advice on how to use troublesome words like *they*. When you are writing, use the words that mean exactly what you intend to say, and that carry exactly the connotations that you intend to express. Think twice about using any word in a way that is not described in a good dictionary, especially if you are writing for an international audience. If you are using a word that you think may be unfamiliar to your readers, define it correctly in text to save them the trouble of looking it up themselves. Also, be sure to explain any special legal or operational definitions that your readers will need to know.

This chapter has covered the basic word-level problems that I commonly see in bad writing. In Chapter 30, I'll start to talk about the sentence-level problems that are common in bad writing.

Reference

1. Nix v. Hedden, 149 U.S. 304 (1893).

CHAPTER XXX

Are Your Nouns Doing Your Verbs?

T he very worst writers are those who write sentences in which the nouns have nothing to do with the verbs. I don't mean that they accidentally use the singular form of a verb with a plural noun. I mean that they use a noun that isn't doing, or can't do, the action described by the verb. They use verbal adjectives made from verbs that those nouns aren't doing or can't do or that can't be done to that noun. Nor do the nouns and verbs in their sentences have any meaningful relationship with the other words in the sentence. As a result, their writing is gibberish. When I'm editing a particularly badly written manuscript, I sometimes wonder whether somebody has accidentally submitted the fake text (often called greeking) that graphic designers use as filler in their designs.

Some writers write gibberish on purpose, for an artistic effect. Here's the first stanza of *Jabberwocky*, a poem from Lewis Carroll's *Through the Looking-Glass, and What Alice Found There*:

> `Twas brillig, and the slithy toves
> Did gyre and gimble in the wabe:
> All mimsy were the borogoves,
> And the mome raths outgrabe.

The poem sounds like real English. You can tell that the words *brillig* and *slithy* and *mimsy* are adjectives. You can tell that *toves* and *borogoves* and *wabe* are nouns, and that *toves* and *borogoves* are plural but *wabe* is singular. You can tell that *gyre* and *gymble* are verbs. However, it's harder to figure out what part of speech *mome*, *raths*, and *outgrabe* are supposed to be.

Jabberwocky is nonsense because it contains meaningless words. Another way to write gibberish is to use real English words but to put them together in ways that make no sense. Consider this passage from Gertrude Stein's *Tender Buttons*:

> If the centre has the place then there is distribution.
> That is natural. There is a contradiction and naturally
> returning there comes to be both sides and the centre.
> That can be seen from the description.

Stein was trying to capture the sound and rhythm of the natural speech of an educated English speaker but without actually conveying any meaning. Reading *Tender Buttons* gives you the opportunity to observe your own mind trying to make sense out of something that sounds as if it should make sense but that really makes no sense at all. Reading *Tender Buttons* is like being aware that you are in a confusing dream.

To write sentences that sound like real English sentences—with real English words—but that don't really mean anything, Stein had to pay careful attention to word meanings and sentence structure. Unfortunately, I have seen many writers achieve a similar effect accidentally—by paying *no* attention to word meanings and sentence structure. Their writing makes so little sense that I wonder what goes on in their minds. However, I have a pretty good idea of what went on in their English classes when they were children in school —nothing of any real value.

A sentence can be grammatically correct but still make no sense. Consider this famous sentence, which Noam Chomsky discussed in his 1957 book *Syntactic Structures*:

> ☺   Colorless green ideas sleep furiously.

This sentence follows the rules for a grammatical English sentence. It has a subject and a predicate. The subject consists of the noun *ideas* modified by two adjectives, *colorless* and *green*. The predicate consists of the verb *sleep* modified by the adverb *furiously*. If you used a Reed-Kellogg diagram to show the structure of the sentence, it would look like this:

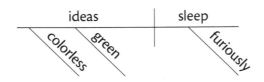

But even though the sentence is grammatical, it is meaningless. Ideas don't really have a color. Even if they did, they couldn't be colorless and green at the same time. Nor can ideas sleep, and nothing sleeps furiously.

Why did the public schools in the United States stop teaching children how to diagram sentences? Some people claim that the diagramming of sentences is a pointless and boring task that makes children unhappy and doesn't help them learn to write better. Of course, those people somehow fail to explain why the scores on the verbal SAT took a nosedive after grammar and sentence-diagramming were stripped from the language arts curriculum. Other people claim that sentence diagramming is pointless because the sentence "Colorless green ideas sleep furiously" can easily be diagrammed even though it has no real meaning. Yet the purpose of the diagram is to show syntax, not semantics. It is to show the grammatical relationships among the elements of the sentence, not to show what the sentence means.

I have found that teaching people how to diagram sentences is an easy way to help them understand the problems in their sentences. The act of diagramming forces them to think about how the nouns relate to the verbs, how the adjectives relate to the nouns, etc. It helps them understand the case of pronouns. It helps them analyze problems with parallel structure, which I'll talk about in Chapter 33.

I use the Reed-Kellogg method, which puts the main words on horizontal lines and the less-important words on diagonal lines.

Linguistics researchers, in contrast, tend to use a different system of diagramming, called a concrete syntax tree or parse tree. That's a more flexible and more powerful system that is particularly useful for computer programmers. However, I think that the Reed-Kellogg system is more useful for teaching people to write better in English because it makes the subject-verb-object relationships and the subject-verb-complement relationship easier to visualize. If I were teaching people to write better in some other language, I might use a different system for diagramming sentences—especially if their language was written from right to left or from top to bottom instead of left to right like English.

The simplest English sentences consist of just a noun and a verb. To show this relationship, write the noun and the verb on a horizontal line. Separate them by a short vertical line that goes through the horizontal line:

Subject	Verb

That's how the diagram looks for an intransitive verb. If the verb is transitive, there will be a direct object. Some verbs can be intransitive or transitive. For example, you could say "I eat" (intransitive) or "I eat pie" (transitive). If you are unsure whether you can use a verb in a transitive or intransitive sense, look the verb up in the dictionary. Here's how the diagram for a transitive verb looks:

Subject	Action verb	Direct object

Transitive verbs raise the problem of the passive voice. If you want to turn the direct object of a verb into the subject of the sentence, you have to put the verb in the passive voice:

☺ Mark Twain wrote *The Adventures of Tom Sawyer*.
☺ *The Adventures of Tom Sawyer* was written by Mark Twain.

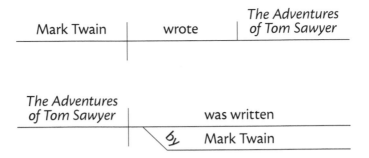

Notice that the subject of the first sentence (Mark Twain) is diagrammed as if it were the indirect object of the second sentence. The direct object of the first sentence (*The Adventures of Tom Sawyer*) is now the subject of the second sentence. The verb has gone from the active voice (wrote) to the passive voice (was written), which is created by using some form of the verb *to be* and the past participle of *to write*. Note that the passive voice also allows you to turn an indirect object into the subject of a sentence: Mary was given an award.

Many English teachers tell their students to avoid using the passive voice, but without telling their students how to recognize the passive voice or why the use of the passive voice is often appropriate. As a result, some people mistakenly think that verbs that express experiences as opposed to actions are in the passive voice.

☺   He believed her story. (Active voice, experiencer subject)

☺   Her story was believed. (Passive voice, agent not specified)

The passive voice means that the direct object of a verb has become the subject; the verb is then expressed with some form of *to be* and the past participle of the verb. The passive voice is useful when you want to emphasize the direct object or when the agent is unknown or unimportant. If the agent is identified in the sentence, think about using the active voice instead of the passive voice.

Some adjectives can be made out of verbs. As a result, some problems with adjectives are really problems with noun-verb relationships. When I see a present participle being used as an adjective, I think about whether the noun that the present participle is modifying is really doing that present participle. The present participle expresses the progressive aspect of a verb, which expresses ongoing action. In English, the present participle is always regular, which means that it is always made in the same way, namely by adding –*ing* to the verb. The present participle can then be used as an adjective that modifies the subject of the participle:

☺   The stone is rolling.

☺   A rolling stone gathers no moss.

In contrast, the past participle expresses the perfect aspect of a verb, which describes a completed action, something that has been done or that has been. Past participles can be a bit confusing because many of them are irregular. (For example, we say "bitten" rather than "bited.") The past participle is often made by adding –*ed* or –*en* to the verb, sometimes with some adjustments in spelling, such as changing the *y* at the end of a word to *i* (as in *worried*). There are also many irregular forms, especially for words of Anglo-Saxon origin. For example, we say "sing, sang, has sung" but "bring, brought, has brought" because of how those verbs were conjugated in Old English. Note also that we add –*en* to some past participles to make the adjectival forms of some of the verbs that came from Old English (e.g., sunken, drunken)

You can turn the past participle of a verb into an adjective only if the verb is transitive, which means that it takes a direct object. The following sentence shows a verb in the present tense, active voice:

☺   This subject bores the students.

Notice how in the next sentence, the direct object (students) has become the subject of the sentence and the verb is now in the passive voice:

☺   The students are bored by this subject.

Notice that the passive voice is made by an auxiliary verb that indicates tense (*are* as opposed to *were*) and the past participle of the verb (bored). The past participle can now be used as an adjective to describe the students.

☺   The bored students became restless.

When I see a participle being used as an adjective, I think about the underlying noun-verb transaction. Is that noun really doing that present participle? Has that past participle really been done to that noun? In other words, does it make sense to use that adjective to modify that noun?

Besides the transitive and intransitive verbs, there are also linking verbs. They are also called copulative verbs. Examples include *to be* (am, is, are, was, were, am being, have been) and *to become*. This category of verbs also includes other kinds of linking verbs, such as *seem* or *feel*. (He seems healthy. I feel good.) Notice that a diagonal line is used between the linking verb and the predicate complement, which can be a noun or pronoun in the nominative case or an adjective (I am I. I am a woman. I am strong.)

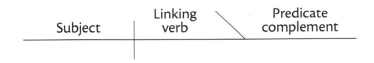

Sometimes, a verb will have an indirect object. For example, if I say "I gave George $20," the direct object is $20 and George is the indirect object. I could also say "I gave $20 to George." It means the same thing, but I had to add the preposition *to* because I changed the word order.

Verbs that can have an indirect object are sometimes called dative nouns because some languages use a separate dative case for indirect objects. (In Latin, the agent of a verb in the passive voice is in the ablative case, not the dative case.) For example, in German you'd use the word *mir* to mean *me* as an indirect object but *mich* to mean *me* as a direct object. That's why when native German speakers speak

English, they sometimes say things like "throw me down the stairs my hat."

Once I teach people how to diagram the subject-verb-object relationship, they stop making mistakes with the case of pronouns. If a pronoun stands for the subject of a verb or the predicate complement of a linking verb, it should be in the nominative case (*I, you, he, she, it, we, they, who, whoever*). If it is being used for anything else, it should be in the objective case (*me, you, him, her, it, us, them, whom, whomever*). That's why it's correct to say "I am I," "this is she" (or he, if you are male), and "between you and me" (please, not "between you and I").

A popular book about English grammar and usage is titled *Woe is I.* Its author complains that some "hypercorrect" people would change "Woe is me" to "Woe is I" because *is* is a linking verb. The problem is that she doesn't explain that *me* is correct because it is in the dative case. The equivalent expression in German is *Weh ist mir,* where the pronoun used for *me* is in the dative case, meaning "unto me." "Woe is me" is perfectly correct. The King James Version of the Bible used the phrase "woe is me" a lot. If that sounds funky to you, you can add a preposition ("woe is *unto* me") to make the objective case sound right.

The pronouns *who* and *whom* follow the same rules. *Who* is used for the subject of a verb or for a predicate complement, and *whom* is used for anything else. If you have any trouble remembering that principle, just think of the old Abbott and Costello routine "Who's on first?" It was about a baseball team whose first baseman was nicknamed "Who," whose second baseman was nicknamed "What," and whose third baseman was nicknamed "I Don't Know." (Who is the subject of a verb? Absolutely. Absolutely is the subject of a verb? No, Who is the subject of a verb! The subject is Who? Absolutely!) Note that I just used the word *who* for the subject of a verb and for the predicate complement. For anything else, use *whom*.

What gets confusing is when *who* (or *whoever*) is the subject of a verb in a clause that is serving as a direct or indirect object. A clause is a string of words that contains a subject and a predicate but isn't standing on its own as a sentence. Every natural human language allows you to embed clauses within sentences. The clauses themselves can have clauses embedded in them, and so on. This feature is called recursion. The following sentences show how the process works:

- He is lost.
- He who hesitates is lost.
- He who hesitates, which means to fail to act quickly, is lost.

As long as a pronoun is the subject of a verb, it should be in the nominative case (*who, whoever*), even if that pronoun is in a clause that is serving as a direct or indirect object. In the following sentences, I have put the embedded clauses in brackets and underlined the subject and verb of the embedded clause:

- Who ate the pie?
- We all know {who <u>it is</u>}. (Who is linked to the subject *it* with the linking verb *is*.)
- Ask not {for whom the <u>bell tolls</u>}.
- I give $20 to {<u>whoever needs</u> it}.
- I give $20 to {whomever <u>I wish</u>}.

One of the lessons that people learn when they are diagramming sentences is that sometimes phrases and clauses can get substituted for nouns. For example, here's an example of a clause serving as a direct object: Lola gets *whatever she wants.* Here's a sentence in which the subject is a clause that contains another embedded clause: *Why people insist that teaching grammar is useless* is a mystery to me. Here's a gerund phrase being used as a noun: *Playing guitar* is no way to make a living.

Some of the people who say that we shouldn't teach grammar in school say that we should teach "sentence combining" instead. However, "sentence combining" deals with the kind of embedding I just described. "Sentence combining" also includes the use of conjunctions, which I'll address in Chapter 33. I don't see how it could possibly be easier to teach someone to "combine sentences" without teaching them about clauses, relative pronouns, and conjunctions.

In English, we have only two real grammatical cases, nominative and objective. We don't mark any of our nouns for case, only the pronouns. Yet our English teachers have been told not to bother teaching children the proper way to mark pronouns for grammatical case in standard English. Maybe it doesn't matter if people say "between you and I" instead of "between you and me." But if people don't develop a clear understanding of grammatical case in their native language in childhood, they will find it far more difficult to learn highly inflected languages like German or Latin later on.

Many of the good editors I've met are native English speakers who tell me that they learned practically nothing about grammar in their English classes when they were growing up. Most of their knowledge of grammar came from studying a foreign language, such as Latin or Russian. They then applied what they learned from those language classes to their independent study of English.

It's not surprising that studying Latin or Russian would have that effect. Those languages are highly inflected. The order of the words in a Russian or Latin sentence tells you very little. To figure out who is doing what to whom, you have to look at the word endings, which indicate which noun is the subject, which is the direct object, which is the indirect object, and which nouns are part of adverbial phrases.

Of course, only a really bright person would be able to learn that sort of thing in college. It's hard to learn grammatical concepts after puberty. Most college students who had never learned about grammatical case in their native language in grammar school would just drop out of Latin or Russian class.

In short, I think that sentence diagramming is an easy way to help students recognize the subject-verb-object transactions in their sentences. You have to identify the subject-verb transactions to ensure that the subject and the verb agree in person and number, but you must also make sure that the subject-verb-object transactions make sense. You also need to be able to recognize when a phrase is being used as a noun or when a clause is being embedded in another sentence or clause. To become a good writer, you must learn to analyze the structure of sentences. Sentence diagramming helps by making that structure visible.

CHAPTER XXXI

Parsing and the Garden Path Effect

S ometimes, the ability of English words to serve as more than one part of speech can cause problems, such as in this headline: Squad helps dog bite victim. The headline writer meant to say that the squad helped the victim of a dog bite, but the sentence could be read to mean that the squad helped the dog bite the victim. This kind of problem is common in English because English doesn't use word endings to show the role that a word is playing in the sentence.

In a highly inflected language, you can tell from the word endings whether a word is a noun or a verb. You can also tell whether a noun is supposed to be the subject or the direct object or the indirect object of a verb. You can tell whether a verb is in the first, second, or third person, and so on. In English, however, it's sometimes hard to tell which words are supposed to be nouns and which are supposed to be verbs. To parse means to break a sentence down into its parts of speech, such as nouns and verbs and so on.

In speech, English-speakers often use prosody, which means rhythm and emphasis in speech, to clarify meaning. Try reading "Squad helps dog bite victim" aloud. Think about how you would make it clear whether the squad was helping the dog or helping the victim. If you put the emphasis on *dog* and ran the words *dog* and *bite* together quickly, it sounds as if the squad helped the victim. However, if you put equal stress on *dog* and *victim,* it would sound as if the squad helped the dog. That's how prosody helps you parse a sentence.

When you speak, you can use prosody to help other people understand what you are trying to say. Unfortunately, prosody is lost when something is written down. Once in a while, someone will use some sort of special typographic treatment, such as italic or boldface type, to suggest how a sentence should be read. You can also use punctuation to make the meaning clear: Squad helps dog-bite victim.

Headlines are typically written in a telegraphic style to make them short and punchy. As a result, they often fail to give you enough clues to enable you to parse them correctly. Ordinary sentences may give you enough clues, but they might give those clues so far along in the sentence that you are initially misled into a false interpretation. To lead someone down the garden path means to mislead them. Linguists use the expression *garden path effect* to describe sentences that initially lead you into an incorrect interpretation. By the time you get to the end of the sentence, you realize that your initial interpretation was wrong. Then, you have to go back to the beginning of the sentence and parse it differently. Here's a classic example of a garden path sentence, from Steven Pinker's *The Language Instinct: How the Mind Creates Language.*[1]

☹   The horse raced past the barn fell.

The first three words in the sentence lead you down the garden path. They make you think that *raced* is the main verb in the sentence. Then, when you see "fell" at the end of the sentence, you realize that your initial interpretation of the sentence makes no sense. You have to go back to the beginning of the sentence and reinterpret the whole thing. Only then do you realize that the sentence means the following:

☺   The horse that was raced past the barn fell.

By definition, a garden path sentence is grammatically correct and can be interpreted in only one way. However, it still qualifies as bad writing because it annoys the reader. People don't like being led down the garden path, and they don't like having to backtrack to figure out what the writer really meant.

Although a garden path sentence is grammatically correct, it is still badly written. Nevertheless, careful attention to some simple grammatical principles can help you avoid sending your readers down the garden path.

The garden path effect often results from the use of a reduced relative clause. In an overzealous attempt to "omit needless words," many people end up omitting relative pronouns: the *wh* words (*which, who,* etc.) or *that.* Using a reduced relative clause will shorten the sentence but may nevertheless end up wasting readers' time by leading them down the garden path.

☹   The cotton clothing is made of is grown in Mississippi.

☺   The cotton that clothing is made of is grown in Mississippi.

☹   Fat people eat accumulates.

☹   The fat that people eat accumulates.

Another way to avoid the garden path effect is to use close punctuation, which means using all of the punctuation that the grammatical structure of the material suggests. Some people complain that all those extra commas make the writing seem "choppy," but close punctuation sometimes prevents the garden path effect:

☹   I kissed Joan and Mary laughed.

☺   I kissed Joan, and Mary laughed.

Garden path sentences are common in English because English words can serve as different parts of speech without being marked as such. Adjectives can serve as nouns, nouns can become verbs, and verbs can become nouns.

☹   The man who hunts ducks out on weekends.

☺   The hunter ducks out on weekends.

☹   The old man the boat.

☺   The elderly people man the boat.

To detect this kind of garden path sentence before it gets published, watch out for adjectives that are being used as nouns and verbs that look like nouns.

When viewed as a whole, a garden path sentence is grammatically correct and unambiguous. However, readers do not view sentences as a whole. They read them one word or phrase at a time. For that reason, garden path sentences should be corrected so that readers will be led in the direction where the writer really wants them to go.

Garden path sentences are easy to find in someone else's writing. They make you stop in confusion and then backtrack to figure out what the writer really meant. It's harder to find garden path sentences in your own writing because you know what you meant!

Reference

1. Pinker S: *The Language Instinct: How the Mind Creates Language.* New York: HarperCollins, 1995.

CHAPTER XXXII

Unscrambling Scrambled Sentences

In Chapter 30, I explained that the worst problem that I've seen in the manuscripts I've edited is nonsensical subject-verb-object relationships. That kind of problem could result from an inability to think clearly. However, it's usually just a result of a careless choice of words. Yet even when writers choose their words carefully, they can get into trouble with word order. Putting a word or phrase in the wrong place can alter the meaning of the sentence. If you fail to pay careful attention to word order, you could end up saying something other than what you meant.

Many writers have problems with word order. These problems generally aren't a matter of taste, or fashion, or dialect. They do make it harder to communicate. If you make mistakes with word order, then your sentences will end up saying something other than what you meant them to say. Of course, if you are writing about simple, commonplace things, your readers may be able to use their background knowledge to figure out what you really meant. But if you are writing about something that they don't already understand, they won't be able to learn about the subject from your writing unless you write well. That means not just using the right words but putting those words in the right order.

Sentence diagramming forces you to think about the subject-verb-object relationships in your sentences. It also forces you to think about modification. What do you really want each of your adjectives and adverbs (and each of your adjectival or adverbial phrases or clauses) to modify? Once you figure out what goes with what, you can use a few rules of thumb to figure out where everything should go in the sentence. First let me explain what modification is and how the various kinds of modifiers work. Then I'll explain the simple rules for solving word order problems.

To modify means to change. A modifier changes the meaning of another word. For example, adjectives modify nouns. Adjectives answer such questions as *what kind, which ones,* and *how many?* In English, adjectives almost always go in front of the noun they are modifying. The exception is the adjective *galore,* as in "we had food galore at Thanksgiving."

Sometimes, a string of words can behave as if it were a single word. If the string doesn't have a subject and a predicate, it is considered a phrase. A phrase that acts as if it were an adjective is called an adjectival phrase. If the word string does include a subject and a predicate, then it is a clause. A clause that acts as if it were an adjective is called an adjectival clause.

Articles (*a, an,* and *the*) are classified as adjectives. The definite article *the* is used to indicate that the noun in question is a particular one that is easily identifiable to the listener. If I say "The book is on the table," it suggests that my listener knows which book and which table I mean. On the other hand, if I say "There is a book on the table," it could be any book, but the listener still knows which table I mean.

The indefinite article *a* has two forms: *a* for use in front of a consonant and *an* for use in front of a vowel sound. Some people use the word *an* in front of some words that begin with the letter *h,* but I think that's because they drop their *h*'s. If you make a breathy sound at the beginning of the word "historic," you should say "a historic" rather than "an historic."

Adjectives can be used to answer the question *which ones?*; to give an opinion about the noun; to describe the size, shape, age, color, origin, of the noun; to describe the material of which the thing is made; and to give some qualifier that is part of the noun. Native English speakers tend to put those adjectives in exactly that order, which is called the Royal Order of Adjectives. The adjectives in the title *My Big Fat Greek Wedding* follow that natural order. So do the adjectives in "her classic little black cocktail dress." Try rearranging the order of those adjectives. Notice how odd it sounds? Putting the adjectives in an unnatural order could create an annoying distraction for the reader.

Sometimes, a single noun will be modified by two adjectives that are more or less equal. Items that are of equal rank are called coordinate. How can you tell whether two adjectives are coordinate? One way is to switch their order and see if they still make sense. Another is to put the coordinating conjunction *and* between them. If it wouldn't sound weird to switch the order or insert the word *and*, separate those adjectives with a comma. (It was a cold, windy day.)

Some adjectives can be made out of other parts of speech. As I explained in Chapter 30, the present and past participles of verbs are often used as adjectives. A noun can also be used to modify another noun, as in the *boy king* or *dog food*. A noun that is used to modify another noun is often called an attributive noun or a noun premodifier. If a particular noun is commonly used as a modifier, the dictionary will generally describe it as "often attrib[utive]." If you are unsure of whether to use a noun or an adjectival form of that noun as a modifier, look carefully at their definitions in the dictionary. After all, a *study* group might not really be a *studious* group.

Adjectives modify nouns. Adverbs are far more versatile. Adverbs can modify verbs, adjectives, other adverbs, and entire clauses or sentences. A phrase that acts as if it were an adverb is called an adverbial phrase. A clause that acts as an adverb is called an adverbial clause. Since adverbs can modify so many different things, you have to think carefully about where the adverbs and adverbial phrases (strings of words that function as an adverb) should go in your sentence. That's especially important when a sentence has more than one verb or has some other verbal element.

Many adverbs end with the suffix *–ly*. Of course, there are also a few adjectives that end in *–ly*, as well as many adverbs that don't end in *–ly*. The word *only* can be either an adverb or an adjective, depending on where it falls in the sentence. That's why changing the position of the word *only* can alter the meaning of a sentence. For example, if I say "Only I ate the pie," it means that nobody else ate pie. If I say, "I only ate the pie," it suggests that I ate but didn't bake the pie. If I say "I ate only the pie," that means I didn't eat anything else.

Adverbs and adverbial phrases can serve several kinds of purposes. They can answer such questions as *where, how often, when,* and *why?* Adverbs can be used to emphasize (he *really* likes this) or to downgrade (I *almost* quit). Just as there is a Royal Order of Adjectives, there's a Royal Order of Adverbs: manner, place, frequency, time, and purpose.

☺   He surreptitiously goes downtown every weekday morning to buy donuts.

Of course, it's a bit awkward to have so many adverbial elements in a row. You can break them up by putting some of them at the beginning of the sentence, even if that means disrupting the Royal Order of Adverbs:

☺   Every weekday morning, he surreptitiously goes downtown to buy donuts.

In English, we usually make a clear distinction between adjectives and adverbs. In German, however, the distinction isn't clear. The German word for good (*gut*) can be used to mean good or well. In standard English, we don't use *good* as an adverb, although *well* can be used as an adjective meaning healthy.

Prepositions are one of the eight basic parts of speech. Prepositions are function words that are used before nouns, pronouns, or noun phrases to form phrases that act as modifiers. There are more than 100 prepositions in English. Commonly used prepositions include *in, on, off, under, over, beside, before, after, with, without,* and *through.* Prepositional phrases can be adjectival or adverbial. Unfortunately, if you put a prepositional phrase in the wrong place, it can modify the wrong thing. Some prepositional phrases can even switch from being adjectival to being adverbial, or vice versa.

When you are reviewing your own writing or editing someone else's, look for the prepositional phrases in each sentence. Try to figure out what each prepositional phrase is supposed to modify. A prepositional phrase that has been put in the wrong place could end up modifying the wrong thing. In particular, a prepositional phrase that follows a noun will sound as if it is intended to modify that noun, whether you want it to or not. Consider this sentence:

☹   This product is available from Acme Distributors in 10-mL bottles.

Really? How did they get the distributors into such tiny bottles?

☺   This product is available in 10-mL bottles from Acme Distributors.

The misplaced prepositional phrase in that example is awkward, but ordinary readers will figure out the meaning of the sentence anyway. That's because they have enough commonsense knowledge to know that products, not distributors, are found in tiny bottles.

Misplaced modifiers may force your readers to take an extra fraction of a second to figure out what you meant; but as long as you are writing about commonplace things, they can usually use their common sense to figure it out. Unfortunately, if you are writing about something that isn't commonplace, your reader may not be able to figure out what you meant to say. In other words, if you write badly, your readers will be able to use their prior knowledge to decipher statements about things they already know, but they might not be able to learn much from what you've written.

Even if a phrase is clearly adverbial, it can still modify the wrong thing if you put it in the wrong place. That's because adverbs are so versatile. They can modify almost anything. To see how much trouble even a clearly adverbial phrase can cause if it's put in the wrong place, look at the following sentence, which I read in a newspaper article:

☹   She decided to stop having sex after going to church.

From other sentences in the article, I knew that the writer really meant that the woman had taken a vow of chastity. Unfortunately, the way the sentence was phrased made it sound as if she was still sexually active, just "never on a Sunday." The prepositional phrase *after going to church* specifies when something happened. It is therefore clearly adverbial because adverbs say when something happened. However, the rest of this sentence contains three verbal elements: two verbs (one in the past tense and one infinitive) and a participial phrase (*going* is a present participle). If you put the adverbial phrase after the participial phrase, it sounds as if you want it to modify the gerund phrase. If you want the adverbial phrase to modify the main verb in the sentence, either put it directly after that verb or put it at the beginning of the sentence.

☺   She decided, after going to church, to stop having sex.

☺   After going to church, she decided to stop having sex.

Although both of these revised sentences are better than the original because they clarify which verb the adverbial phrase is modifying, they still leave something to be desired. They simply explain *when* she made a decision, not *why* she made it or how well she followed through with it. Did she stop having sex, or did she merely *decide* to stop? There's a difference.

Adverbs can be found in many different places within a sentence. Sometimes, if an adverb is placed between two verbs, it's not clear which of the verbs the adverb is supposed to modify. That problem is called a squinting adverb. Notice that in the following sentence, it's unclear whether *often* is intended to modify *exercise* or *are*:

☹   People who exercise often are thin.

This problem can easily be solved by moving the adverb:

☺   People who often exercise are thin.

☺   People who exercise are often thin.

Prepositional phrases aren't the only kind of phrase that can end up in the wrong place in the sentence. Participial phrases are also often misplaced. Sometimes, they are even left to dangle. Most people have heard of dangling participles, but few people seem to know what a participle is, or what it means if a participle dangles.

Participial phrases are phrases that contain a participle and a complement, along with any associated modifiers. As I explained in Chapter 30, the present participle is formed by adding -ing to the end of a verb. The present participle is used to express the progressive aspect (ongoing action) of a verb. Past participles are often formed by adding -ed or -en to a verb and are used to express the perfect aspect (completed action) of a verb. A participle is dangling if its subject is missing from the sentence.

☹ Walking to school today, my book fell in the mud.

Who was walking? I was walking, not the book. Yet the word *I* does not appear in the sentence. Thus, the participle *walking* is dangling. To solve the grammatical problem, you can turn that introductory participial phrase into an adverbial clause: add the participle's subject, plus the auxiliary verb and a subordinating conjunction:

☺ *While I was* walking to school today, my book fell in the mud.

The sentence is now grammatically correct, but it doesn't really tell the whole story. Here's a solution that is more satisfying. Not only does it connect the participle to the correct noun, it explains why the book fell into the mud, and who was responsible.

☺ While walking to school today, I accidentally dropped my book in the mud.

Of course, some participial phrases aren't really dangling, they're simply misplaced. Consider this example, which came from an old edition of the *American Medical Association Manual of Style*:

☹ Organized into 13 chapters, the reader of this book will benefit from an extensive appendix.

Normal people know that books, not readers of books, are organized into chapters. Thus, a normal person would be able to figure out what the writer intended this sentence to mean. However, when you are writing about complicated, unfamiliar subjects, your readers might not always be able to use their background knowledge to compensate for that kind of sloppiness.

The AMA's original suggestion for fixing this sentence was to make it clear that the book, not the reader, is organized into chapters. But why mention the reader at all? Why use the word *organized*?

☺ The book has 13 chapters and an extensive appendix.

Another common grammatical problem is the use of a participial phrase as if it were an absolute phrase. An absolute phrase isn't intended to modify something within the sentence, or even something that's missing from the sentence. An absolute phrase modifies the sentence as a whole, or perhaps an entire independent clause.

An absolute phrase normally contains a noun or pronoun and a participle and perhaps some modifiers.

☺ His muscles quivering, the sprinter crouched on the starting blocks.

If the participle is from a linking verb, it is sometimes omitted.

☺ His face white with rage, the writer looked at all of the changes the arbitrary, mean-spirited editor made in his flawless manuscript.

An absolute phrase contains a noun or pronoun that serves as the subject for the participle. In contrast, a participial phrase doesn't contain a subject for the participle. If you put a participial phrase at the beginning of a sentence, it will modify the subject of the sentence.

☺ Blushing in embarrassment, he realized that the manuscript he submitted was riddled with errors in syntax.

Unfortunately, the participial phrase will modify that subject, whether you want it to or not. Here's an example of a participial phrase (*based* is a past participle) that is incorrectly being used as if it were an absolute phrase:

☹ Based on my experience, near-sighted people make excellent proofreaders.

Based on my experience doesn't qualify as an absolute phrase. Instead, it sounds as if it is an adjectival phrase modifying the subject, which in this sentence is *people*. However, it makes no sense to say that near-sighted people are "based on my experience." If you want to modify the entire sentence, you might use a prepositional phrase, such as in the following example.

☺ In my opinion, near-sighted people make excellent proofreaders.

You could also make *I* the subject of the sentence.

☺   I have found that near-sighted people make excellent proofreaders.

Of course, the statement that near-sighted people make excellent proofreaders is clearly an opinion. If the reader can tell from context that the opinion is yours, you might just say it like this:

☺   Near-sighted people make excellent proofreaders.

Some of the people who think that grammar shouldn't be taught in grammar school think that the proponents of grammar instruction "link 'correct' grammar to propriety and even morality." Some even go so far as to say that "Grammar is politics by other means." Yet when I, as a technical editor, correct writers' dangling participles and move their prepositional phrases around, I'm not trying to dominate anyone or to impose my culture or political views or to police anyone's morals. My goal is to make the authors' sentences say exactly what the authors intended them to say, so that readers can understand what the writers are trying to convey. My job would be much easier if the writers had learned about modifier placement in seventh grade.

After I teach people how to diagram a sentence and teach them a few simple rules about word order, their writing tends to improve dramatically. They start putting their prepositional phrases in the right places. Their adverbs stop squinting. They stop dangling their participles. Their writing becomes far more understandable. These principles have nothing to do with propriety or social class or morality, but they have a huge effect on clarity. These principles are easy to learn if they are directly taught, so why have our schools stopped teaching them?

CHAPTER XXXIII

Making Big Sentences
From Little Sentences, and Vice Versa

In my career as an editor, I've seen a lot of bad writing that came from educated people. Some of it came from people who claimed that they had a bachelor's degree or even a master's degree in English. From what I can tell, bad writing results either from sloppy thinking or from sloppy sentence structure—or perhaps from some combination of the two. I'm not even sure that sloppy sentence structure and sloppy thinking are two separate problems. I believe that grammar lessons can help people clarify their thoughts as well as their writing.

Many of the self-proclaimed experts on how to teach writing claim that grammar lessons are not only a waste of time but are probably harmful. What some of these authorities recommend instead is an exercise that they call sentence combining. The teacher generates a set of simple, "kernel" sentences and then has the student combine those short sentences into a long, complicated sentence. But why not teach students the principles of sentence structure directly? Then, the students can analyze their own sentences and figure out how to rearrange the pieces to say exactly what they mean.

Sentence combining is supposedly fun, presumably because it is a game with no rules. Yet every single game that normal human beings think is fun has rules. Football has rules. Poker has rules. Video games have rules that the computer ruthlessly enforces. Part of the fun of a game is figuring out a strategy that doesn't violate the rules. So why should I believe that learning the rules of grammar would ruin the fun of writing? People don't necessarily object to rules, per se. What they hate is to be punished unpredictably for violating rules that were never properly explained.

Sentence combining seems to me to be just another application of an educational theory called constructivism. Years ago, some psychologists argued that learning is a process in which people actively try to make sense out of their perceptions and experiences. That idea makes sense to me, but some educators have extended the idea to mean that children cannot learn anything worthwhile from direct instruction. Supposedly, children must discover all human knowledge for themselves from their own, first-hand experiences rather than from reading books or having things explained to them by grownups. In other words, some educators think that adults shouldn't directly teach children anything. Instead, they think that adults should simply "facilitate" while the next generation wastes time reinventing the wheel.

Rather than having children waste time puzzling out how to combine the teacher's "kernel" sentences, why not just teach children the names for the various parts of a sentence and the rules for putting those parts together? Then students can apply the rules when they want to make big sentences out of little sentences or little sentences out of big ones. The underlying concepts really aren't difficult. I learned them in seventh grade. However, many college graduates and even some English majors write badly because they have never learned these concepts or don't understand how to apply them.

It's far easier to combine small sentences into larger yet still clear and meaningful sentences if you know what a phrase is and what a clause is and how conjunctions work. Good writers know how to use conjunctions, relative pronouns, and conjunctive adverbs. Bad writers do not. As a result, bad writers make annoying errors of parallel structure. Bad writers also often fail to distinguish between restrictive and nonrestrictive clauses. As a result, many of their sentences are confusing or misleading.

If you doubt that proper use of conjunctions is important for logical writing, consider this: most of the words that are used as logical operators in computer programming—such words as *and, or, if,* and *then*—are actually conjunctions. (*Not* is an adverb.)

In the rest of this chapter, I'll explain how to recognize and fix some of the problems of sentence structure that are common in bad writing. I'll use Reed-Kellogg diagrams to help you see the structure of the sentences.

A phrase is a string of words that can act as if it were a single word, such as a noun, an adjective, or an adverb. A clause is a string of words that contains a subject and a predicate but is part of a larger sentence. Some kinds of clauses can act as if they were adverbs. Others act as if they were adjectives.

A conjunction is a word that connects words, phrases, clauses, or sentences. Coordinating conjunctions (*and, or, but, nor, for, yet, so*) are used to connect things that have equal importance within the sentence. (Note that *but* can also be used as a preposition or an adverb.) Correlative conjunctions also connect things of equal importance within the sentence, but they work in pairs (*either...or, not only...but also, neither...nor, both...and, whether... or, just as...so*).

The correlating conjunctions are often used to link nouns or noun phrases. When you use the conjunction *and* to make a compound subject, the verb in the predicate should be plural, even if all of the nouns in the compound subject are singular:

☺ Jack and Jill are going up the hill.

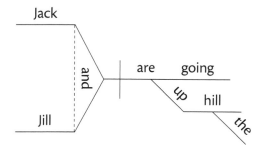

When you use *or* or *either...or* to make a compound subject, then the verb will agree in person and number with the last element in the list:

☺ Jack or Jill is going up the hill.

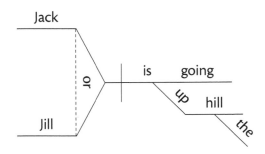

You can also use coordinating conjunctions to make compound predicates as well as compound subjects. A compound subject contains two or more nouns. A compound predicate contains two or more verb phrases. The following example has two nouns and two verb phrases:

☺ Jack and Jill went up the hill and got a pail of water.

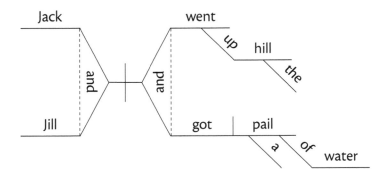

Notice that both the subject and the predicate of the sentence are split into two branches. Notice also that there are no commas in that sentence. There's no comma in the compound subject because it has only two branches. There's no comma in the compound predicate because it, too, has only two branches. Nor would you use a comma to separate the subject from the predicate.

In contrast, I would use commas in a list of three or more items:

☺ Jack, Jill, and Keisha ate lunch together.

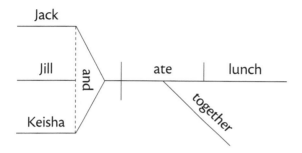

The comma before *and Keisha* is called the serial comma. A serial comma (or Oxford comma or Harvard comma) is the comma before the coordinating conjunction before the last item in a list of three or more items. Some style guides tell you to use the serial comma. Others tell you not to use it. I prefer to use the serial comma because it helps to clarify sentence structure. The publishing companies where I've worked have used close punctuation, which means using punctuation exactly according to the structure of the sentence. As a result, they've all required the use of a serial comma.

I also use a comma before a coordinating conjunction that connects two independent clauses, which are clauses that could stand on their own as sentences. In close punctuation, you do this even if the clauses are short:

☺ Jack tripped, and Jill stumbled.

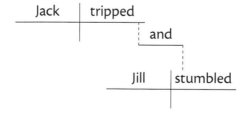

Notice that in the following sentence, the first clause has a compound predicate:

☺   Jack fell down and broke his crown, and Jill came tumbling after.

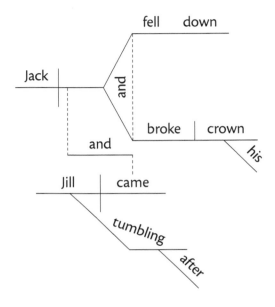

The use of coordinating conjunctions raises a problem called parallel structure. If two or more items in a sentence are of equal rank, they generally should be in the same grammatical form. In other words, look for the coordinating conjunctions in your sentences. If those coordinating conjunctions are connecting words and phrases, try to make those words and phrases match each other. Look at the following example:

☹   He likes bicycling, canoeing, and to go on hikes.
☺   He likes bicycling, canoeing, and hiking.

Why have two gerunds (-ing nouns) and an infinitive phrase (to go…) when you could have three gerunds? There's no reason to make them different. Your reader's brain will be able to process this sentence more quickly and easily if all of the coordinate elements are in the same grammatical form.

Learning how to diagram sentences really helps you understand parallel structure. That's because the things that are parallel in the sentence often appear on parallel lines in the diagram. Here's a diagram that shows some parallel direct objects.

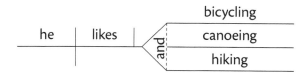

Here's a sentence with parallel modifiers: Lee types slowly but accurately. Here's how it would be diagrammed:

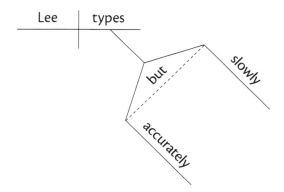

I think about parallel structure whenever I see any of the following:
- Sentence elements that are joined with a coordinating conjunction
- Items that are being listed, either within a sentence or in bulleted lists or tables
- Items linked by correlative conjunctions
- Verbs of being
- Comparisons

Verbs of being include the various forms of the verb *to be* (am, is, are, was, were, etc.). It's sometimes nice to put the things that are being connected by a verb of being in parallel form:

☺   What you see is what you get.

☺   Seeing is believing.

When I see correlative conjunctions, I worry about the placement of prepositions, as well as about parallel structure.

☹   Injustice can result **from** either stupidity or **from** malice.

☺   Injustice can result either **from** stupidity or **from** malice.

☺   Injustice can result **from** either stupidity or malice.

Note that *either* always goes with *or* and *neither* always goes with *nor.* You can use these correlative conjunctions to link more than two elements:

☺   Neither snow nor rain nor heat nor gloom of night stays these couriers from the swift completion of their appointed rounds.

Comparisons often involve the conjunction *than,* the construction *as… as,* or a verb of being. These sentences can be marred by faulty parallel structure and/or faulty comparison. Faulty parallel structure means that the items that are being compared are not in the same grammatical form. Faulty comparison means that the items being compared are not what the writer really meant to compare.

Here's a good example of a faulty comparison that involves a verb of being. Notice how the use of a demonstrative pronoun (*those*) improves the sentence:

☹   The results of this study are similar to the Nurses' Health Study.

☺   The results of this study are similar to the results of the Nurses' Health Study.

☺   The results of this study are similar to those of the Nurses' Health Study.

Faulty comparisons often result from an elliptical construction, which means that words have been left out of the sentence.

> Ambiguous: He is closer to his father than his mother.
> Clear: He is closer to his father than **to** his mother.
> Clear: He is closer to his father than his mother **is**.

Be particularly alert for the word *than*. You might want to search your document electronically for all instances of *than*. Look at the elements that are being compared by *than*. Watch out for faulty parallel structure and faulty comparisons. Also consider moving the items that are being compared as close as possible to the word *than*:

☺ You can catch more flies with honey than you can catch with vinegar.

☺ You can catch more flies with honey than with vinegar.

To find other comparisons, search for the character string *compar,* which will turn up all instances of the words *compare, compared,* and *comparison.* Note that "compared with" phrases are adjectival; thus, they will try to modify whatever noun they directly follow. Sometimes it is better to say "than in" as opposed to "compared with."

☹ Heartworm infection is more common in dogs compared with cats.

☺ Heartworm infection is more common in dogs than in cats

The coordinating conjunctions connect two or more things that have equal rank within the sentence. In contrast, a subordinating conjunction joins a subordinate clause to a main clause. Words that can be used as subordinating conjunctions in English include *if, though, although, because, when, while, after, before.* A relative pronoun can also be used to connect a subordinate clause to a main clause. Examples include *who/whom, whoever/whomever, whose, that,* and *which.* Sometimes, *what, when,* and *where* can function as relative pronouns. The relative pronoun serves as the subject of the relative clause.

A subordinate clause contains a subject and a predicate but can't stand on its own as a sentence. In the following examples of subordinate clauses, I've used an ellipsis (the three periods that indicate that something has been omitted) to show that the subordinate clause isn't a complete sentence:

- Because of the terrible weather ...
- If I were king of the forest ...
- ..., which is ridiculous.

Some people are afraid to start a sentence with the word *because.* Perhaps it's because they've been punished for starting a sentence with *and, or,* or *but* (even though good writers have been doing that since Anglo-Saxon days.) However, there's absolutely no reason to avoid putting a subordinating conjunction at the beginning of a sentence. If you can put *if* at the beginning of a sentence, you can put *because* at the beginning of a sentence. They're both subordinating conjunctions.

I always use a comma to set off an introductory clause, just as I'd use a comma to set off an introductory adverb or phrase.

☺   Because the weather was bad, the picnic was postponed.

But what if the subordinate clause occurs inside the sentence or at the end of the sentence? Should it be set off with commas? The answer to that question depends on whether the subordinate clause is restrictive or nonrestrictive. (British grammarians refer to them as defining or nondefining subordinate clauses.)

Relative clauses are adjectival. Like adjectives, they modify nouns. Adjectives answer such questions as "which ones?" or "what are they like?" If a relative clause is specifying which ones, it is restrictive (or defining). The clauses that begin with the relative pronoun *that* are always restrictive. Restrictive clauses are **not** set off from the sentence with commas.

☺   He threw away the potatoes <u>that were rotten</u>. (In other words, some of the potatoes might not have been rotten. He threw away only the ones that were rotten. The underlined relative clause is restrictive because it implies that the sentence is about only the rotten potatoes.)

If a relative clause is just saying what something is like, not restricting the action to a subset, then it is nonrestrictive (nondefining). I think of nonrestrictive clauses as parenthetical elements. They should be set off from the rest of the sentence with punctuation. You can use a comma before and after the relative clause. You can also use dashes or parentheses instead of commas.

☺ He threw away the potatoes, <u>which were rotten</u>. (The relative clause tells you something about what the potatoes were like, but it doesn't specify which ones were thrown out. The underlined phrase is therefore nonrestrictive. It's not restricting the action to a subset of the potatoes.)

If you want to be wishy-washy, you can use *which* without a comma. Then, it won't be clear whether you want it to be restrictive or nonrestrictive.

☹ I oppose death sentences which are inhumane.

Does this mean that you oppose all use of the death penalty, or only death sentences that strike you as inhumane? If you oppose the death penalty as a matter of principle, you'd say "I oppose death sentences, which are inhumane." If you think that only some death sentences are inhumane, you'd say, "I oppose death sentences that are inhumane." Using *which* with no comma enables you to weasel out of taking a stand. I don't trust people who use *which* with no comma.

If the relative clause refers to one or more human beings, you should probably use *who* or *whom* instead of *which* or *that*.

☹ Everyone that attends will get credit.
☺ Everyone who attends will get credit.

Note that *whose* is the possessive form of *what*, as well as *who*. You can use *whose* to explain that something belongs to places, things, or ideas, as well as to persons.

☺ No one can resist an idea whose time has come.

Sometimes, you can collapse a nonrestrictive relative clause into an appositive, which is a noun or noun phrase that simply restates another noun.

- ☺ Neil Armstrong, who was the first person to set foot on the moon, was born in Wapakoneta, Ohio.
- ☺ Neil Armstrong, the first person to set foot on the moon, was born in Wapakoneta, Ohio.

Be careful about using the word *or* to introduce an appositive. An appositive restates another noun; but if you use *or* to introduce the appositive, it may look as if you are talking about two separate things.

- ☹ *Streptococcus pneumoniae* or pneumococcus is a common cause of ear infections.
- ☺ *Streptococcus pneumoniae*, or pneumococcus, is a common cause of ear infections.
- ☺ *Streptococcus pneumoniae*, which is also called the pneumococcus, is a common cause of ear infections.

If you are talking about things that your audience already understands, then you can get away with that kind of sloppiness. But if your audience doesn't already know that *Streptococcus pneumoniae* is also called pneumococcus, they could end up totally confused.

Adverbial clauses can also be restrictive or nonrestrictive. A restrictive adverbial clause limits the action of the main clause and is not set off by commas:

- ☺ I take antihistamine when the ragweed pollen count is high. (The "when" clause is restrictive because it specifies that the action is taking place at a particular time.)

Occasionally, you may want to put a comma before a restrictive adverbial phrase, just to make it clear which verb is being modified. Here's a classic example:

- ☺ He didn't run, because he was afraid. (He was too afraid to run.)
- ☺ He didn't run because he was afraid. (He ran, but for some other reason.)

However, it would be better to rewrite the sentence so that its meaning is unmistakable:

☺ He didn't run; he was too afraid to run.

☺ He ran, even though he was not afraid.

A nonrestrictive adverbial clause provides some other information about the main clause but doesn't change the meaning of the main clause:

☺ He tried to get more sleep, as his doctor recommended.

Sentence adverbs also have no effect on the meaning of the main clause. A sentence adverb is a disjunct, which means that it doesn't actually modify anything in the sentence. In English, sentence adverbs are used to express the speaker or writer's opinion about what the sentence is saying. If you know how to use sentence adverbs, you can turn a complicated sentence into a simpler sentence. Consider the following sentence:

☺ It is obvious to me that grammar lessons are important.

Here's how that sentence looks in a Reed-Kellogg diagram:

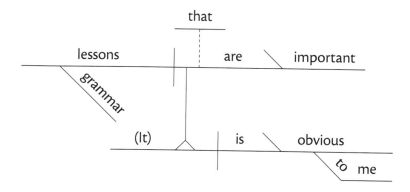

I can collapse the meaning of that main clause (*it is obvious to me that*) into a single word, the sentence adverb *obviously*. I can then turn the subordinate clause into a main clause, modified by the sentence adverb:

☺ Obviously, grammar lessons are important.

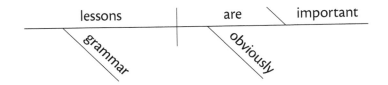

You can even move the sentence adverb inside the sentence:

☺   Grammar lessons are obviously important.

Which version would you rather read? I think most people would prefer the third one.

Obviously isn't really modifying anything in that sentence. Instead, *obviously* expresses my opinion about what the sentence is saying.

Sentence adverbs have been used in English since the 14th century. Words like *fortunately, unfortunately, clearly, evidently, curiously,* and so on have been used as sentence adverbs. The one sentence adverb that some grammarians complain about is *hopefully.* Curiously, they complain about the use of *hopefully* but not about the use of *curiously.*

A sentence adverb expresses a feeling or opinion about the content of the rest of the sentence. When you are speaking or writing, it's important to keep in mind that other people might not share that opinion. Something that seems obvious to you might not be obvious to someone else. Similarly, something that is fortunate for you might not be fortunate for someone else. Readers should also realize that sentence adverbs generally express the speaker or writer's opinions, and nothing more. What seems obvious to one person might not even be true.

Sentence adverbs are not the only kind of adverb that you can find at the beginning of a sentence. Sometimes, you can find an adjunctive adverb (i.e., one that does modify something in the sentence). In Chapter 34, I'll discuss another kind of adverb that is often found at the beginning of a clause or sentence: conjunctive adverbs, which are used to link clauses and sentences to one another. As I'll explain, careful use of pronouns and conjunctive adverbs can help you write coherently. Even if each of your sentences is meaningful, your writing won't make sense unless your sentences work together like the members of a relay race team.

CHAPTER XXXIV

Unity and Coherence in Paragraphs

fter I teach writers how to solve their problems with word choice and sentence structure, I teach them how to solve their problems with paragraph structure. Even if you choose the right words and put them together into grammatical sentences, your writing will still be bad if the sentences in each of your paragraphs don't work well as a team.

The effects that I strive for in writing and revising paragraphs are unity and coherence. By unity, I mean that the paragraph contains no irrelevant details. By coherence, I mean that the reader can easily follow my train of thought. A good paragraph is like a good relay race team. Each sentence in a paragraph is like an individual runner. Each member of the team runs one leg of the race and then hands the baton smoothly and securely to the next runner. To get the paragraphs in your sentences to work well together, you have to think about how they relate to each other. Once you have eliminated the irrelevant details and put your thoughts in a logical order, you can use some simple grammatical tricks to clarify how these sentences relate to each other.

There are many good ways to structure a paragraph. One way is to use a topic sentence to sum up the main message that you want the paragraph to convey. Then you can add other sentences to support that topic sentence or to handle objections to it. The topic sentence is often the first or last sentence in the paragraph. The topic sentence could represent the conclusion of an argument, while the other sentences represent the premises that support that conclusion. The topic sentence could express a general principle, while the other sentences provide specific examples. The topic sentence could also express an overarching concept, while the other sentences provide definitions or clarifications. To maintain unity within the paragraph, you may wish to remove anything that doesn't relate to that topic sentence.

Notice that the previous paragraph doesn't have a topic sentence. The first three sentences serve as a topic sentence. I used repeated elements (the word *way* and the term *topic sentence*) to tie them together. The other sentences are connected by the repeated phrase *topic sentence,* as well as by repetition of sentence structure. Notice also the repetition in the verbs: "could represent, could express, could also express." Don't be afraid to use repeated elements to tie the sentences in a paragraph together, and don't be afraid to use the same sentence structure repeatedly if the ideas are parallel.

I don't generally worry about whether my paragraphs have a topic sentence. My main concern is that my paragraphs are often too long. I try to keep my paragraphs short enough that I can see the entire paragraph at once on my computer screen, even if the text is fairly large. The breaks between paragraphs give people a bit of breathing room so that they can process what they've just read. To keep my paragraphs short enough to fit on one computer screen, I have to eliminate needless words as well as irrelevant sentences. I also look for opportunities to break larger paragraphs into smaller paragraphs. If you tend to write long paragraphs, the discipline of keeping your paragraphs short will probably also help you achieve unity in your paragraphs.

The advice to repeat words may strike some people as strange. Also, some English textbooks specifically tell you to avoid monotonous sentence structure, which suggests that it's bad to use the same sentence structure repeatedly. Personally, I don't worry about monotony of sentence structure. When I fix all of the inevitable problems with modifier placement and parallel structure, the problem of monotonous sentence structure goes away on its own.

English textbooks also warn people to avoid "primer language," by which they mean a relentless series of short, simple sentences. If your writing sounds too much like primer language, then you need to learn how to use subordinating conjunctions and relative clauses. You might also benefit from learning how to use conjunctive adverbs. I have the opposite problem. If left to my own devices, I'd write long, overly complicated sentences. I force myself to break my thoughts down into shorter, simpler sentences. To alert me that I'm writing sentences that are too long and complicated, I use the Flesch-Kincaid Grade Level score and the Flesch Reading Ease score in my word processor's spell checker. I tried to keep this book at a ninth- or tenth-grade level.

A conjunctive adverb is an adverb that serves as a conjunction —it joins two clauses or sentences. Conjunctive adverbs can express similarity (*likewise*) or contrast (*however, nevertheless*). Some conjunctive adverbs can be used to express timing (*afterward, meanwhile, finally*). Conjunctive adverbs can also be used to express cause-and-effect relationships (*consequently*) or logical relationships (*therefore*). My younger sister, who is respected as a scientist and as a writer, posted an extensive list of conjunctive adverbs next to her desk. This list helped her think about how to connect the sentences in her writing.

To use a conjunctive adverb or conjunctive adverbial phrase correctly, you must first think clearly about the relationship between the sentences that you wish to connect. For example, you can use the conjunctive adverbial phrase *for example* to indicate that you are about to give specific examples of some general principle that you have just stated. The word *however* is used to introduce a statement that conflicts with or seems to contradict something else that you have just said. *Therefore* is used to mark the conclusion of an argument, after the premises that support that conclusion have already been stated. You can also use the words *first, second, third* and so on as conjunctive adverbs to show how the minor sentences in a paragraph relate to the topic sentence:

☺   There are three reasons why we need to buy a new computer. First, our current computer is slow. Second, …

You can also use words like *first, second,* and so on as adjectives within the sentences of a paragraph for the same purpose.

☺   The first rule of Fight Club is that you don't talk about Fight Club. The second rule of Fight Club is that you do not talk about Fight Club.

I think it's important for people to know the difference between a conjunctive adverb and a sentence adverb. Conjunctive adverbs connect a clause or sentence to another clause or sentence. In contrast, sentence adverbs (e.g., *obviously, evidently, fortunately*) express the speaker or writer's feelings about the rest of the sentence, as I explained in Chapter 33. In other words, these two different kinds of adverbs perform completely different functions, even though they both can either be used at the beginning of the sentence or positioned so that they look as if they are modifying the main verb of the sentence.

☺   It's raining. <u>Fortunately</u>, I brought my umbrella. (*Fortunately* is a sentence adverb.)
☺   It's raining. It was <u>obviously</u> a good idea to bring my umbrella. (*Obviously* is a sentence adverb.)
☺   It's sunny right now. <u>However</u>, it will rain this afternoon. (*However* is a conjunctive adverb.)
☺   It will rain this afternoon. It will <u>therefore</u> be a good idea to bring an umbrella. (*Therefore* is a conjunctive adverb.)

It's easy to punctuate conjunctive adverbs and conjunctive adverbial phrases. If the conjunctive adverb or adverbial phrase is at the beginning of a sentence, put a comma after it.

☺   His alarm clock failed. <u>Nevertheless</u>, he made it to work on time.

If a conjunctive adverb or adverbial phrase appears at the beginning of an independent clause within a sentence, put a semicolon in front of it and a comma after it:

☺   His alarm clock failed because of the power outage; <u>as a result</u>, he overslept and was late to work.

Pronouns can also help show the connections between sentences. Pronouns are one of the eight basic parts of speech in English. A pronoun is a function word that has no meaning of its own. It takes on its meaning from its context. A pronoun stands for some other noun, which is called the antecedent (because it usually appears before the pronoun) or the referent (because the pronoun refers to it). In good writing, the meaning of each pronoun is obvious. I think it's important to deal with pronouns on a paragraph level because the antecedent of a pronoun may occur in an earlier sentence.

☹   A pronoun is a function word that has no meaning of the pronoun's own. The pronoun takes the pronoun's meaning from the pronoun's context.

☺   A pronoun is a function word that has no meaning of its own. It takes its meaning from its context. (Note that the referent for the pronoun and possessive adjectives in the second sentence is in the first sentence.)

To make sure that all of my pronouns have clear referents, I use a computer macro that highlights all of the pronouns and possessive adjectives (*my, your, his, her, its, our, their*) in turquoise. I then go through the document and make sure that the reader can easily tell what each pronoun is supposed to mean. I like to make sure that the antecedent for each pronoun occurs at least once in the paragraph. After I confirm that the antecedent of a pronoun is clear, I remove the highlighting from that word.

A pronoun should match its antecedent in person, gender, number, and case. Person is easy. The first-person pronouns are used to refer to the speaker or writer, the second-person pronouns are used to refer to the person whom the speaker or writer is addressing. Everyone and everything else is in the third person.

Gender is a bit trickier in English. In English, only the singular third-person pronouns are marked for gender. There are three genders: masculine (*he, him, his, himself*), feminine (*she, her, hers, herself*), and neuter (*it, its, itself*). The easiest way to get around problems with the gender of pronouns in English is to convert the antecedent to a plural. Then, you can use some variant of *they* without any trouble. I dealt with the problems related to the gender of pronouns in Chapter 25.

The fact that English third-person pronouns are declined for gender and number makes it easier to identify the antecedent of a pronoun. If you are talking about one woman, one man, and one thing, then the feminine pronouns (*she, her, hers, herself*) will have something to do with the woman. The masculine pronouns (*he, him, his, himself*) will have something to do with the man. The neuter pronouns (*it, its, itself*) will have something to do with the thing. Singular pronouns get confusing if there is more than one possible antecedent of that gender. Plural pronouns aren't marked for gender in English. As a result, there's no gender to give you clues to the identity of the antecedent.

Paying careful attention to the pronouns and conjunctive adverbs helps you achieve unity and coherence within each paragraph. However, unity and coherence are in the mind of the beholder. If you use words and concepts that your readers don't understand, your writing will seem incoherent to them. If they have to stop reading to look up words in a dictionary, then you have failed to achieve unity and coherence.

To achieve unity and coherence in your paragraphs, you will have to think about what your readers already know, and what they will need to learn as they go along. Think about what background information your readers will need to have before they can understand what you are saying. Be sure to provide that information at the right time. Also, whenever you introduce any unfamiliar words, or any words that will be used in an unusual way, be sure to define them. Look those words up in a dictionary to make sure that your definitions are accurate.

Just as the individual sentences within a paragraph must work together as a team to achieve a purpose, the paragraphs must also work together to achieve a common purpose. The writer must think carefully about what that purpose is, and how best to achieve it. In Chapter 35, I'll explain how to approach the work as a whole.

CHAPTER XXXV

Composition

Before you can start planning a piece of writing, you must ask yourself what you want to say, to whom you want to say it, and why you want to say it. The approach you take to writing will depend on your answers to those questions. For example, the approach that you'd take to writing a cookbook would be far different from the approach you'd take to writing a work of science fiction. Even the approach that you'd take to writing a cookbook depends on whether the cookbook is intended for a consumer audience or for students at a culinary institute. In this chapter, I explain the basic approaches that I take toward writing nonfiction.

As I described in Chapter 11, classical authors outlined five canons of persuasive speech: invention, arrangement, style, memory, and delivery. Of these, invention, arrangement, and style are important for writing as well.

Invention meant that one should find out the available means of persuasion. That could mean the arguments that you want to make and the kinds of evidence you could provide to support them. Invention involves study not just of your subject but of your intended audience. In school, you may be asked to write papers that will be read only by your teacher. In those cases, your teacher is the only person in your audience.

In school, you are supposed to learn the research skills that will help you learn about your subject and find the evidence you need to support your arguments. However, I also think it's important to have some ordinary conversations with people who represent your intended audience. Find out what they know about your subject and what they want to know. From them, you can find out what's important and what's likely to be persuasive.

If you are doing a big research project, you may end up taking a lot of notes, to keep track of not only the facts themselves but the information you'll need for footnotes. Back in the old days, I used to use index cards for that purpose. Now I keep my notes in a word processing document and use a citation management program to keep track of the footnotes. That way, I can just copy blocks of text from my notes into the draft of an article, and the citation management program will take care of renumbering and formatting the footnotes. If you decide to do that, make sure that everything you put into your notes document either is in your own words or is clearly marked with quotation marks. Otherwise, you might accidentally commit plagiarism.

The second canon of rhetoric is arrangement, which means selecting and assembling arguments effectively. Many years ago, I taught a teenage friend of mine how to do that when she had to write a paper for English class. Her teacher had asked the students to write a paper about the impact that some American writer had had on American society. My friend chose Dr. Seuss, a choice that intrigued me. My friend was having some trouble figuring out how to organize her paper, so I gave her a few pointers.

I asked my friend if she could express her main point in a single sentence. She could, so I told her to write that down. Then I asked her if she could give me reasons why she had come to the conclusion that she just explained. She gave me several reasons, and I told her to write those down. Then, we went through the various reasons, and I asked her if she could show me evidence to support each of them. She assured me that she could. Then I explained that each of those reasons should be a topic sentence in a paragraph. The supporting statements, along with footnotes, should be the other sentences in those paragraphs. In other words, she had already done so much invention that the next step was arrangement. She could build the outline for her essay by putting those topic sentences in a logical order. To write her essay, all she had to do was flesh out those paragraphs and then add an introduction to explain what she was setting out to prove and a conclusion to sum it all up.

When I was in school, we were taught to use an outline to plan an essay. Unfortunately, that approach doesn't work for many people. I think it's because they want to write the outline from beginning to end, instead of laying out everything they want to say and then organizing it. Many people seem to panic if they have to put their thoughts down in an organized way before they have even had a chance to think things through. They need guidance in how to do that other kind of planning. They need to think about the main point that they want to make and the arguments that they want to make in support of that main point. Once they've thought all those things through, then they can use an outline to put those things in order.

When I have to teach people how to write an essay, I teach them a mind mapping technique. Rather than having them put things in an outline, I have them sum up the main point of the essay in a single sentence. I have them write that sentence in a circle in the center of a piece of paper. Then, I have them summarize each of the supporting arguments in a single sentence. Those sentences go in other circles surrounding that central circle. Underneath each supporting argument, they can make notes about the evidence that they will cite. They can then draw lines to show how the various ideas are connected to each other. Sometimes, it's helpful to use some system of color coding, such as different colors to represent the evidence for and against an idea. After you have mapped out an idea in this way, you can then use the numbers and letters of an outline to indicate the order in which you'll deal with these ideas in your essay.

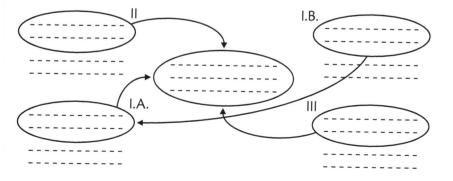

This kind of mind mapping is particularly useful for writing position papers or some other work where you have to draw on many different kinds of support for a main conclusion. In contrast, many kinds of scientific and technical documents follow a predetermined format. Reports of scientific experiments generally follow the AIMRD format: abstract, introduction, methodology, results, discussion. I once helped a friend get started on her thesis for her master of fine arts degree by showing her how to follow this formula, which is seldom used in the fine arts.

My friend's master's thesis was a report of a large performance event with public participation. She'd already organized and staged the event, but she was having trouble writing the report about it. I had her open up a word processing document and showed her how to view it in outline mode. Then I had her type the words Abstract, Introduction, Methodology, Results, and Discussion—each on a separate line. I showed her how to promote them all to Heading 1. Then I showed her how to make subheadings, should she need them. Then I had her tell me what the purpose of the event was. After she explained that, I said, "That goes under introduction." As she told me more about the event, I would say "That goes under Methodology" or "That goes under Results." I showed her how easy it is to move bits of text around in Outline mode. Just a few minutes of that kind of coaching enabled her to overcome her writer's block. She quickly finished writing her thesis and got her diploma.

If you are writing something that is supposed to follow AIMRD format, follow the format religiously. Say everything that you have to say about your methodology in the methodology section. Save everything you have to say about your results for the results section. Use the discussion section to discuss what you learned from the results. This may seem like silly advice, but you'd be surprised how often I've had to move bits of text around to put them under the proper heading when I'm editing AIMRD-format articles.

Style is the third canon of rhetoric, and it is as important to writers as it is to speakers. Style meant presenting the arguments in an appealing way, through word choice, sentence structures, and figures of speech. As I mentioned above, it's important to know your audience. If you have done your homework in invention, you will already know what your intended audience already knows about the subject, and what kinds of evidence will persuade them. If you have done your homework in arrangement, you have already put your arguments in an appealing order. Now you must apply that knowledge in the actual writing.

The points about word choice, sentence structure, and paragraph structure that I have discussed in the preceding chapters are all important to style. Yet they are oddly invisible. If you follow all the rules I spelled out in Chapter 28 through Chapter 34, people won't necessarily notice that you are following the rules. They'll just know that your writing is clear and strong. George Orwell once wrote, "Good prose is like a windowpane." It doesn't call attention to itself. It just gives a clear and undistorted view of its subject. If you violate the rules of sentence structure, your readers won't necessarily realize that you are violating rules. They'll just know that your writing is annoyingly confusing and vague.

Questions of style are particularly important to medical writers. I use a completely different style when writing for medical doctors than I use when writing for a consumer audience. When writing for consumers, I use shorter and simpler words, and shorter and simpler sentences. I also explain some basic biological concepts that medical doctors would already know. Even when I'm writing for a consumer audience, however, I make sure that the scientific facts are presented accurately. In fact, I feel that it's even more important to maintain scientific accuracy when writing for a consumer audience than when writing for a scientific audience. Scientists can easily tell if you don't know what you are talking about, and they won't waste their time on you if they think you are stupid. Consumers, on the other hand, aren't always able to figure out how reliable you are. As a result, they may have to take what you say at face value.

My high school English and history teachers taught me and my classmates how to write papers and how to give speeches. Today, children are learning how to put together multimedia presentations. Fortunately, the approach that I described for how to plan an essay is exactly the same approach that people use for planning Web sites.

Regardless of whether you are building a Web site or just tweeting, the classical canons of persuasion (invention, arrangement, style, memory, and delivery) still matter. In other words, the liberal arts that have been taught for a few thousand years are no less important in the electronic age.

In this book, I have explained why we have such problems in teaching children how to read, and why those problems have been perpetuated for political reasons. I've pointed out that our problems with reading instruction are just the tip of the iceberg. In addition to our epidemics of dyslexia and functional illiteracy, we have a pandemic of general ignorance about important academic subjects, including history, geography, and the natural and social sciences. Even people who have been trained in some of those academic subjects have not necessarily been trained in logic and argumentation. As a result, our political discussions tend to be so ugly and unproductive that democratic decision-making becomes practically impossible. From studying the history of educational policy, I think that that outcome is no accident.

The problems I described in this book stem from widespread failure of our social institutions to serve the general public. These problems can be corrected. However, they won't be corrected until we get a critical mass of education activists who understand the nature of the problems and are willing to work together effectively to solve them.

The main problem I focused on in this book is the curriculum and the overall approach to teaching. I think that we should use intensive phonics to teach children to read and then teach them the liberal arts (grammar, logic, rhetoric, mathematics, geometry, music, and astronomy), along with giving them a strong background in other academic subjects, such as history and the sciences. In Chapter 36, I explain how you can provide an enriched curriculum to your own children and the children in your local school district, as well as how to fill in the gaps in your own education.

CHAPTER XXXVI

Educate Yourself, Educate Others

In the late 1960s, an antipoverty program called VISTA (Volunteers in Service to America) used the following recruitment slogan: "If you're not part of the solution, you're part of the problem." I believe that everyone has an individual responsibility to take charge of his or her own education. Yet at the same time, I believe that everyone has a responsibility to promote good public education. There's no contradiction between those two responsibilities. They are merely the private and public aspects of being a wise and good person. Besides, each of us depends on other people for at least some aspects of our education. My friend Tony East, who is a chemistry professor with 46 patents to his name, insists that no scientist is self-educated. He says that to make a contribution to modern science, you must learn some kinds of things that individuals simply cannot learn on their own.

I think that it's foolish to expect people to learn those things on their own. Nevertheless, advocates of constructivist educational theory claim that children learn only what they discover for themselves. Unfortunately, it took humanity thousands of years to develop the sciences. Nobody could be expected to discover even a sliver of that knowledge through their personal experiences in a single lifetime. Instead of expecting schoolchildren to re-create all human knowledge from the ground up, adults should be providing children a solid foundation upon which they can climb high enough that they can see further than anyone has before. In this chapter I'll talk about a mixture of things that you can do to educate yourself and things that you can do to improve education for other people.

You must take responsibility for your own education, yet you must also learn from others. From what I can see, the biggest danger in self-education is that self-schooled people end up grading their own papers. They end up judging their own knowledge and abilities. Unfortunately, people who have poor intellectual and social skills are often unaware of how poor their skills are. As a result, an uneducated or self-educated person can easily end up ignorant, overconfident, and obnoxious. With a combination of ignorance and arrogance, they can be dangerous to themselves and to others. To avoid this pitfall, you must make sure that your education includes a heavy dose of discipline, which means studying a discipline or two.

By "discipline," I don't mean punishment. I mean training that corrects, molds, or perfects the mental faculties or moral character. When I talk about "a discipline," I mean a field of study in which there are some objective standards for determining what is true or false or what is good or bad. Mathematics is a discipline. So is judo. In mathematics, there are clear rules for figuring out whether an answer is right or wrong. In judo, there are clear rules for deciding who wins a match. When you study a discipline in a social setting, you get clear feedback about whether you are right or wrong about something, and how your skills measure up to other people's. This kind of study teaches you to accept that you are sometimes wrong. It also enables you to base your self-confidence on real achievement, not on vanity.

In a discipline, the students can eventually surpass their master. In fact, that kind of progress is expected in an academic discipline. In contrast, military discipline just involves obedience and subordination. Many kinds of religious discipline likewise involve permanent subordination, often to a guru who plays some sort of "heads-I-win-tails-you-lose" type of dominance game. Both military discipline and that kind of religious discipline are based on the idea that some people are inherently and permanently superior to others for no discernible reason—that all men and women are not created equal in a political sense. Both easily lead to human rights violations and to intellectual stagnation.

If you already have a lot of well-earned self-confidence, I think it's good to study some discipline for which you have no natural talent. That experience will help you develop humility, and it can teach you that the world won't end if you make a mistake or fail at something. Thus, it can help you develop empathy for people who don't have your natural gifts or your educational advantages.

What does it mean to take charge of your own education? It means taking the responsibility to be an active learner. Progressive educators are always talking about active learning, but they typically imagine that active learning must involve some sort of physical activity. Yet active learning is essentially a mental activity. It means engaging mentally with your schoolwork. It means figuring out what you need to learn and working out strategies for learning it. It also means taking advantage of whatever learning opportunities are offered to you. If you are in school, it means actively studying what you are being taught. It also means thinking critically about what you are being taught, instead of being a passive receptacle. In this chapter, I'll provide an overview of how to fill in the gaps in your own education. Once you've done that, you can get involved in improving education for other people. By working together in this way, we can make ourselves wiser and our society more humane.

Whether you are in school or not, you should think about what should go in your curriculum vitae, or lifelong course of study. The first step is to take stock of what you know and what you still have to learn. That's a difficult task because human beings are notoriously bad at judging their level of skill in things like grammar and logic. People with poor skills tend to overestimate their skills. Only after they develop good skills can they start to recognize their mistakes. Thus, in this chapter I am offering a plan that can help you avoid the pitfalls of self-education. It also provides a starting point for improving the curriculum in public schools and even colleges.

You shouldn't have to rediscover all of the world's knowledge from the ground up. Nor should you have to create a curriculum entirely by yourself. Fortunately, you can make use of the materials that have been developed for homeschoolers and for people who are preparing for standardized tests, such as the Scholastic Aptitude Tests (SATs) and the Advanced Placement examinations (AP exams).

I also recommend the Schaum's Outline series, which includes books on many academic subjects.

The SAT prep materials provide a good basic review of many of the things that you should have learned in grade school through high school, such as vocabulary words and mathematical problem-solving. The SAT prep materials do cover a lot of grammatical concepts. However, I think that there's no substitute for getting a good English grammar and composition textbook that explains the underlying linguistic principles of grammar and shows you how to diagram sentences. Once you understand those principles, you can use them to improve your writing, as I've explained in this book. After you have a good grounding in basic grammar, you can start to study logic.

People who have poor skills in logic are seldom aware of how poor their skills are. They may not even realize that there are any objective standards that they are failing to meet. To study logic, you must get some sort of objective feedback about whether your answers are right or wrong. That's why books like the *Schaum's Outline of Logic* are so useful. Not only do they explain the subject, they provide problem sets with answers, so that you can test your comprehension and skills.

In junior and senior high school, the math teachers and the English teachers should work together to make sure that the students develop good skills in logic. Then the English teachers can help the students develop skills in rhetoric. In other words, I think that students should learn grammar in grammar school and should learn logic and rhetoric as soon as their brains are physically mature enough to grasp the underlying principles.

Once you have developed your basic skills through using those materials, you can start studying the materials that were designed to help people pass the AP exams. The AP examinations are the best value in education in the United States today. They were designed to allow high school students to get college credit for doing college-level work. They also represent a cheap and easy way for any high school or family or labor union or church or other group to set up what is essentially its own junior college, just by helping high school students or adults prepare for the AP exams. I feel that the AP exams can even provide a guideline for designing the public school curriculum. If the public schools improved their curricula, then a large percentage of young people would end up doing college-level work in the junior and senior years of high school. The AP examinations are a cheap and easy way for them to get college credit for doing that work.

The high school teachers I talk with are thrilled by this idea. They would love for their students to achieve at a higher level. Most of them are frustrated that their students aren't even prepared to do high school work. To understand this problem, imagine a relay race at a track meet.

In a relay race, each runner is supposed to carry the baton to a specified point and then hand it to the next runner, until the person running the final leg of the race carries the baton across the finish line. Many high school teachers feel that their students weren't adequately prepared in the earlier grades. It's as if the baton is not being delivered to that teacher's starting point. It's as if the teachers must backtrack to where the baton has been left by the previous runner. Then they must struggle to carry the baton as far forward as they can. Meanwhile, many of the batons are so frustrated and alienated that they struggle to escape from the runners' grasp. Punishing the people who run the later legs of the race for losing the race won't solve the underlying problem. To solve this problem, we must improve how the race is being run from the start. That's an important point that is always glossed over in movies like *Stand and Deliver.*

Stand and Deliver tells the story of Jaime Escalante, a Bolivian immigrant who worked as a math teacher at Garfield High School in East Los Angeles, California. When Escalante arrived at Garfield in the early 1970s, the school was performing so poorly that its accreditation was threatened. Escalante himself was threatened with dismissal because he came in too early, stayed too late, and raised funds without permission from the administration. Fortunately, a new principal gave Escalante his full support, and Escalante remade the math program. He started by helping to improve the math curriculum in the junior high school, so that the students would be ready to study higher math when they got to Garfield. In 1982, Escalante made national headlines when 18 of his students passed the AP Calculus examination. They did so well that they were accused of cheating. The Educational Testing Service asked 14 of the students to retake the exam, and all 12 of those who did so passed.

Unfortunately, the movie focuses on Escalante's personality and compresses the events at Garfield to a smaller timeframe, for dramatic purposes. Thus, it fails to convey what I think is the real lesson that we can learn from Escalante's achievement: that an enriched curriculum starting at least in junior high school is crucial to students' success in higher mathematics, and that the teachers in the math program must work like a relay race team.

Of course, the movie cannot show what happened after it was made. Escalante's supportive principal took a sabbatical year to finish his PhD but then was not allowed to go back to Garfield. Escalante was then stripped of his chairmanship of the math department. Thus, he was unable to keep his successful math program from being dismantled. He eventually quit in disgust.

Why did the administration work to undermine Escalante's successful math program? I think it's because it was in East LA, not Beverly Hills. Remember what Rockefeller's General Education Board said back in 1913:

> We shall not try to make these people or any of their children into philosophers or men of learning, or men of science. We have not to raise up from among them authors, editors, poets or men of letters. We shall not search for embryo great artists, painters, musicians nor lawyers, doctors, preachers, politicians, statesmen, of whom we have an ample supply.

In other words, John D. Rockefeller Sr.'s General Education Board felt that the purpose of higher education was merely to produce an adequate supply of professionals and court jesters to serve the likes of John D. Rockefeller Sr. It certainly wasn't to provide higher education and social uplift to the sons and daughters of the working class.

Providing an excellent education to even a small group of working class Latino children could raise expectations throughout the working class, leading the families in other school districts to demand improvements in their schools, too. This could lead to the development of a truly egalitarian educational system, which means that the children of the well-to-do would no longer have unfair advantages. The public schools that successfully serve disadvantaged populations thus set a "bad example" and tend to get suppressed by the educational establishment.

I believe that education should do far more than train people for work. I believe that education should prepare the people to govern themselves, instead of allowing themselves to be governed by a privileged elite. Thus, it's important for individuals to gain more knowledge and skills than they will need just to make a living.

I think that the public school curriculum is going to have to be redesigned from the top down and the bottom up. By "from the top down," I mean that we need to set the goals that we will expect young people to achieve before they leave public school. By "from the bottom up," I mean that we'll have to figure out a roadmap, starting in kindergarten, for enabling children to achieve those goals. For example, I believe that the K-12 art curriculum should provide at least as much instruction in art history as a student would get in an introductory art history class in college. That's really not too much to ask. Likewise, the K-12 music program should give children enough training in music theory to pass the AP music theory exam. I know dozens of singers and instrumentalists who can play from a printed score but who cannot compose anything or improvise—they even have trouble with sight reading and memorization—because they have had no training in music theory.

I believe that the art and music curricula should also be coordinated with each other and with the science and history curricula. Likewise, language arts teachers should coordinate with the history teachers, so that their lessons reinforce each other. For example, children should learn why and how certain kinds of art and music were created in particular historical periods, and the social and political purposes for which art and music have been used. This means gaining an understanding of social institutions and the role of the artist in different historical periods. It means gaining an understanding of how language is related to mathematics; how music is based on acoustical theory; and how art is based on geometry, chemistry, and physics. In other words, the things that students learn in one class should resonate in other classes. Thus, students would learn about the history, purposes, and applications of the things that they are being taught. In short, I'm advocating a highly enriched, highly coordinated curriculum that shows how the arts and sciences and history and politics are interconnected. In other words, children should be able to see that the things they are learning really do matter.

As I explained at the beginning of this book, children must learn to read before they can read to learn. That's why bad methods for teaching reading have been so destructive, and why those methods have been promoted for political reasons. Starting in kindergarten or at least first grade, children need direct instruction in intensive phonics so that they learn to read phonetically. They also need direct instruction in spelling and writing. I don't think that the teaching of reading can be separated from the teaching of writing and spelling. Poor reading and bad spelling are both the result of the use of whole-word methods instead of phonics to teach reading.

One of the reasons why so many teachers were attracted to the "whole language" philosophy was that it meant that they wouldn't have to correct children's mistakes. Fortunately, the development of personal computers means that teachers can now let the computer do much of this correcting. My word processing program has a spell checker and a reasonably good grammar checker. It even has a voice synthesizer. The spell checker indicates whether a word is in its dictionary. The voice synthesizer can read the word aloud, which often helps children recognize that the word they wrote is not the word they meant.

Electronic dictionaries even make it easy to look up how to use and pronounce a word. I teach people to go through their writings backward word by word and look up everything in the dictionary—even the words they think they know. The dictionary gives the spelling, pronunciation, and definitions of each word. It also shows how the word can be used in a sentence. In particular, the dictionary indicates whether a noun can be used as a verb, or whether a particular word can be used as either a conjunction or a preposition. This information can help you solve many problems with sentence structure.

I also think that it's good for children to learn to touch-type. There is software for teaching touch-typing. The main challenge is to get the typist to stop looking at the keys. I see the same problem among piano students. They use their eyes instead of their ears and their sense of body position to guide their hands. Likewise, some beginning trombone players use their eyes to guide their slide hand; as a result, they tend to play out of tune! The solution is simple. Put tape on the computer keys so that the typist cannot read the letters on the keys, and have the musician practice blindfolded.

Once children can read and write fluently, they need to expand their vocabularies and learn lots and lots of basic facts about the world. This should happen in school, but it should also happen outside of school and beyond school. The rise of the homeschooling movement and the Internet means that people have an incredible wealth of options for self-education, at least if they can already read.

Children should be encouraged to read more and better books. They need to get in the habit of looking up unfamiliar words in the dictionary, unfamiliar place names in an atlas, and unfamiliar historical persons on the Internet. In fact, they can look up all of these things online if they aren't too distractible. All of this is solid advice for continuing education for adults as well. Read books about science and history and politics, and especially books about the history and politics of science.

It's hard to understand serious books or even the stories on the television news if you don't know the meanings of words and the locations of cities and countries and other basic facts about the world. There's no substitute for knowing who's who and what's what and what happened where and when it happened. These are the kinds of facts that used to be drilled into children's heads in kindergarten through eighth grade. This kind of knowledge will help you make sense out of what you see and hear and read. Knowing who did what—and when and where they did it—is the first step toward figuring out *why* people do things. If you have no working model of why people behave as they do, then you will have no hope of playing a meaningful role in shaping your own future or that of your society. In grammatical terms, you will be an object rather than a subject.

How can we get children to engage in learning these things? I think we have to alter the social environment in our schools. The first step is to stop the bullying that targets the smart kids and that persuades everyone else to disengage from academic interests. Educators should also think about how to make use of a powerful force that they have systematically ignored: the positive influences that older children can have on younger children. Children would much rather learn from other children than from adults. Children are particularly interested in impressing children who are a few years older than they are. The traditional one-room schoolhouse let the older children help the younger ones. The strict age-segregation that we have in a typical school strikes me as unnatural and infantilizing.

I would like to see as many students as possible pass as many AP exams as possible. To make that happen, we have to improve the K-10 education so that most students will be prepared to take the AP classes in their junior and senior years of high school. To use a sports analogy, the K-10 grades should be regarded as a farm team for the AP program. If schools did a good job in K-10, then many students could get one or even two years' worth of college education by the time they leave high school.

The AP examinations are a worthwhile target, but aiming for those targets will be beneficial even for students who decide not to take the exams. That's because the entire curriculum will have to be enriched to enable the average student to be able to do advanced placement work in high school.

One of the best-kept secrets in American education is that you can take the AP examinations without necessarily having taken an AP class in school. Thus, even adults who have left high school can take charge of their own education by preparing to take AP exams. (To get college credit for some of the AP science courses, you have to do laboratory work and submit the laboratory notebook to your college.) Even if you decide not to take an AP exam, you can learn a lot of important lessons from reading the materials that have been published to help kids prep for that exam.

Which AP classes should students take? At the very least, we should be preparing the main stream of high school students to pass the AP exam in English Language and Composition and the one for United States History. I think that students should also prepare to take one of the AP courses in a foreign language, such Spanish or Chinese. That means starting foreign language instruction in kindergarten. Given the number of Christian high schools and Christian home schoolers and the number of young people who have a bar or bat mitzvah in the United States, I'm surprised that there is no AP exam in Greek or Hebrew, although there is one in Latin.

I think that high school students should be expected to take at least one of the AP exams in science. During the days of the Space Race and the Cold War, there was a lot of pressure for the smarter boys in high school to study physics and calculus, to prepare them to become engineers. For the average person, however, I think that biology and statistics are far more useful because they can prepare you to read and understand medical and environmental research. Thus, these studies can equip you to make informed decisions about your own medical care and to participate meaningfully in debates about healthcare and environmental policy.

We also need for a large percentage of young people to take the AP examinations in micro- and macroeconomics. Economic issues are supposedly the most important issues that Americans are supposed to consider before casting their votes in political campaigns. Yet only a tiny percentage of American voters have had any real training in economics. For example, few Americans know why the stock market crashed in 1929, or why there was a major financial collapse in 2008. More importantly, Americans are generally unaware that major financial collapses and panics used to happen every few years.

Few people realize why the US economy was so strong and stable between the end of World War II and the 2008 collapse in the financial markets. They don't know why the financial markets collapsed in 1929 and 2008. They don't know why the policies that were followed in the wake of the 1929 collapse caused the Great Depression to be so severe and long-lasting. Nor do they realize how and why the earning power of the American worker has been eroding since 1973, even as worker productivity has been going up. Right now, this kind of knowledge is generally reserved for the upper middle class and the very rich. It should be taught to everyone.

I believe that every labor union should be encouraging its members to prepare to take the AP exams in macro- and microeconomics. If a substantial portion of the working class knew the basic facts about political economy, then working people would demand economic policies that served their interests, instead of serving the interests of the filthy rich. Another benefit is that we'd have a huge constituency of knowledgeable people who can insist on improvements in the high school history curricula.

The problems that plague our public schools aren't inevitable, and they didn't happen by accident. They are the predictable result of political decisions that have been made at the highest levels of society for the past 100 years or more. Other countries manage to teach all of their children to read.

If we are failing to teach our children to read, it's because the people who are at the top of our educational establishment are happy with the dismal results. They are knowingly training our teachers to use teaching methods that don't work. They are knowingly selecting bad textbooks. They are knowingly creating a toxic school environment that alienates instead of educating. They are knowingly destroying the careers of the teachers and principals who succeed by deviating from the approved methods and curriculum. These people at the highest levels of the educational establishment create the problems and then blame the problems on the teachers and the students and the students' families. This will go on as long as we let it.

To solve the problems of our public schools and our society and even the world, we must find some way for the general public to become informed and to use its strength in numbers to solve these problems. As Orwell wrote in *Nineteen Eighty-Four,*

> If there was hope, *it must* lie in the proles, because only there, in those swarming disregarded masses, eighty-five percent of the population of Oceania, could the force to destroy the Party ever be generated.

In the United States, we supposedly have a two-party system, yet neither party really seems to be on the side of the swarming disregarded masses. Otherwise, they'd solve simple problems like an underperforming school whenever they managed to get the upper hand in a local school district. They'd solve bigger problems as soon as they got control of Congress and the White House. As long as neither of the major parties is working on behalf of that vast majority of the population, then we can't really claim to have a true democracy in the United States.

In this chapter, I've talked about how to get yourself educated, and the kind of curriculum it will take to educate others. Marxists tell me that this kind of change cannot take place in the United States without some sort of revolution. They point out that major literacy drives took place in the Soviet Union, Cuba, and Nicaragua only in the wake of a revolution. They tell me that Paolo Freire's literacy movement in Brazil was aborted by the 1964 General's Coup, which was supported by the United States. They remind me that the United States supported the Contras, who suppressed the Sandinistas' literacy programs by harassing and sometimes murdering schoolteachers in Nicaragua in the 1980s. Yet I don't believe that it will take a revolution just to get good public schools in every neighborhood in the United States. We had extremely high rates of literacy in New England before Horace Mann introduced whole-word reading instruction and Prussian educational philosophy. What we need is a well-informed and well-organized democratic political movement aimed at improving education.

As Victor Hugo once wrote, "One cannot resist an idea whose time has come." I'm hopeful that the time for real educational reform is now. In this book, I've outlined the problems and their causes. The solution to our problem of illiteracy is as simple as A, B, C—intensive phonics. The solution to our problems of widespread ignorance and irrationality are simple, too—an enriched curriculum and a more humane social environment in schools, along with more opportunities for continuing education for adults. Only one question remains: What role will you play in the movement to bring these things about?

About the Author

Laurie Endicott Thomas taught herself to read at age four, by studying the rhyming words in *Green Eggs and Ham* by Dr. Seuss. Thanks to that head start in reading, she was able to get an excellent education in the public schools of Ohio, Wisconsin, and New Jersey. Her classmates who did not figure out the phonics code on their own before they entered school were not so lucky.

After receiving a bachelor and master of arts degree in regional science at the University of Pennsylvania, Thomas spent more than 20 years working as an editor and writer in medical and veterinary publishing. She has also copyedited college textbooks on education and philosophy.

Although Thomas has never worked in a school, she has essentially taught remedial writing to some of the most highly educated people in the United States: medical doctors. She is also the author of a column on grammar and usage in the *American Medical Writers Association Journal*. Thomas is a popular speaker on education and healthcare reform.

A Special Thank You to You!

On behalf of everyone at Freedom Of Speech Publishing, thank you for choosing *Not Trivial: How Studying the Traditional Liberal Arts Can Set You Free* for your reading enjoyment.

As an added bonus and special thank you, for purchasing *Not Trivial: How Studying the Traditional Liberal Arts Can Set You Free*, you can enjoy discounts and special promotions on other Freedom of Speech Publishing products. Visit: www.freedomeofspeech.com/vip to learn more.

We are committed to providing you with the highest level of customer satisfaction possible. If for any reason you have questions or comments, we are delighted to hear from you. E-mail us at cs@freedomofspeechpublishing.com or visit our Web site at: www.freedomofspeechpublishing.com/contact-us-2

If you enjoyed *Not Trivial: How Studying the Traditional Liberal Arts Can Set You Free*, visit www.freedomofspeechpublishing.com for a list of similar books or upcoming books.

Again, thank you for your patronage. We look forward to providing you more entertainment in the future.

Made in the USA
Lexington, KY
27 September 2013